# NAKED ON THE INTERNET

## Hookups, Downloads, and Cashing in on Internet Sexploration

1010110010010110010010 **Audacia Ray** 0110010010110010010010110010

SEAL PRESS

NAKED ON THE INTERNET
Hookups, Downloads, and Cashing in on Internet Sexploration
Copyright © 2007 Audacia Ray

Published by Seal Press
1400 65th Street, Suite 250
Emeryville, CA 94608

ISBN-13: 978-1-58005-209-2 (alk. paper)
ISBN-10: 1-58005-209-6 (alk. paper)

Library of Congress Cataloging-in-Publication Data

Ray, Audacia.
Naked on the Internet : hookups, downloads, and cashing in on Internet
sexploration / Audacia Ray.
p. cm.
Includes bibliographical references and index.
ISBN-13: 978-1-58005-209-2 (alk. paper)
ISBN-10: 1-58005-209-6 (alk. paper)
1. Internet and women. 2. Computers and women. 3. Women's computer
network resources. 4. Sex–Computer network resources. 5. Internet
pornography. 6. Computer sex. I. Title.

HQ1178.R39 2007
306.770285'4678082–dc22
                    2007004269

Cover design by Rodrigo Corral Design
Cover image courtesy of nerdpr0n.com
Interior design by Tabitha Lahr
Printed in the United States of America

For my parents and
for Rob, my superbuddy

# 0110010100001 01**Contents**0100100010010

**AUTHOR'S NOTE ON METHODOLOGY**

The women I interviewed for this book were found—where else?—on the Internet. I started my research with a short list of women whom I wanted to interview, and over time the list grew. The initial group of women I set out to interview suggested other women they knew who would be interesting interview subjects. I placed ads, posts, and notices on sites I haunt regularly: my own site, Waking Vixen; Craigslist; MySpace; as well as on Listservs and message boards I belong to. I asked everyone to forward my calls for interviews far and wide.

It has not been my goal to give a comprehensive history of women's sexuality and the Internet, and there's no doubt that I have left out women who were key players in the development of various movements, styles, and ideas online. However, I don't subscribe to the "great men" notion of history, so the Internet junkies will certainly notice the mix of key figures with more-peripheral women who offer up different kinds of experiences. Though, of course, this book is very much about the women I have interviewed, it's more about the ideas and cultural development of the Internet with regard to women's sexuality and less about all-inclusive biographies.

For the actual interviews, I gave the women a choice as to the medium via which they wanted to be questioned. They could respond to my questions by email, telephone (or Skype), in an instant messenger (IM) conversation, or in person for those in the New York City metropolitan area. Preferences varied widely and seemed to be based on different factors: the way a woman was most comfortable communicating and thought she could give the best answers, the degree to which a woman wanted her identity protected, and both of our schedules and time zones. Although I knew at the outset that doing interviews in so many different ways would mean that I would sacrifice a certain level of consistency, the trade-off seemed worth it to make my interviewees comfortable. Even for the many women I interviewed who are doing exhibitionistic things on the Internet, talking about, describing, and analyzing their experiences was often difficult.

Having frequently found myself on the interviewee side with people who were not particularly sensitive to my experiences as a highly sexual woman and as a sex worker, I found myself being perhaps overly sensitive to the needs of the women I was interviewing; when listening to intense truths, I kept thinking about whether the woman was telling me her story as part of our conversation, or if she really wanted this story in print. Although it's true that anything said in an interview is fair game, my own experiences with being misquoted and misrepresented by writers whose sole intention was to get a good story have led me to believe that sometimes it's important to be conservative with what one chooses to reveal. As a result, there are a few places in this book where I paint a less-than-complete picture of particular women. This is done intentionally to protect identities.

When doing a real time interview (i.e., not email), my training in oral history comes out: I listen a lot, and though I have general questions in mind, I try not to rush from one point to the next and instead let the interviewee tell her story the way she wants to tell it. In general, an interview is not a conversation; it is one person getting information and insight from another person. For the most part, I tried to stay in active-listener mode, though sometimes I shared a personal tidbit or perspective with my interviewee, which was usually rewarding and served to open the conversation up in a new way. After all, I'm not an outsider to this whole naked-on-the-Internet thing, and at any time, my interviewees could search out any number of interesting details on my blog and much would be revealed. I found that being transparent instead of professionally removed was a good thing—and ultimately an essential thing for writing this book.

I do think writing books about the Internet is an important and useful thing to do, and there are myriad reasons why this is a book and not a website, but I also recognize that the Internet moves faster than any other form of media (especially publishing), which is just one reason why I love it. But this fact is also probably going to make me look foolish to some readers who are up on all the latest technology and new innovations. As I write, the world of user-driven content, particularly video, is becoming the next big thing on the Internet; while I highly doubt that online moving images will make text extinct, they will definitely shape the future of the Internet. By the time this book is in print, some of the websites I discuss here will have gone dark, but thankfully, there is more thought going into the preservation of digital culture these days. The best public tools for seeking out information about any website (other than search engines, of course) are Archive and Alexa. Both of these sites, though certainly imperfect tools, help to provide a better picture of any given site and how it fits into the web. Archive's Wayback Machine shows sites as they once were before going dark or having undergone design changes, and Alexa traces comparative web traffic trends.

# INTRODUCTION
## How I Got Naked on the Internet

You know you spend way too much time looking at Internet porn when you Google "cream pies" and are surprised when the top results are all recipes for banana-and-chocolate cream pies. These days, Googling dirty phrases, which include the less-family-friendly version of "cream pies," is a normal part of my day, something I do unblinkingly while sitting in my home office in my underwear.

I wave my nerd flag high—I'm curious and a little bit obsessive when it comes to information, especially about sex. This all started innocently enough (well, kinda) back in college, when I began to research the hell out of gender and sexuality issues and spent lots of hours in the library at The New School for Social Research, where I was doing my interdisciplinary BA at Eugene Lang College. The card catalog was slowly being digitized, but it still had some real, tangible, yellowed cards in it back then at the end of the twentieth century. In college, while most of my fellow students got really into parties or activism or sports, I got really into New York City libraries. Words and information about sexuality, radical politics, and ways people live their lives became my calling, and after a few years of interning for a small publisher and an academic journal and discovering my penchant for spending time in neglected archives, I got my first real research job at the then-nascent Museum of Sex in the fall of 2001, my senior year of college. I began to spend even more time at various branches of the New York Public Library, carefully sorting through old dirty pictures. I relished the opportunity to look at fading photos of burlesque superstars and their forgotten lesser-known sisters as well as Zagat-like guides to areas of ill repute in nineteenth-century New York City; there was a trove of pornographic filth, ironically preserved for my research (and prurient) pleasure by moral crusaders opposed to such things.

But as intrepid a researcher as I am, I'm also shy. It's this shyness, in addition to my propensity for sitting in my office and working without shoes (the library frowns upon such things, not so the Museum of Sex), that brought me to the world of online research—and research about sexuality in particular. Online, I could check out people's websites, lurk on their blogs, look at whatever photos they had posted, and follow their links to a seemingly infinite and interconnected world of content; most importantly, I could learn a whole lot without having to talk to anyone (or wear shoes). Later, when I started working from home, I would decide that wearing pants wasn't necessary either.

Ah, the Internet—land of information, procrastination, and copious photos of boobies, populated by people with obsessions to which they devote entire websites and online communities. I could suddenly see the world from my desk chair—even better than that, I could see what the people of the world had in their pants and in the dark, pervy recesses of their brains. I was hooked.

## The Debauchery Begins:
## From Casual Encounters to Sex Work

In the winter of early 2003, several months after the Museum of Sex opened its doors to the public, my monogamous relationship of nearly five years fell apart. From the moment I moved out of our shared apartment in Queens and into a new place with a stranger in Brooklyn, my Internet exploration escalated from browsing to active participation—yes, including hooking up with strangers for sex.

Having been with the same person throughout college and for a year afterward, I had no idea how to go about dating. More than that, I was terrified of speaking to strangers and couldn't conceive of picking someone up in a bar or chatting up a person at a party. In fact, on the rare occasions when I went out on the town and got hit on, I was all but oblivious to it. I was genuinely surprised when my friends teased me about someone they'd seen flirting with me.

But on the Internet, I was moving from being a studious academic with a voyeuristic twist to being a participant not just in online flirtation but in the pursuit of offline, real-life encounters of the sexy kind. My first stop was Craigslist's Casual Encounters (the section is referred to as CL CE by those in the know) because I was fascinated by the free-form, text-only (though they've since added pic capabilities) postings on the site. Also, I am a cheapskate and Craigslist is free.

But really, more than the appealing financial nonburden of this exploration, the words were what got me. On Craigslist, I wasn't so fascinated by the old (old in Internet time, anyway, in which things older than six months are ancient) axiom that "on the Internet, nobody knows you're a dog," from a 1993 *New Yorker* cartoon in which one dog sitting in front of a computer says this to another dog. Rather, I was seduced by the ability to be myself—the person I am in my brain, not in my awkward social moments. I had also started to further develop an awareness of the ways in which I was different from your average dog on the Internet (opposable thumbs, for one).

The things I wanted were not what lots of other people wanted, and having worked at the Museum of Sex for going on two years, I had learned that even on the rare occasion when I was able to carry on a conversation with a stranger, the mere mention of my job usually had two potential outcomes: abject horror or lecherous interest wrapped up in assumptions about the degree of my personal sluttiness. When I added to that my desire for lots of interesting and varied casual sex with likewise interesting and varied people, along with my gradual realization that I wanted my next relationship to be honestly nonmonogamous, the wilds of the Internet seemed like my best bet. True, this decision was made in part because I was becoming familiar with that expression on a date's face when I started talking about my peculiar vision of great sex and the perfect relationship, and I hated that sinking feeling of knowing that regardless of what we had in common, my ideas of the perfect sexual relationship were bound to get in the way.

On Craigslist, I could multitask. If I saw a relationship-oriented post, I could respond to it if the mood struck me, or I could post my own ads and get hundreds of responses to peruse, laugh at, and maybe select a partner (or two or three) from. As a bisexual, I tried to play the field evenly to begin with, but I quickly realized that the W4W (women for women) section was rife with drama, and that it was much easier to get a man to be at my beck and call, because horny men on the Internet greatly outnumber horny women.

For someone with flexible morals like myself, the line between casual hookups and sex for hire was very thin, and my curiosity about sex for hire, coupled with my disappointment with my casual hookups, got the better of me. After about a year and a half of being on the prowl, during which time I'd developed a full-blown open relationship with a man I'd initially met for sex while also maintaining a number of more-casual guys on the side, I had a two-night stand with a guy I genuinely liked—and who was good at fucking. Then he disappeared into the mist. I was a bit distraught, since I was used to being the one to disappear. As I thought about it more and talked to a few friends who were sex workers, it became clear to me that if I was going to be having hit-or-miss casual sex anyway, I should probably consider getting paid for it. Combined with the sketchiness of my employment at the time and the ease of the hop, skip, and jump from posting for cas~~~ ~~~ ~~~ to including the words "seeking generous man," s~ ~ ~.~ ~~ined like a logical next step.

I don't know that I ever would've had the guts to become a sex worker were it not for the ease of advertising on the Internet and the fact that initially, it didn't feel all that different from a casual encounter, save for the difference in green. The options for sex workers before the Internet—working for a madam at an escort agency, placing an ad in the back of the *Village Voice,* or standing on a street corner—would've scared me away from the sex industry. Advertising my services online somehow seemed much more palatable, and much like the hookups I'd already become comfortable with. I didn't have to work for or answer to anyone, and my word count was flexible, unlike print advertising.

After spending so much time on various webpages, reading blogs, surfing porn, and peeking in at other people's lives through the window of the Internet, I jumped in feet—or maybe tits and ass—first. Forget camming, cybersex, and dirty emails—I knew what I wanted: real experiences with real people, facilitated by a sometimes-surreal medium.

## DIY Porn: Freeing My Ass

Hookups and hooking, as it turned out, were just the tip of the iceberg.

After the downsizing of my job at the Museum of Sex, in the fall of 2003 I started doing public relations for a small Manhattan porn website, where I was getting paid to keep up with trends in the online adult industry and develop what I thought was an already immense and obsessive knowledge of the subject. However, I quickly learned that my knowledge was largely theoretical: I had an understanding of the feminist issues around porn, for sure, and when I was at the Museum of Sex, I had sat at the feet of the grandes dames of 1970s porn, Vanessa del Rio and Annie Sprinkle, hanging on every word they said. But I didn't know much about the mechanics of making porn. The daily realities, as it turns out, are more mundane than exciting, though it took me a while to get my sea legs, and even longer to get jaded about seeing close-up penetration shots with my morning bagel. What working in porn did offer me, though, was the chance to continue working in an officelike environment with foul-mouthed colleagues, kicking off my shoes and surfing porn for hours.

I had an inkling of the amount of money that could be made off people's sexual desires, but I was initially more intrigued by the sexual politics of the porn industry, and I began to envision in it a unique space for fucking the system, challenging sexual stereotypes, and clearing the way for all kinds of freedoms. As I worked away on more than just public relations and got a hand in model management and productions, I could see how easy it was to make different kinds of porn on the Internet, both in terms of the simplicity of getting content online and in terms of the variety of sexual tastes and body types that different websites cater to. Still, I was too green to fully grasp so many aspects of the industry: the financial and technical differences between film, video, and digital video; the nuances of credit card processing for an adult business; the fact that digital images exist and are sold in perpetuity. Learning all of this firsthand, plus seeing the influx of all kinds of content and people into the adult industry, gave me insight into what was newly possible at the beginning of the twenty-first century.

I had always thought of the porn industry as one that's run by men who, like my then-bosses, hit forty and realized they couldn't get chicks like they used to and so decided to start a porn site. So when I actually started working in the industry, I was most captivated by the women who were running their own careers within the industry. True, there were female porn directors and adult-business owners before the advent of the Internet, but the web opened the floodgates for women, not solely as models but as business owners who were in control of how their wares (as it were) would be marketed, how their bodies would be shown, and which markets and fetishes they would cater to.

While I had immediate respect for the business-minded women who were pushing the envelope of so-called amateur as well as professional porn, I was mostly taken with the newly emerging subset of alt porn sites, which featured young women (and sometimes men) who looked like me—and read the same books and listened to the same music. The models were personalities, not just body parts. Moreover, these women appeared to meld porn and sex-positive politics in a way that had me swooning. The idea behind alt porn sites was to blend hip youth culture, music, and politics with porn, or at least with softcore nude pictorials.

I found this self-awareness refreshing, and these sites' predilection for community boards, blogs, and other kinds of participation added a kind of attitude that I felt was lacking from more-mainstream porn. Prior to this point, I had felt alienated from the women in porn and even slightly afraid of them. From the inside, I got to build professional relationships with porn performers who were funny, sweet, sexy, and real live people.

During college I had modeled nude for my photography student roommate, but at the time I hadn't considered making images like these available for public consumption, mostly because I didn't think I was sexy, and I didn't think anyone would like (or pay) to see me naked. Years later, watching the parade of beautiful imperfections move across my computer screen and through my office on a daily basis, I started to rethink my assumptions and consider getting naked on the Internet. Although my bosses were mildly creepy, they were good guys, and the work itself seemed pretty easy. Plus, I found it gratifying to know that lots of people would be looking.

I banded together with that old college roommate and my then-boyfriend (the casual-sex-cum-open-relationship guy), and we set forth to develop an alt porn website. The site was to be laced with hardcore content, unlike many other alt porn sites at the time, plus sex education demonstrations; it would be a paysite, which we hoped would make us money, and our mission was to contribute to a positive view of sexuality. We started creating content, which roughly translated to my boyfriend and I fucking a lot, and my best girl photoing and videoing it. A few weeks short of launch, things started to go sour. My boyfriend decided he didn't want to be naked on the Internet, and the crumbling of our various relationships ensued.

Looking back now, I know that that first collaborative porn/sex-ed project would have failed financially, partly because we didn't consider any financial aspects beyond our very naive assumption that all nudity on the Internet would make money in short order. After those relationships disintegrated and I considered my options, I decided that I did indeed want to get naked on the Internet, and I branched out on my own and began to model for a small handful of alt porn websites. Some of these gigs paid, others did not. Alt porn modeling didn't feel as much like work as the other kinds of sex work I'd done: The money was terrible, for one. But I felt like I was part of a community of brilliant and beautiful women with whom I was creating some kind of naked-lady kinship. Modeling brought all the glory that running my own paysite would have—without the headaches, but also without the continued profit and control over the content I took part in producing, which will forever float around the Internet without a financial return to me.

## Back to Solitary Pleasures: Blogging

As my porn group project began to tank in the late summer of 2004, I started feeling anxious about what I was doing with myself and searching to figure out exactly what fruit more than a year of buying outfits, producing content, writing web text, and stressing over web design had borne. Certainly it was a learning experience—or at the very least, an experience that made it clear to me that I knew very little about the technological and financial aspects of making a porn site move forward, much less make a profit. The detritus of failure around the project left me wanting something to do with my glorious Internet knowledge, research, and contacts. I didn't want to slip off the radar, but I didn't have any desire to collaborate on another porn project, so I struck out on my own, not just as a model, but as a writer.

I was at an interesting place in my life—moving into my midtwenties, plucking casual sex partners off the Internet, exploring polyamory, doing public relations and production management for a porn website, beginning my master's at Columbia, starting a nude modeling career of my own, and trying to find my niche in the world of commercial sex (and the world at large). I had always been a journal keeper, and having developed a sex blog reading habit, I signed up for an account with Blogger in July 2004. Thus, Waking Vixen was born. The blog was a place where I could sort all this stuff out, or at least begin to tell the many pieces of my tale.

That tale included the hilarious and weird details of working for a porn company, as well as raw emotional outpourings about my relationships (I had both a boyfriend and a girlfriend at the time, plus miscellaneous lovers), erotic tales of lust and group sex, and stories of my sensual massage and foot fetish clientele. I was aware of my audience and that the secretive but not private nature of the writing I was doing stirred something in people, prompting readers to comment on my posts, both publicly on the site and privately to my personal email.

In the first eight months of this endeavor, I became entirely seduced by the power of my written words. But offline, in my so-called real life in which I had to talk to people, I was doing a less-than-stellar job of communicating. Instead of talking to my boyfriend about our relationship, I blogged about it. I poured all of my thoughts into my blog, which he didn't read until after we'd broken up. Meanwhile, I was blogging about my newer relationship with my girlfriend, who was also blogging about me; we read each other's blogs and comments obsessively. The seduction of the writing, the instant gratification of comments, emails, and links to my posts, created a sense of elation—not just that I wasn't alone, but that people related to me and my struggles. In many ways this elation became entirely unreasonable, and my blogging habit became a lot more important than other things in my life—and sometimes I felt as though I were living, or at least fucking, just in order to blog.

Even though there were moments when it seemed like it would be wise to give blogging up entirely, my decision to continue was largely determined by a choice to become more private. By blogging about my private life, I realized the differences between secrecy and privacy. It was a wake-up call when I figured out that my blog was not anonymous or going unnoticed. It is, in fact, read by people I know in real life, people who don't necessarily need to know all the nitty-gritty details of my sex and love life. Over time, my blog has become less personal; emotional rawness still peeks through on a fairly regular basis, but I no longer detail the emotional and sexual content of my relationships.

## Lures, Snares, and Glorious Moments

My most solitary endeavor—blogging—was responsible for bringing me to the darkest places in my Internet travails, because it brought me deeper into my own head. Ironically, it also brought me the most comfort and community with other women. Perhaps this is because many women come to blogging—especially sex and relationship blogging—with a sense of restlessness, aloneness, and the general frustration of being misunderstood—plus a serious compulsion to write.

The Internet, like a city, can be an extremely isolating place to exist and take up space, or it can provide a wealth of opportunities to connect with other people and to develop means of self-expression. Very often it can do both for the same person, as it did for me. True, the Internet can be a place to hide and to avoid talking to people and interacting, but it also has an extraordinary power to foster connection. I made connections through casual and commercial sex ads and more-indirect connections by choosing to get naked on a variety of porn sites and blog about my life.

Though at first I had no intention of developing real relationships, community, and a support network online, over time it simply began to happen, and more importantly, I began to seek these things out both on- and offline. Meeting other women through the Internet has been crucial and life changing: I've forged friendships with other sex workers through the Internet and discovered a kind of camaraderie among the ever-expanding network of friendly sex bloggers in New York City that I never knew could exist. The staff members of *$pread Magazine,* the magazine by and for sex workers that I first read about on a sex workers' Listserv in the fall of 2004, and of which I'm now executive editor, taught me about activism and the power of collective action in a project that was conducted mostly on our home computers and Internet connections until recently. While I may have found these women and these communities eventually, without the Internet it probably would have taken me a few more lonely and potentially self-destructive years to do so.

Participating in sex culture online and hearing other women's stories have made me sit up and pay attention to the ways women are pursuing and developing their sex lives both on- and offline, often combining both in complex ways. Most of the current writing about the Internet, especially when it comes to sexuality and particularly with reference to women, falls into two polarized camps, both of which have the propensity to quickly escalate toward hysteria: (1) Sex on the Internet is evil and responsible for bringing down social and communication structures as we know it! The children, think about the children! Especially your daughters! (2) The Internet is an amazing and positive tool for the future of communication and connecting people! If you can think of a kink, other people are also into it, and you can find them through Google! Both of these statements are true. Both of them are false, as well.

Although there are certainly many unsavory things about the Internet and the ways that people use it, there are many unsavory things about the ways people treat each other, Internet aside. The evils of the Internet aren't necessarily separate from the evils that linger inside people, though the Internet manifests these evils in new and interesting ways. For women online, many interactions are immediately sexualized—and women are harnessing the power of this sexualization for themselves, using the Internet as both a playground and a workspace. Over the past few years of my own personal and professional experimentation, my eyes have been opened to the vast possibilities and infinite challenges that women confront as they choose to express their sexualities online. It was this firsthand experience, combined with meeting, watching, and interacting with extraordinary women who bare themselves online, that inspired me to write this book.

Women who experiment with their sexualities on the Internet can't help but get tangled up in the complex issues of self-representation, commodification, and commerce, even if they're not paying for or being paid for what they're doing online. There isn't really a way to opt out of this mess, but there are ways that women can challenge and question what it all means, while also enjoying themselves (and sometimes profiting). This is essentially what *Naked on the Internet* is about: the ways that women connect with themselves and others to explore the Internet as a communication and lifestyle tool as well as a valuable, though sometimes risky, sexual space. I address a wide range of ways that women experience the Internet: cam-ming, chatting, and making websites; dating, hooking up, and forming friendships; sex blogging; porn and other forms of sex work; sexual health and online support communities; and technology that enables physical sexual encounters.

Ultimately, these issues extend beyond the World Wide Web and into the physical world—hence the general absence of the words "cyber" and "virtual," words that crop up in most pieces of writing about the Internet. This book is written on the assumption that the Internet affects the women who use it in real ways that extend beyond the screen and that can't be powered off with the press of a button. Many of the communities I detail are communities that I'm also part of in some way, and my criticism of them, though sometimes harsh, is rooted in my deep belief in the power of women's communities and communication—however they're facilitated.

# 010101000CHAPTER 1: GIRLS GONE WIRED01 00
## A Short History of Women,
## Computers, and the Internet

W hen I Googled the combination "women + computers," many of the results that popped up were organizations and groups designed to support and encourage women who are interested in computers. Googling "men + computers" turned up nothing of the sort. Those results led to random websites that happened to contain text with the words "men" and "computers" mixed in somewhere; these words didn't really produce a targeted search because a relationship between men and computers is assumed. These Google results, though of course very unscientific, reveal that the idea of women using computers is still regarded as something of a novelty, a career choice that needs support from other women in the form of support groups, professional organizations, and online forums. Hence the existence of easily-discovered-by-Google organizations like the Association for Women in Computing, which was founded in 1978 and offers support and professional growth opportunities for women who work with computers.

There is a gender gap that first appeared between male and female computer users, which then transferred over to Internet users. In the not-so-long but very rich and hectic history of computers, networks, and the Internet, women have generally been overshadowed, pushed around, and ignored. Despite—or perhaps because of—this, many women have banded together to create support organizations, art projects, theoretical frameworks, and communities in which they flourish as women who use computers and have access to the Internet. Though these gender gap issues still exist today, and many studies show that women use the Internet in different ways and with different expectations than men do, there has been a cultural shift brought about by women's determination and commitment to being visible and capable users of computers and the Internet. Female computer programmers and users certainly existed before the 1981 introduction of the IBM PC, followed by the Gavilan SC laptop in 1983 and Apple's Macintosh in 1984, but women didn't begin to strongly fight for or create their places in the digital landscape until personal computing became ubiquitous.

*Naked on the Internet* is entirely consumed with the effects of personal computers and the things women get up to when they are alone with their machines, their Internet connections, and their desires. My personal area of interest is the world of the Internet and personal computing in the dozen years since the user-friendly revolution. It's easy for newcomers to the scene to forget that the ease of creating websites, interacting with computer users around the world, and creating and occupying female-friendly sexual spaces is a relatively new phenomenon. In the worlds of computer technology and Internet content, changes happen so fast that one offline year is the equivalent of ten Internet years. For women, these shifts in technology have gone hand in hand with a lot of work, which has paid off in visible changes to the shift in gender balance and accessibility.

## Boys Only, Girls Keep Out?

Feminist criticism and activism around issues involving the media, representation, and the presence of female and feminist voices was in full swing in the 1980s, and the world of computers didn't escape its scrutiny. Sherry Turkle, the founder and director of the Massachusetts Institute of Technology (MIT) Initiative on Technology and Self, has done extensive academic studies and writing on computers, the Internet, identity, and gender. Her work started as personal computers began to nestle their ways into people's workplaces and homes. She was quick to note the gender gap, but rightly pointed out, in the first line of a 1988 essay entitled "Computational Reticence: Why Women Fear the Intimate Machine," that "The computer has no inherent gender bias."[1]

Computers were largely developed by men, so one might make the leap to say that they were created in man's image, and if you believe, as many do, that men are becoming evermore like machines—with their systems and their hardware—then the synchronicity between man and machine is compelling. And while popular culture might have us believe that men and women are different creatures intellectually and emotionally, in the real world women of course have the ability, if not always the desire, to understand technology created by men, as well as to create new technologies. Biological determination of behavior aside, Turkle is correct that computers themselves aren't coded male or female.

It was, instead, the culture around computers starting in the mid-twentieth century that kept them in the realm of men who were computer scientists, burgeoning hackers at universities, and self-taught programmers. If you want to get heavy about it, for men, making technology—computer programs, systems, and networks—was a Promethean act of creation, an act of creation that could be performed and maintained without women.

In her essay, Turkle goes on to say that when women look at computers, they don't see devoid-of-gender-politics machines, they see the culture of men that has sprung up around computers.[2] Men who are into computers are perceived, wrongly or rightly, as weird hacker types, pale and fragile from lack of exposure to the elements, unable to make social connections when they are away from the computer screen. These men, ultimately, prioritize computers over flesh-and-blood interactions—and this threat to human interaction is what women have found abhorrent about computers, especially in a pre-Internet era when people who sat at computers weren't using them to connect with one another. It's not the technology on its own, rather its potential to wreck havoc on human interaction.

This is in many ways a perfectly good explanation for why women have historically steered clear of computers in greater numbers than men. To take Turkle's idea one step further, the culture of men that surrounds technology is tied into women and technophobia, as though men's desire to explore and/or conquer technology were distinctly antifemale. In the 1980s, the gender gap that fostered this type of antifemale vibe was a very real thing, but this has shifted and changed over the last twenty-plus years. Women are moving away from the dubious designation of protectors of the hearth against the invasive evils of technology and are expressing curiosity about technology, if not already downright embracing it. This is a larger measurable trend among regular computer users, and also quite visible and growing among small groups and individual women who have begun to raise hell and engage with gender, sex, and technology in a passionate way, especially since the Internet started to become more widely available in the 1990s.

When Macintosh was released in 1984, Joy Callan, a professor of Management in the Department of Women's Studies in the Raymond Walters College at the University of Cincinnati, began to study the different attitudes that male and female students had toward computers. She mapped the students' changes in attitudes over a period of ten years and attempted to identify the essence of what the gender gap was about. Callan focused on something she calls the "Fear Index." In the first phase of the study, Callan found that women scored much higher on the Fear Index than men did at the beginning of the semester when both groups were inexperienced in working with the computers. However, by the end of the semester, the women's comfort level was on par with their male counterparts.[3] By the conclusion of her study in 1994, Callan found that the gender gap had closed and women were less anxious and apprehensive about computer use at the beginning of the semester, before they'd had formal computer science training, though both men and women shared concerns about their knowledge base and ability to operate computers and troubleshoot problems.

Different types of anxieties have sprung up since the infiltration of computers and technology into our daily lives.

The anxiety around the mechanics of computer use is shared by men and women who may feel intimidated about the incessant growth of technology that they can't keep up with. It's common to note a generation gap here, where younger people feel more confident and are more likely to roll with the changes than their elders. The anxiety about the culture that has sprouted up around computers is a quite different thing, one that continues to be debated as psychologists, teachers, and parents question the impact of our online interactions, the pervasiveness of video games in young people's day-to-day lives, and the wide-scale changes that our culture has witnessed as technology continues to boom. Over the past twenty years, both of these anxieties have influenced women's decisions about the role of computers in their professional and personal lives. Despite the fact that the gender gap closed significantly between the mid-1980s and the mid-1990s, women and men still tend to use computers in different ways—particularly when it comes to the Internet. A 1996 report on women and online marketing concluded that the best way to get women online and buying was by providing them with content or interactive capabilities that create a sense of community, promoting benefits that extend into their lives offline, and offering services that are personalized and friendly.[4]

Interaction and human connection have consistently been pinpointed as the primary benefit that women want from the Internet—and actually, what women want from life in general. A 2005 Pew Internet & American Life Project study called "How Women and Men Use the Internet" confirmed these findings yet again. The study shows that while men have long been using the Internet for a wide variety of activities, women are just beginning to catch up and adopt more uses themselves.[5] Since the previous Pew study in 2002, women's enthusiasm for and experimentation with the Internet became more varied, and women became more willing to try a wider range of offerings on the Internet, especially when it came to entertainment like downloading music and watching videos online. To a certain extent, the Pew study pits men's and women's Internet usage against one another, but it makes clear that their uses are and will continue to be different: Women are more likely than men to use the Internet to send and receive email, search for health information, and use websites for support for personal problems, while men use the Internet to get news, find do-it-yourself information, listen to music and watch videos, and check for sports statistics.

As women's enthusiasm for and willingness to experiment with the Internet has grown, their suspicions about its dangers have held steady. More women than men express concern about crime facilitated by the Internet. Statistically, women are significantly more concerned about crimes like child prostitution (86 percent of online women versus 74 percent of online men) and wide-scale fraud (55 percent of online women versus 49 percent of online men). These fears are likely to affect women's web surfing habits as well as the amount of personal information they are willing to provide about themselves online, especially when coupled with the increasingly widespread articles about how to protect oneself both online and when meeting people off the Internet.

Women online must continue to make decisions about the spaces they want to inhabit, and if they do choose sexualized spaces (or choose to remain when a space becomes sexualized), they must decide how to manage their identities and degree of personal information so as to be able to function online to the best of their abilities and explore in the safest and most rewarding way. This is not to say that the Internet is a vast, evil, and hostile frontier for women but that different and gendered challenges exist for women than for men online, and some of them are indeed hostile.

## Hello over There:
## The Evolution of Internet Interaction

Internet fads come and go, and traffic is easily deflected from one site and attention drawn to another. Internet users tend to have short attention spans, partly because there are just so many damn things clamoring for our attention. Before elaborate graphics and moving images populated the Internet, text-based chat and message boards ruled the scene. Even today, with much more colorful and distracting things available—like video blogs and entire realms of three-dimensional games with computer-generated graphics—discussion boards and chat rooms remain a favorite among many people. Textual interactions in public forums and often in real time are part of the early stirrings of user-generated content (UGC), which is sometimes also called "consumer-generated content," targeting Internet users not as people interested in participatory culture but as buyers of goods and services. UGC has become the cornerstone of the contemporary Internet and a major part of what, since 2004, is being called Web 2.0. Web 2.0 is a way for Internet users to feel more engaged in the online cultures they are interested in. It's also a way for companies that create and own sites with these features enabled to have access to content that costs them nothing to produce. Most successful and highly trafficked websites of the past few years contain at least some amount of user-generated content, which can take the form of message boards that exist as an offshoot of the main content of the site (many alt porn sites have this feature), site visitors' ability to post comments (as on blogs), or user-uploaded photos (Flickr exists solely for this purpose), or video (YouTube's raison d'être).

One of the first semipublic spaces where conversations happened between participants and remained accessible to visitors long after they were over was the bulletin board system (BBS), one of the first iterations of a means of communication through a network, which was made available to the public in 1979 by Chicagoans Ward Christensen and Randy Suess. Their BBS, like the ones that would quickly follow, was an electronic message-posting system that was accessible through phone lines. BBSes were more democratic in form than traditional forms of media and information dissemination: Anyone with a computer, a modem, and a phone line could access them and post their thoughts. Some BBSes that flourished in the 1980s were operated by companies and organizations engaged in computer programming and research, but the majority were run by systems operators (quickly shortened to "sysops") who ran BBSes from private servers as something of an obsessive pastime rather than a for-profit venture. Many BBSes were free to use, though the dial-up expenses could be considerable if the BBS sysop was a long-distance phone call away. BBSes that got away with charging were the ones that existed to exchange pornography—in the form of written erotica, GIF (Graphics Interchange Format, image files introduced by CompuServe in 1987) images, and images constructed using American Standard Code for Information Interchange (ASCII prOn). BBSes required that their users dial up, at which point they logged on with a username (or "handle"), which then allowed them to create and reply to various "threads," or conversation topics, that were posted on the boards. From the outset, BBSes ranged in topics—some were specific and technical and others were more general and social in nature.

By the mid-1990s the BBSes were in decline—the emergence of the World Wide Web opened up a whole new level of interactivity that superseded their more limited scope. Though there are still a few BBSes, they've adapted to the broader capabilities of the web. The dial-up and entirely text-based functionality of BBSes seems foreign and antiquated to today's computer users, while the basic idea of message boards is something that's proved to be an enduring feature of online communities. But because the web brought the technology to make messages more private and in real time, many Internet users opt for real-time chat rooms and instant messenger services over message boards.

Chat spaces are universally functional on most computers since they're primarily text based (though many also include photo- and video-sharing capacities that may not work on all platforms). Today there are a profusion of chat programs that specialize in one-on-one communication, including AOL (America On Line), Yahoo!, MSN, Google Talk, ICQ, and Jabber. Each has a slightly different interface and only allows communication with other people who are within the same network and on the user's "buddy list." Though most people have a favorite service, many maintain accounts with several different services. It's also common for people who use chat services to maintain different handles for different purposes: one for chatting with family members, another for friends, still another for forays into the world of anonymous sex chatting or for testing the waters of online dating. There are also web-based services that bring all the different chat programs together in one space without the need for downloading any software. One such popular service is Meebo, launched in 2005, which allows users to avoid downloading chat services and instead use the services directly through the website and within the web browser window so that chat windows don't litter the user's desktop as they tend to do when several different conversations are happening at once.

Chatting is the most rudimentary form of online social networking, which refers to any website or online service designed to connect people to one another through networks or otherwise-linked user identities and handles. Some forms of chat, like Yahoo! Messenger, are linked to a profile or email address on a larger site, which makes it easy for people to browse and search for other users. Though chatting once served as an initial form of contact or online introduction, today it's more common for chatting to be a later part of the getting-to-Internet-know-you process. Though one-on-one private chatting is very popular and common, it's still the case that people chat and get to know each other in public forums—virtual spaces where many users hang out—before moving into a more private online space.

Though AOL's instant messenger has become very popular, AOL chat rooms can take credit for introducing many people to online chatting. Chat rooms are loosely structured around topics of interest, which can range from extremely general to extremely specific. Kis Lee, an erotica writer from San Francisco who got her start in online dating through AOL chat rooms, was unsure where to begin her online odyssey. She says, "I popped in and out of local chat rooms that had names like 'SoCal people' or 'LA 20–30,' and that was the way I got involved in the Internet in 2000." Chat rooms exist entirely because people have the desire to socialize with (hopefully) like-minded strangers, and many chat rooms are open to the public (others are invitation only). And while random passersby may wander in to check out various spaces, chat rooms tend to have a more or less static group of visitors who get to know each other over time.

Although BBSes, message boards, chat rooms, and instant messenger seemingly fill the recommendations offered by the 1995 NIKAinteractive study that encouraged online services to be more interactive and communication focused if they wanted to attract women, these formats have nevertheless often felt hostile to women. BBSes of the past and message boards of the present seem to encourage one of the less-savory aspects of online communication—"flaming." Flames and their resulting flame wars are the product of deliberately hostile and offensive postings that are designed to get a rise out of other participants. People who initiate flames are sometimes referred to as "trolls"—board participants who may sign up for the sole purpose of harassing other members and posting inflammatory remarks. When a pattern of trolling or flaming becomes apparent on a bulletin board, common wisdom says, "Don't feed the trolls," meaning avoid posting responses that give the trolls what they want—sustained attention. Though jerks abound in offline communications as well, being one on the Internet involves invading spaces that other users consider safe and intentionally using that space to subject others to some degree of directed bitterness that the trolls most likely wouldn't express in their day-to-day offline life.

Many women's experiences with flame wars are particularly intense, because in addition to having their ideas and words attacked—which happens as often to men as to women—their physical attributes are often criticized and used against them, despite the fact that these interactions are purely text based. Paige, an Internet security researcher, first got her introduction to the Internet through BBSes and email discussion lists. She was thrilled to become part of a community where her ideas were the first point of contact for the (mostly) men in her area of specialty, and says, "I immediately liked the Internet because as a woman walking around in public, I was always treated according to my appearance." Unfortunately, when conflict arose, she noticed immediately how insults and flames often involved her physical attributes, something that never happened to her male counterparts. Men who disagreed with her on the message boards would call her ugly when countering an opinion she had made over something that was strictly professional. Even when circumstances were less hostile, Paige's participation on the boards often spurred her male colleagues to wonder in public postings and private messages alike what she looked like: Men sent her messages detailing their fantasies of what she looked like on several occasions. These types of responses led Paige to wonder, "Do guys need to sexualize me because they need to put me in my place?" Though the answer to this question is most likely yes, it's probably more complex than that. Paige's and other women's "place" is not simply sub-ordinate to men's, but entails the broader ways in which men sexualize women's space, even when the conversations don't approach the sexual realm in any way whatsoever.

Even though physical female bodies aren't a presence online, women's presence is intensely delineated in interactive online spaces. Being male online is the default, while being female inspires comments and attention. Though both Kis Lee and Paige began their online explorations on message boards and in chat rooms that were vastly different, they each discovered that the moment their femaleness became known, they attracted a whole other level of attention, ranging from hostile to sexually suggestive, and sometimes both at the same time. Women's presence on bulletin boards and in chat rooms is both highly desired and reviled because female presence changes the meaning of the space for the men who occupy it. To be more precise, it's really men's *knowledge* of women's presence that changes the meaning of the online space for them, not women's presence itself.

Online spaces create the potential for difference-blindness, at least to the degree to which a person who is different from the average community participant (or to make things more complex, the *assumed* average community participant) wishes to remain unknown. Of course, the Internet is full of people who are experimenting with identities other than who they are or appear to be offline, but for many women, the struggle to be the person they want to be without all the projections of other participants is the biggest challenge, one that's fraught with the sexism of the spaces they enter online, as well as their own assumptions about their limitations and expectations.

## The Sexy Dance of the Cyborgs

Although the concept of humans combining with machines in utopic and dystopic ways has existed since the advent of industrialization, and since science fiction writers and moviemakers have embraced it as one of their most beloved recurring story-lines, the concept of the cyborg only gained cultural currency in the 1980s. "Cyborg" is an abbreviation of "cybernetic organism"—essentially humans who have added technology into their body that makes them better able to function. "Better" in this case can mean both better functioning than people in general or better than they had been functioning due to illness or disability. While in popular culture cyborgs bring to mind a kind of souped-up Tin Man with wires and microchips (and probably also sex appeal because of movies like *Terminator*), in more simple and realistic terms, a man with a pacemaker or a woman with an artificial leg could be defined this way. Cyborgs are envisioned both as a threat and as a complement to human culture and existence. Though cyborg technologies that combine human bodies with mechanical and computerized parts are not inher-ently linked to the Internet, they exist in the same cultural space in that they both enhance and threaten life as we know it.

Thinking about cyborgs is useful in a book about women and the Internet because cyborgs have visible bodies in a way that women sitting in front of their computers don't. Cyborgs, after all, are visual representations of what happens when body meets technology, and the Internet, with all its photos and videos, still offers users a chance to engage with the more mindful (less visual) part of sexuality. Whether we're talking about body or mind, female cyborgs and women on the Internet are both the stuff of fantasy. After all, sexy cyborgs don't roam the earth glinting with their shiny modifications, and women who express themselves sexually on the Internet don't wear special identifiers that denote them as members of the naked-online tribe.

Whereas online exploration is a means of breaking away from the body or coming to understand the body and desire in a different light, the cyborg is a physical body, albeit a modified one, that demands consideration. Women carry their baggage, their experimental nature, and their limitations online with them into a space where, if they like, they can reimagine and recast themselves as different sexual beings. They can explore more deeply what it means to be themselves in their own physical trappings, or they can explore the possibilities that someone else's body might provide them. Women on the Internet, when freed from the bodies they live in offline, can try out other skin in role-playing games or in chat, presenting themselves differently than the person they are in life: A woman who is slim and blond might present herself online as a curvaceous woman of a different race; a straight woman might present herself as a gay man; a monogamous woman might present herself as a wanton slut. This act of imagining oneself in another's body and life pushes online experience beyond the trappings of a single body or single gender.

Even though cyborgs and the Internet itself have created spaces for people to postulate about the arrival and consequences of things like transhumanism and postgenderism, in which the trappings of bodies and the ways bodies are interpreted by people in the world are eroded, notions of gender and bodies have, in fact, remained pretty limited (even in imagining cyborgs and life online). In the popular imagination, cyborgs end up being hypermasculine or hyperfeminine, within the confines of the binary gender system, featuring big muscles or big boobs respectively. As a result, female cyborgs in popular culture are a technofetishist's wet dream. Often stripped of more-nurturing female characteristics, they're generally outfitted in sleek, sexy garb that emphasizes their shiny curves and technological additions, like Seven of Nine, a character in the *Star Trek: Voyager* television series. The character, played by Jeri Ryan, is a human female who has been assimilated into Borg culture and has taken on attributes of a cyborg; she's outfitted in a shiny catsuit with a corset built into it. Sex appeal reigns supreme with these popular culture cyborgs—in the technofetishist's imagination there probably isn't much of a leap from "ass-kicking lady cyborg" to "lady sexbot."

But technologically enhanced beauty (and brawn) standards aside, the idea of cyborgs calls many boundaries into question. Donna Haraway, the premier theorist of technology, gender, and the relationships between them, says in her groundbreaking essay, "A Cyborg Manifesto," that one of the "boundary breakdowns" of late-twentieth-century science and culture is that "the boundary between the physical and the nonphysical is very imprecise for us."[6] This is one of the biggest conundrums of the Internet and of women's interactions with and through it. Though cyborgs in many ways have things to add to human culture, they also detract from it in some ways—and their existence in science fiction as well as in reality symbolically underscores the tension between the glories and horrors of the Internet for women.

## Cyberfeminism and Struggles of Difference

Take the tensions between technology, culture, and nature and pile them on top of the tensions produced by the gender gap that came out of the early years of personal computing, and the result is predictable—women getting wound up and itching to make their own mark. Women now use computers and online technology to forge ahead in their careers, join support organizations (or not), participate in online communities (despite the communities' being sometimes hostile toward them), hone their skills to be able to do their computer-related jobs better or to be better able to explore and experience the social aspects of the Internet (or both), and to turn the challenges of the Internet into a medium of expression. The women at the forefront of this highly self-reflexive, technically adept and aware movement of artists, activists, and academics began to dub themselves cyberfeminists.

The Old Boys Network (OBN) was perhaps the first group to claim the identity of cyberfeminist. The group was founded in Berlin in 1997 and became the first international alliance of cyberfeminists. In their special tongue-in-cheek, resistance-fueled way, the group refused to define cyberfeminism—this in itself was part of the fun—but they conceded to the demands of others by creating a list of "100 Anti-Theses." The list is in both English and German, and starts with the phrase "cyberfeminism is not . . ." and includes such statements as "cyberfeminism is not about boring toys for boring boys" (my personal favorite). The primary focus of the OBN is on women's agency online; its approach to cyberfeminism supports women in the different permutations their online explorations may take. And that's key—women experience the world of online expression in ways that are diverse and interesting, and that should also be limitless and judgment free.

Cyberfeminism is most often expressed in theoretical writing, web projects, and art that explores the possibilities of the Internet joyously and looks at its repercussions with highly critical and wary eyes. The artist Praba Pilar, who produced the 2005 chapbook *Cyber.Labia: Gendered Thoughts and Conversation on Cyber Space,*[7] is in the wary-eyes camp. Her written, visual, and performance work investigates the actual lived experiences of women whose lives are entangled with or otherwise affected by the Internet. Pilar is highly critical of cyberculture and Internet ventures and the ways they affect the culture and the environment at large. As one of the few women of color who's engaged with cyberfeminism and issues of the Internet, she confronts head-on the issue of the "digital divide" in race and class.

In her conversation with academic writer and researcher Anne Balsamo, Pilar dives straight for the very thing that's so cherished about the Internet—the promise of democracy: "Part of the mythology of global communications is that it's inherently democratic, because you can open up access to the inputs and outputs. This has not proven true given the digital, racial, and class divide around the world—there are persistent issues of access. Women make up two-thirds of the world's illiterate. Most of the Internet is still in English. It's inaccessible—what's democratic about that?"[8]

Pilar and Balsamo discuss the fact that democracy is regarded as a nearly universal good—therefore if something like, say, a technology promotes democracy, it becomes infallible. The democracy of the Internet in turn becomes a concept that can't be argued against—everyone loves democracy, and so a democratic technology should make people happy. However, the Internet only gives voice to people who have access to it, who are able to learn the foibles of both computers and the Internet. In order to really express their voices, these democratic participants need to also be able to develop a website, self-publish writings on a blog, moderate and participate in a Listserv, prepare and distribute podcasts, or edit and post video blogs. The production of and interaction with user-generated content relies on basic computer literacy and comfort with the Internet and related concepts like uploading, downloading, and file sharing. And while many of these functions are increasingly user-friendly—publishing and uploading media is possible with a few clicks and no understanding of coding whatsoever—it is certainly *not* democratic.

Democracy in the true sense is inclusive regardless of class, race, ability, and other issues that oppress people. Although in theory the Internet frees people from cultural and societal constraints that would register if online correspondents were face-to-face with one another, there are barriers to more-diverse populations even getting online to have these kinds of identity-neutral encounters. Though today young black women are getting online at higher rates than people in other demographics,[9] there is still a major gap between the racial and class makeup of the general population and those using the Internet. This disparity is represented throughout this book, as the majority of the avid Internet users I interviewed were young and white with middle-class backgrounds, though many of them fall into the lower-income creative class by virtue of being female, young, and in a position to opt out of "better" ways to make a living. The demographics of the women I interviewed are not just a function of the book being about the Internet, but about the sex work and exploration part of it as well. The study and obsession with sexual pleasure remains the domain of middle-class white women, women for whom other obstacles (like jobs and housing) are not top concerns.

As a woman of color who is interested in these issues of democracy and who wants to enact social change, Pilar sees the Internet as a tool that perpetuates the corporate, white, middle-class hegemony of American consumer culture rather than a tool for revolution. Instead of viewing the Internet as a new outlet for activism that opens up a world of communication, Pilar sees online communication and activism as an escape valve, a way to remove oneself from interactions with people. Although I disagree with her on this point, I'm also very much aware that my ability to see the Internet as revolutionary comes from a place of privilege, in which I can think of the Internet as a sexual, political, and intellectual arena because I'm in a place (geographically and economically) where these are the very things that are my primary focus and concern. Although some of Pilar's criticisms overlap with those technophobes who view the Internet as the devil's playground, her observations come from a very real, intense place of political and personal discomfort with the forging ahead of digital culture and the casualties this "progress" may leave.

Cyborgs and cyberfeminism carry the type of controversy that tends to bring forth the theory monkeys from their philosophical caves—but where does that theory leave us? Are all women who plug in to their computers and log on to the Internet battling with or against something? And must that something have an "ism" at the end of it? Clearly, most women who explore online spaces—whether sexual or not—are not picking their way through Donna Haraway's "Cyborg Manifesto," but reading theory as a backdrop for the hijinks women have been getting up to lately is important because it provides a structure for understanding all the different elements at work. Women who explore their sexuality online tend to be introspective about their doings (or at least the eighty women I interviewed were introspective in their interviews with me), but I suspect that the very act of exploring sexuality online, especially through creating and interacting with user-generated content, brings up social, moral, and cultural questions that lead to introspection and create a high degree of self-awareness and self-reflexiveness.

## Cam Girls: Online in Real Life

The debate over the difference between online and "real life" has been a hot topic since the Internet came to be—and it's still alive and well, even as the Internet has become a nearly ubiquitous presence in people's professional and personal lives. Email, instant messages, and personal blogs, as well as posting and exchanging nude photos, are activities that happen online and not in the physical world. (Though, yeah, keystrokes and mouse clicks are happening in the physical world, if you want to be a smart-ass about it.) Yet, they are real activities that hold real emotional weight for the women involved in them. The division between online and "real life" has worn thin in recent years, if indeed it ever existed. But still, especially with respect to friendships, people tend to distinguish between relationships that are exclusively over the Internet and relationships that are "in real life" (IRL in Internet shorthand). The overlap and interconnection between online and offline life begs the question: Does something have to be physically present and palpable in order to be real?

The answer is more complex than a simple yes or no. Just as documentaries evoke real responses and emotions in their viewers, so do representations of lives, stories, and sexualities on the Internet. While film and television offer a kind of buffer zone between audience and culture makers—you can see them but they can't see you—the Internet breaks down this divide to a great extent, as audience members become participants and producers of online culture in the Web 2.0 world of user-generated content.

Though message boards and chat rooms heralded the participatory culture that's so much a part of online communities as we know them today, the webcam brought things to a whole other level. When webcams first began to nudge their way into Internet culture, they were little more than low-res, refreshable still cameras that were small and durable enough to install in a corner of a room. Early webcams took a picture, or "refreshed," once every thirty to sixty seconds; today many webcams capture moving images or refresh their still images quickly enough to give the illusion of a moving image—albeit choppy. Most Mac laptops now come with a built-in cam, a tiny little eye that can broadcast the computer's user to whomever she chooses to show herself to.

As in many kinds of media, the best way for a cammer to get attention is simple: Be a girl. Internet users, as a population, seem to pay much more attention to girls online for the same reasons girls and women get attention offline—because of the sexual/sexist element of looking at women. We are trained as a culture to girl-watch ("girl" meaning both younger and full-grown women), and the Internet enables that kind of voyeurism on a whole new level. One of the most popular early home/life webcams, JenniCam, was run by Jennifer Ringley, who launched her website and cam in 1996 and maintained it until the end of 2003. Her first domain was Jennicam.org, and after a few years she also bought Jennicam.com.[10]

The site was a chronicle of Jenni's daily life through the entirety of her early twenties. She began running what came to be known as a lifecam, which took pictures of her everyday life twenty-four hours a day, seven days a week from one vantage point, in her dorm room in 1996, when she was a student at Dickinson College. In its earliest incarnation, the site only had one cam, which was set up to take a picture every three minutes. As Jenni's fan base grew—and when she moved out of the dorms and into her own apartment with more than one room in Washington, D.C., she set up more cams to monitor life in the different rooms of the apartment. As a freelance web designer, Jenni spent a lot of time at home and in front of her computer, so much of her life was pictured online. Therefore, most of what was captured online was mundane, often featuring Jenni doing the work that made her website possible—answering emails, designing webpages, and doing server maintenance. At the height of her Internet fame, Jenni reported that her site had three to four million hits a day—and though many of these hits were brief looks at the free sections of her site, some were or became paid subscribers. She was making at least enough to support her lifestyle, which included increasingly nicer furnishings and better living spaces. Though the site started out as a fun web project, it quickly became all-consuming as the traffic to her servers required her to take the cam off her college servers and onto servers dedicated only to her site. When the rising popularity of the site escalated her monthly hosting bills, Jenni began charging for access to a member's section of the site, where image updates were more frequent.

JenniCam and the rise to popularity of other webcams roughly coincided with the emerging popularity of reality television—but with important differences, the fact that Jenni didn't have to go to a casting call being among them. One of the principal differences was that webcams were completely unedited, while reality television shows like *The Real World,* which first aired in 1992, pulled together a week or more of interactions and footage into a tightly edited hour-long weekly episode. There isn't anything especially "real" about condensing a week of life into an hour-long show, but it's a hell of a lot more interesting and dramatic than a webcam that shows life twenty-four hours a day, seven days a week. But the webcam's implicit invitation ("watch me, you know you want to") drew viewers who often became fixated on the cam's subject and who held out for the inevitability of eventually catching something interesting.

One of the concerns that camming raises—some would say confronts—is the issue of surveillance. Though the 1990s saw the increase in popularity of the consumer-grade cam mostly for the purpose of entertainment and titillation, prior to that it had mostly been used as a surveillance tool. It's not uncommon to see signs warning that your activities are being filmed posted in areas where security cams are used, though posting this information isn't required and people are often filmed without their knowledge. A woman who runs a webcam site and interacts with her viewers is obviously doing so consensually, but the issue of privacy persists. In the FAQ page that was on Jenni's site in 1999, she answered the question about privacy by writing, "I don't feel I'm giving up my privacy. Just because people can see me doesn't mean it affects me—I'm still alone in my room, no matter what. And as long as what goes on inside my head is still private, I have all the space I need."[11]

Jenni makes her feelings clear here, and in addition to sharing images of her day-to-day life, she also shared an online journal (when her site first launched, the term "blog" hadn't yet become widely used) with her site's visitors. The difference between the visual and written representation was striking—the cam offered up an unedited look at what Jenni was doing all day, while the journal provided filtered access to her thoughts. But in both mediums Jenni was allowing a level of access to her personal life that seemed like violation to the average person, for whom living a life under the surveillance of millions of unseen people on the Internet was unimaginable.

Though Jenni was focused on simply living her normal life but doing it on cam, other women have explored and experimented with the experience of living their lives on cam in more-direct and sometimes aggressive ways. Ana Voog launched her Anacam in 1997, a little more than a year after JenniCam went online. Ana takes credit for being the first 24/7 art/lifecam; her cam has stood the test of time and has been online for ten years with no signs of stopping. Ana's camming practice is much more stylized than Jenni's was, and because she started her cam at age thirty, her sense of art and self has always been more developed than many of the younger (and in some cases barely legal) women who have flocked to sign up for webcam accounts on a variety of cam hosts in the years since. Ana represents the first generation of cam girls whose cams capture their daily lives in their entirety, and she remains a pioneer in the genre.

While Jenni made it a point to live her normal life and basically ignore the presence of the cam, Ana often orchestrates elaborate performances for her cam, using the many peculiar props she stashes in her apartment. Like Jenni, Ana makes the distinction that the cam allows visitors to see a picture of her life, but doesn't give access to a complete understanding of who she is. On the bio page of her free site, she reminds the visitor that the cam "is not a surveillance thing or a peeping thing, because I have invited you." However, a few sentences after declaring that the images of her don't give the viewer access to her inner life, she says that "sometimes it is more about showing you what is going on *inside* me than what is going on in my actual physical surroundings." Ana's internal contradictions are very much a part of her art. She plays with subjectivity and teases out the complexities of being watched, adored, and puzzled over from a distance.

While Jenni never offered camshows because she thought they were antithetical to the nature of her lifecam, and Ana plays to the camera but doesn't schedule shows, Melissa Gira, whose lifecam went online at her site Beautiful Toxin in late 2000, did scheduled camshows on both her own site and on Nakkid Nerds, an alt porn site. Camshows tend to be associated more with porn performers who are cam girls, but Gira blurred the lines between lifecam, art, and porn in her work. Unlike Jenni and Ana, Gira never made her site into a paid-membership site; instead, she saw the lifecam as an experiment in surveillance and the camshows as an opportunity to make money. Though Jenni and Ana didn't take direct requests from their viewers, Gira sometimes did. The window into a cam girl's life is a one-way portal, but all cam girls have relationships to and with their viewers. "I always had a sort of ambivalent, if not adversarial relationship with my viewers," says Gira.

## Everyday Porn

While neither Jenni nor Ana considered themselves to be the webmistresses of porn sites, and Gira skated the edge of this a bit more, many people have watched their cams obsessively for brief glimpses of the women's sexualities. Both Jenni and Ana agree that because their cams were and are 24/7, it's inevitable that at some point they'll be naked and possibly enjoying sex with a partner. However, they are adamant that the focus of their sites is not erotic—after all, the amount of time they spend engaging in any activity that could be viewed as remotely sexual is a mere fraction of the time they spend doing everything else. Their declarations that sexuality is part of the package and not the main point aside, this is one of the most frequently obsessed-over aspects of homecams. In some respects, this is puzzling—from the time cams first became popular through today, explicit porn has been rampantly available on the Internet, so cam viewers' focus on the erotic aspects of homecams isn't for want of material to fuel masturbatory reveries. Instead, this fixation is likely the result of the obsession with the idea of the girl next door—a good girl who occasionally does bad. The very fact that women who operate lifecams are good girls who go about their lives in an orderly fashion and then occasionally get naked and have sex is what makes these erotic moments all the more appealing to viewers. The degree to which women who operate lifecams have had to be on the defensive about their choice to keep their cams uncensored (hence the entries in their FAQs and blogs that speak to this issue) is indicative of the fact that many people feel conflicted about seeing sexuality as part and parcel of the scope of a woman's life. Porn represents only women's sexual aspects, while many documentary portrayals of day-to-day lives leave it out; lifecams fall somewhere in between, which seems to confuse and even outrage people.

Both Jenni and Ana have spoken out vociferously about the value of uncensored cams, and both are certainly aware that censoring themselves would negatively affect their traffic. However committed each has been to showing sexuality as a slice of life, it remains a complex issue when other people are involved in the sites as well. When Ana announced her pregnancy in late November 2006, she immediately began to think about the ways she could capture the birth with her cams and started asking for viewer and reader feedback to this ethical and logistical question on the LiveJournal she writes in as a supplement to her cam activities. This brought up a number of issues for her—the logistics of bringing cams with her to the hospital, as well as the problems she could face if she shows her birth on a site that has previously been known as a site that sometimes provides sexually explicit content. It's much easier for the viewing public—especially those who criticize cam girls' choices to share the most intimate details of their lives—to hang on to the notion that sex is a nonthreatening part of life when the woman baring it all is a single woman who's responsible for only herself and her own choices.

But bring a baby into the picture, and suddenly people are up in arms about whether a woman who's making homemade porn (even if that's not what the women themselves choose to call it) is fit to be a parent. Suddenly issues of child pornography and abuse are brought into play. Giving birth or breastfeeding a baby on a site that draws the attention of men hoping to catch the cam girl nude or in sexual acts might well be the fodder that critics (and child services) need to launch a crusade against Ana. There's no shortage of moral crusading when it comes to choices that are perceived to be harmful to others—particularly innocent babies. Ana will therefore have to decide how important it is to her to be the test subject for this matter.

## I Can See You: Webcams and Chat

Regardless of the testaments that lifecammers put forth saying that their cams are not mainly about sexuality, people have and will continue to associate cams with sex. This association has plenty to do with nudity, but also has do with intimacy—or at least perceived intimacy. As both Jenni and Ana concur, their cams offer just a slice of their lives—the visual pieces. However, plenty of people use cams to increase both sexual and emotional intimacy with people who they don't get to have "face time" with on a regular-enough basis, either people they know offline and can't see often or people with whom they've developed online relationships. Personal, one-on-one cams often complement text-based chat so that two people can see each other while they write back and forth. These interactions are not always explicit and erotic, but they certainly can be.

For Madeline Glass, a sex blogger and a single mom from the Midwest, the webcam added a human dimension to her 2005 interactions with now-boyfriend Jefferson, who lives in New York. The couple's first point of contact was through their blogs, and their connection evolved through the written word. After several weeks of email, chatting, and reading each other's blogs, Jefferson asked Madeline if she had a cam, because he felt that a key ingredient to building a connection with someone else—eye contact—was missing from their interactions. She did indeed have a webcam, and she accepted his invitation to cam because, she says, "We both wanted to see how the other looked and have conversation that included facial expressions instead of just text."

Though both Madeline and Jefferson are quite adventurous sexually, neither had a desire to get naked and sexual on cam. Madeline says that it "just never seemed that appealing—sexy words are much more interesting anyway." Though they have since had a number of in-person dates and weekends together, their cams remain part of weekly chat dates in which they pour themselves a glass of bourbon and talk about their lives face-to -face. Although the cam is a major part of their interaction, they also sometimes treat it the way that the lifecam girls do. Madeline says, "Sometimes we wouldn't be chatting on cam; we'd just keep it on and go about our business—it's kind of like sharing a desk and working together."

For Madeline and Jefferson, their webcams create what Madeline calls a "private and secret space"—a space of words and images that exists just between them and is transient because neither of them save their chat transcripts or make screen grabs of particular frames of the cam transmissions. Madeline was never interested in webcams before using one to communicate with Jefferson, and she still can't imagine regularly incorporating one into chat with casual online acquaintances, but she appreciates the intimacy it brings her long-distance relationship.

Though also in a long-distance relationship, Pam, who's in her late thirties, uses her webcam in a much more sexual way than Madeline and Jefferson use theirs. Because she and her partner are unable to see each other in person with much frequency, he suggested extending their BDSM relationship into the realm of webcams. After playing with sexy chat and phone sex for a while, Pam's partner, the dominant one in the relationship, bought her a webcam. On the cam, he would ask her to masturbate for him and tell her which of her toys he wanted to see her use. Though Pam got a thrill out of the exhibitionist aspects of the experience—she had never before been naked and looked at without being in close proximity to a lover—ultimately she found the experience less than satisfying. Compared to phone sex or erotic chat, Pam says, "There was much less interaction between us. I felt as though he viewed it as some kind of a video game he was playing, and instead of being interested in my brain and my words, he was only interested in my cunt." Despite this, Pam does think that under the right circumstances, webcamming with a partner could be lots of fun, just not as the primary means of interaction in a relationship.

## Evolution of the Camshow

Lifecams like JenniCam and AnaCam attract people who are acutely interested in the cam girls' sexualities, but in the real time of the cams, daily life and personality take precedence while the rarity of the sexual material adds to its appeal. As with anything remotely sexual, porn producers had their antennae tuned in to lifecams before these types of sites' traffic started to skyrocket. In light of the popularity of homecams, many porn sites added cam features. Some independent performers installed lifecams in their homes or shooting spaces; other sites added the now-ubiquitous scheduled camshows, and entire networks were founded on the basis of cams alone. The porn industry quickly whittled the appeal of cams down to their perceived essence: naked girls doing naughty things to themselves and others. Although adult cams are big business and the Internet is now littered with them, the appeal of lifecams that aren't solely devoted to adult content persists. Try as they might to capture the girl-next-door feel of lifecams, many adult cams are very transparent in their pandering to prurient interest.

One of the largest cam networks, iFriends, was established in 1998 and has grown tremendously since then. Though a quick glance at the iFriends homepage may lead the viewer to believe that adult cams take up only a fraction of the site, it's the cams and their adult material that provide most of the site's profit. The site is membership based, and it hosts cams and provides bandwidth to cammers ("hosts" in the parlance of the site) who sell their time on cam. Women who run cams through the site create a username and build an identity around it. When it comes to camming, the more literal and descriptive the handle the better. Identities based on obscure literary references are better reserved for dating sites. A username is essentially the cam girl's brand. Beyond that, she has her profile, which often includes her sexual (at least professionally) preferences, her physical statistics, and options for contacting her, to advertise herself to potential clients ("guests" in the phrasing of the site). The most populated profile section on iFriends is the "women home alone" section, where potential clients can search by preferred characteristics, like age, build, ethnicity, and amount of body hair. Performers work in two online formats—camshows and private sessions.

Camshows usually last anywhere from thirty minutes to an hour and occur at regularly scheduled intervals. Many women who run their own paysites offer memberships to iFriends as part of their membership package so that their members can attend their scheduled camshows. These shows offer a structured setting in which the woman can interact with many fans at once, text chatting as she performs. The shows generally include anything ranging from costumed role-playing to striptease to explicit play with toys.

Private shows are the much less structured of the two camshow options, and a woman who gives private shows, regardless of whether she runs her own site, can easily log on to iFriends and wait until a customer (usually a guy) expresses interest in "going private." A man's decision to go private is sometimes based on nothing more than the cam girl's profile, but often women need to hustle to get a client to take that step—by offering a little more. This might entail the promise of phone chat or a show that is explicit and caters to a specific fetish. While the fee for camshows is a flat rate, or is included as part of a membership to a performer's site, private shows are paid by the minute—and rates escalate as sex acts get more acrobatic or include things that not every cam girl will do (like anally penetrating herself with toys).

Most of the women who work through iFriends run their cams inside their homes, but the ease of setting up a cam business has also spawned bigger companies that rent out spaces, set up cams, and hire girls to come play online. These businesses, known as cam studios, have mostly shady reputations because they take most of the profits to cover their costs while doling out a fraction of their earnings to the women who spend time naked on cam. Cam studios are easily recognizable because their camming rooms are sparsely furnished and don't look at all lived in (because they aren't). Although this setup is a far cry from the lifecams that inspired this trend, it doesn't necessarily mean the service is bad—just more streamlined and professional. It's a little harder for the cam girl set up in a studio to dupe her customers into believing that she's just a fun-loving college student who happened to find this site and thought it would be a scream to get naked on the Internet.

Although cam sites market the idea that the man can tell a cam girl what to do—the customer, after all, is always right—the reality is that a performer can cut her client off and block him from contacting her again at any time during their session if he gets too pushy or demanding. The exchange of bang for buck is certainly more explicit on cam sites than it is on the paid-membership portions to lifecam sites, but women who do cam shows and women who have lifecams have something in common:

Both have invited viewers into their realm, and they can rescind this invitation if they want to.

Trixie Fontaine, whose career in online porn is extensively detailed in Chapter 4, started her adult industry career on the iFriends network and used the site as a springboard into the world of self-run paysites. While she earned money on iFriends doing private shows, she honed her skills at managing clients and learned web design well enough to launch her own paysite, Tasty Trixie, which then blossomed into several related sites, including SpyOnUs, which now has a 24/7 spy cam that displays the lives of Fontaine and her live-in boyfriend, Tucker. Doing private camshows on iFriends was something of a gateway drug for Fontaine: Though it demanded that she commit to learning basic Internet technology and the best methods for promoting herself online, she didn't have to commit to buying a domain name or developing a website until she was ready. It also helped her to build up a reliable fan base that would follow her links to her new site and (hopefully) sign up for the monthly membership. Her website branched out from being just a cam and now includes regularly updated hardcore photo sets in addition to scheduled camshows and the lifecams that give a window into Fontaine and Tucker's lives.

## For Fun, Profit, and Orgasms

Since personal computing has taken center stage in so many people's everyday lives, and the Internet has created a new space for communication and commerce, women have faced myriad challenges creating and maintaining safe spaces for themselves to explore their own and other people's sexualities, and the lines between exploring sexual expression and commerce have often been blurry. The Internet and its sound-bite-ready, commodification-driven culture and user-generated content creates a tension between commerce and freedom by its very nature. Meanwhile, the so-called Internet "users" are happily producing content that quickly turns into a commercial entity and most often slips away from its producers to become profitable for someone else. This is most true when it comes to representations of women and their sexuality online.

Women avidly use technologies like chat, blogging, and photo- and video-hosting services as recreational ways to explore their sexuality and meet partners for all kinds of sexual play, as well as for relationships. They use these online tools to build and strengthen relationships and to capitalize on their sexuality in big and small ways—from making significant money to maintaining a weekly date with a long-distance lover. But these exact same tools can also endanger relationships if they are abused or used without regard for other people. Chatting and camming with abandon can complicate relationships, especially if those spaces are where most of a relationship is taking place.

User-generated content has seemingly opened up the Internet to many more voices, while also perpetuating the cultural silencing of many more voices—specifically those of women of color. Essentially: Computer technology is a mixed blessing. The very things that are empowering and useful to women can also be harmful and problematic. Yet, using the same technologies for different purposes can't help but make the boundaries between useful and harmful more fluid in ways that are problematic but also empowering.

# HAPTER 2: HOOKUPS, MATCHES, AND SEX PLAY 01

## The Trials and Tribulations of Online Dating

In the past five years, Internet dating has gone from being the domain of desperate people with something to hide to being socially acceptable for people who like to shop for dates the same way they shop for pretty much everything else—on their computer, in their pajamas. With the advent of major mainstream paid dating services like Yahoo! Personals, Match.com.com, and the Spring Street Network, as well as niche services that cater to targeted populations like H-Date (for people with herpes), Adult Friend Finder (for people interested in purely sexual relationships), Lesbotronic (for lesbians), and Alt.com (BDSM personals), a whole new culture of dating and selectivity has emerged.

Then there are the free sites, which have a more ambiguous and sometimes casual nature, like the public boards on Craigslist and the free social networking sites like MySpace, Friendster, and Tribe. These are venues that allow women to experiment with and experience their sexuality in unprecedented ways. Women use many different kinds of sites to experiment with their sexuality, oftentimes starting out on a path of sexual exploration somewhat unintentionally. This is common when women start lurking in communities and blogs that they're curious about or when they participate in chats that may only be tangentially (or not at all) related to sexuality. Dating sites have a clear structure and intent behind them: They are made for people to meet, date, and have sex with each other. However, there are plenty of spaces beyond these clear, commercial enterprises that welcome and foster deliberately vague intentions.

Seeking relationships (I use "relationships" in the broadest sense—any kind of interpersonal interaction between people, whether it's a date or a lifetime) online pushes women to articulate their needs and desires in the hallmark of membership sites: the profile. Personal profiles, whether for dating sites or some other kind of site (high-profile blogs, for instance, increasingly require profiles of their commenters), provide a (sometimes) carefully crafted snapshot of who a person is through text and photos, and increasingly through short voice and video recordings. Profiles are infinitely updatable, so if something in a person's life changes (like hair color or religion), she can change her profile to reflect that. Or, if a dating profile isn't getting hoped-for results, it can be recrafted to emphasize different aspects of her personality.

Though dating professionals have long given the somewhat ridiculous advice of approaching a first date the way you would a job interview, this notion of putting your best foot forward has become infinitely more like public relations in the age of online dating, as online daters are encouraged to pitch themselves and put a spin on their assets that makes them appear enticing. The signals someone sends through an online profile are intentionally composed to reflect the person that any given poster would like to be seen as. As much as this is true of in-person interactions, online profiles offer posters the opportunity to choose to conceal or reveal things that are more immediately obvious in person (like height), or only obvious after more-intimate interactions (like sexual tastes). Beyond the basic statistics of the profile, which typically include age, height, weight/body type, hair and eye color, education, religion, and smoking and drinking habits, most sites also provide more free-form spaces where the profile writer can enhance her description of herself and get across a broader picture of what she's like. At the very least, these essay-encouraging spaces prompt something to the effect of "a little more about me" and "what kind of person I'm looking for," though websites also pose other creative questions that encourage witticisms, like Spring Street Network's "Best or worst lie I ever told" and "Five things I can't live without." Each category is searchable, which means that online daters can select the desired characteristics of their ideal date, plug those things in to their dating service of choice, enter their geographical requirements, and be rewarded with the profiles of people who match that description in their chosen area. Or not—depending on how specific the demands and where they live.

Susan Mernit, an executive at Yahoo! Personals, says that "16 percent of people who use the Internet use online dating services," and that online dating is "targeted behavior": People go into it with a goal and usually a time frame for achieving that goal. Despite the claims of success from sites like eHarmony, which boasts a high marriage rate among people who meet through its services (though it also advertises marriage counseling on its homepage), it's pretty impossible to figure out what percentage of people who have profiles on dating sites actually go on to meet potential dates in person.

Estimates for the ratio of men to women on dating sites vary from fifty/fifty to seventy/thirty, and though it's difficult to confirm a precise ratio, according to Mernit, men and women use dating sites differently. While women tend to carefully consider matches before approaching them, or wait for men to approach them if they haven't shaken traditional ideas of who should do the pursuing, men tend to cast their net wide and contact many women, often without scrutinizing the match statistics very closely. For this reason, women tend to find online dating frustrating. They often feel that their efforts at carefully crafting a profile that represents them go ignored. Men also express frustration with online dating, but for different reasons: They feel that it's next to impossible to get a woman to even write back to them. It can be exhilarating, though, just like real-life dating. As with in-person interactions, the choice to accept or reject a suitor's advances rests with the person who is being contacted, so for women who are in this position—since women are usually the ones who get to make this choice, the thrill of being pursued and desired is enough to keep them at it.

Though these patterns of dating assume a heterosexual model, women who are not straight, vanilla, or traditional in any way also use the Internet to facilitate meeting like-minded and like-desired people. Online dating is especially powerful for women whose desires or life situation makes it difficult for them to meet viable partners in person: older women who are divorced and out of the practice of dating, women with particular sexual tastes and fetishes, women interested in or already involved in polyamory. Shandee, a recently out lesbian in her midtwenties who lives in rural Ohio, says, "On the Internet it's easier to meet people. Where I live, the bi/lesbian population is few and far between." For Shandee and others like her, the Internet offers a safe space to explore desires—oftentimes providing a venue to explore before a person is completely ready to act on them. Speaking about her process of coming out, she says, "When I was in a relationship with a man, I had to lay it all out to the women I was talking to online. I was confused about my sexuality, and I wanted to resolve it. But they had to have the understanding I wasn't ready to make any life-changing decisions at that moment."

Dating through the Internet is also useful for people who have a clearly delineated idea of what they want and need out of an encounter. Jean, a woman in her twenties who lives in Boston and is involved in BDSM, says, "I have a relatively unusual hobby and sexual proclivity: I like to tie people up and hurt them. On the Internet, I can readily find people whose desires complement my own. This isn't my sole reason to use the web for dating, because there are events for people who do BDSM to get to know one another. However, online etiquette permits more bluntness and encourages greater precision than one generally sees offline, even at kink events." Instead of going the standard route of meeting people and then piecing together their sexual tastes and sussing out whether they are a good match, online dating allows these women to be forthcoming about their proclivities. For women whose desires are viewed as abnormal or outside of the mainstream, the Internet fosters a certain level of comfort and creates spaces in which they know that they won't be rejected for their most basic desires.

The Internet, of course, offers its own unique space for rejection. Because women are often socialized to please, and because many do genuinely take pleasure in doing so, it's sometimes difficult for women to say no, especially to positive attention. Even if women don't start out with the intention of becoming attention hogs, sometimes all the online attention can stroke their egos and become a source of pride and self-esteem. Revealing and sultry photos encourage this attention, and most women who use sexy photos in their profile, regardless of their shape and size, do get a lot of short and to-the-point messages of the "u r hott!" variety. These messages might seem trite and irritating to some, but plenty of women find them flattering and exciting.

It's true, however, that many women find it easier to say no to unwanted suitors online. And some women, like Shandee, prefer the Internet for this reason: "It's easier to deny people who you know won't work. I've had bad experiences with this in person, which is why I prefer to use the Internet." Whereas the Internet makes it easier for women to do the rejecting, it also makes it easier for them to take rejection. Women have increasingly begun to approach men on dating sites because they feel that the risk of rejection is less humiliating in an online space. Many of the women I interviewed told me that it's much easier to deal with rejection online, where they don't have to make eye contact with someone who is clearly not interested in them; some even suggested that they pretend there isn't a real person on the other end of the exchange. Certainly one way to assure self-protection.

Although so far I've been writing about people meeting on the Internet under the auspices of "dating," the Internet holds opportunities for women seeking many different kinds of relationships: the serious, long-term types that may lead to marriage and babies, short-term types that are based around fun and don't involve emotional commitment, relationships structured around the mutual desire for sex or other kinds of play, and, of course, relationships that begin with one set of intentions and evolve into something different. Though people who pay to use sites like Yahoo! Personals and Match.com profess to have particular goals in mind for their online dating adventures, goals can certainly shift over time, and many people move between several different modes of partner seeking, where serious dating, casual sex hookups, and nonsexual social interactions overlap.

Just as a woman may shop online for items she might be too embarrassed to buy at a brick-and-mortar store (like crotchless panties, fist-shaped dildos, and porn), many women "shop" online for the kinds of sex they might not have the courage to ask for when they meet partners in other contexts. Kis Lee, a thirty-year-old Asian woman who lives in the San Francisco Bay Area, began to explore her sexuality via the Internet in her midtwenties. She started out using chat rooms for reasons that weren't explicitly sexual—she wanted to meet new people—but then progressed to sites like Adult Friend Finder (commonly referred to as AFF) and Alt.com to meet people for sex and BDSM play, about which she says, "I would say that my experiments with AFF and Alt.com were like my sexual awakening. I went from being really dorky and shy to being more comfortable about my body and sexuality. I seriously doubt that would have happened without the

Internet. The computer was like my filter to the outside world. I could be as sexy, flirty, and kinky as I wanted to be without being self-conscious about whether I looked dumb or desperate." The Internet wasn't just a portal for Lee; it also provided spaces where she could try on sexiness for size and learn about what suited her tastes and desires, without worrying about how she was perceived by others.

## Free-Form Socializing

Membership-based dating sites aren't the only places where people meet each other online. Just like in life offline, Internet users who aren't explicitly looking for love or sex meet people online in various ways who turn out to be promising potential dates and hookups. It's not unusual for people who are engaged in groups structured around their interests—whether that be knitting, robots, or collecting soap dishes—to end up talking and flirting with someone they meet on those forums. However, regardless of the type of community—and this was especially true in the 1990s—chat rooms are overwhelmingly populated by men. Therefore, once a woman (or a man posing as a woman) enters the space, she's bombarded by messages.

Kis Lee spent a year exploring chat rooms before formally joining Alt.com. She enjoyed the attention she got in those chat rooms to a certain extent, saying, "I could just pick and choose from the comfort of my home." In 2000, when Lee first started using chat rooms, online dating seemed a bit taboo to her. Her friends thought it was weird, so chatting and developing online relationships seemed like a compromise that would satisfy her curiosity without stepping too far out of bounds. It wasn't too long before chatting led to a meeting, and to dating and having sex with a man she met through AOL Instant Messenger. It was in the course of her conversations with him that an interest in BDSM and bondage play was sparked, spurring Lee on to sign up for Alt.com, mainly with the intent of meeting kinky friends who shared her proclivities.

Paige, a mom and academic in her thirties, first got online in the mid-1990s. Though she was married at the time, and not seeking out in-person meetings, she was immediately drawn to text-based chatting. She was fascinated by the ways people in sexually oriented chats expressed allure and attempted seduction. She says, "Sometimes I hit it off with guys who were more witty and verbal. I would catch people's attention because I had a good command of language. I met a guy who was an English teacher and married, and he would confess things to me."

The Internet allows a confessional kind of honesty because of the exhilaration of offering up secrets without direct, real-life consequences, but it also makes it easy for users to conceal things about themselves. For many people, this is about experiencing the world in a different way. Online role-playing can take many forms: It can happen as straight-out lying about age, height, weight, or marital status, or it can be without the intention of hurting someone. On the worst end of the spectrum are people who disguise themselves to lure underage children into compromising situations; on the more fun end are those who are simply posing as someone else for the sake of having harmless conversation and engaging in fantasy role-play.

Paige, for example, engaged in some chat room conversations posing as a gay man—a role she could clearly never pass for in life offline—and claims that this gave her permission to be more direct in her sexual encounters. It also allowed her to fantasize in the realm of the cerebral, leaving her body behind. She was able to break free of what being a woman means for her and to others. Although this kind of fantasy can be liberating, it can also have the consequence of revealing the limits of other people's sexual imaginations. This is what happened to Paige, in fact, emphasizing the fact that even in a space that could theoretically be free from the constraints of sexual scripts and assumptions, gender roles are firmly adhered to. Paige found that gay men gruffly cyber-bang each other like men are "supposed to," with little small talk or other encouragement, while men woo women with flowery language that they probably assume the women want to hear.

The out-of-body experience that the Internet provides can help quell anxieties about actual bodies and assist an explorer in tapping in to the biggest and best sexual organ: the brain. Although bodily experiences aren't completely impossible online—after all, no one's stopping you from touching yourself— being free from the assumptions people make based on bodies offline all but disappear online. At the same time, people carry their baggage with them wherever they go, so online explorations are limited by the sexual and social imaginations of the people doing the exploring.

After her marriage broke up and she moved to a new state, Paige put a profile up on Match.com and met three different guys through the site. But it would ultimately turn out to be

Paige's other foray into online culture—a discussion group for geeks and hackers—where she met her current partner. Paige was attracted to Cameron for the same reasons she was drawn to other men she'd had encounters with online—for his intellect and well-crafted writing. For several years, Paige and Cameron forged a relationship over a six-thousand-mile physical divide, keeping weekly voice-chat dates when they'd read each other sections of books they were interested in and then discuss the books and life. "It was like regular dating, but we were six thousand miles apart," Paige says, "and we'd wear headphones and share our lives with each other. The things we did online and now in real life ended up being very much the same: We'd talk while cooking dinner, watch movies, read." Though the physical aspect of the relationship wasn't possible in the beginning, they found that there were many other ways to express themselves and be sexual. They never used webcams due to the fact that Paige just didn't find them as sexy as the written and spoken word.

## Reach Out and Fuck Someone

Paige and Cameron's online interactions—both sexual and nonsexual—were affected by the context of their larger relationship, which has been as loving and supportive offline as it was online. The portrait of their relationship seems mundane, and many relationships initiated online are just that. But what about all the raunchy emails and florid descriptions of desire? Well, the fact is that sex and relationships online are as varied as relationships offline. They're not all about pornographic desires, though certainly there are plenty of people whose online relationships with the objects of their desires are exclusively down and dirty. And for those folks, sex is often the sole focus of their relationships.

In many ways, sex online, often called cybersex, is a natural progression of phone sex, because it uses available technology for the purposes of sexual interaction. Unlike phone sex, cybersex doesn't have to happen in real time. People who are separated by many time zones can write each other dirty emails at any hour. However, for people who like instant gratification, there are a variety of instant message and chat programs that do the trick. Instant messaging affords some privacy and one-on-one contact, while chat rooms are more public and can become group play spaces. If things start to heat up in a public chat between two users, they can do the equivalent of "getting a room" and can either move their chat into an instant message program or create a private room within the chat for just the two of them. Sex online is, generally speaking, much less conspicuous than phone sex. The only sound one needs to make is the clacking of keys on a keyboard, whereas the words and sounds of phone sex are difficult to conceal if someone's trying to be discreet. Anonymous email accounts and instant message handles also make cybersex easier for the person with something to hide—or for a person who's hearing impaired.

Sex conducted through emails and instant messages is a lot like phone sex in other respects. It tends to be richly descriptive of fantasies and tactile sensations. The basic rule is this: If you're not there to do it yourself, you should be able to describe what you would be doing very thoroughly. This descriptiveness doesn't come easily to everyone, not only because there are cultural taboos around talking about sex and giving voice to desires, but also because describing sex can feel downright silly, especially if you're used to just doing it. "Now I'm running my fingers lightly up your leg toward your wet pussy" taken out of context is just giggle-inducing. Cybersex is an adventure best undertaken by people with a decent sense of anatomy, as well as a good vocabulary.

## Craigslist: From Text to Sex

Craigslist, the website with the eleventh-highest hit count on the English-speaking Internet, is considered by many to be the mother lode of the erotic free-for-all experience. Because posting a personal ad is completely free and requires little or no premeditation or spell-checking, and because posters can post anonymously (which essentially means they aren't accountable for anything they say), Craigslist is a playground for people's most basic desires. If female posters, profile makers, and chat room participants are bombarded by suitors in other forums, women on Craigslist experience this onslaught on a whole new level. Depending on the city and what she's seeking, a woman can expect to get several hundred responses to a posting, most of which will be short emails stating the responder's stats (e.g., six feet, white, brown/blue, eight inches cut, athletic) and probably suggesting what kinds of things he can do to her.

There are several different personals boards on Craigslist where women can post: W4M (women for men, for dating and serious relationships), W4W (lesbian and bisexual women interested in both dating and casual hookups), Misc Romance (your guess is as good as mine), and Casual Encounters (wanton free-for-all for all genders and orientations). Despite the variation of these boards, the emails from responders in all categories are remarkably similar. The fact that men quite often reply to W4W postings highlights the totally indiscriminate nature of some men's search for potential dates and hookups. The effects of this are something of a self-perpetuating problem: The more men respond to postings where the mismatch is obvious, the more women (if they are even looking for a man) get frustrated by men's responses, and the less likely they are to respond, which means that the men's chances decrease, increasing *their* frustration and tendency to say, "Ah, fuck it—I'll go with quantity and I'm bound to hit the jackpot eventually."

For their part, men who hope to meet someone on Craigslist are often wary of the process and of the validity of the ads. It's ridiculously common for men to respond to a woman's posts by asking her if she's "real." Whether it's due to Craigslist urban myth or personal experience, lots of men assume that the vast majority of Craigslist postings are either made by porn companies or girls looking to make a quick buck. Also prevalent among the stereotypes of people who frequently post on Craigslist are gay men trying to ensnare a horny and desperate straight man (which I am told works more often than you might think) and men posing as women because they are curious to see what kinds of emails women receive. So really, you can't blame those men for assuming that there's probably only a small majority of "real" women posting personals.

Like many women, Ruth was hesitant to try Craigslist, though she'd been meeting people on JDate—a dating site specifically for Jewish people—before moving to New York City from Michigan in 2003. "JDate seemed to me to be the safest place to meet someone for what I was hoping to be a pretty sterile experience. But CL was not for sterile experiences," she says. Though the lack of "sterility," as Ruth puts it, was what deterred her from exploring Craigslist initially, it ultimately proved to be the very reason she was drawn to the site when she got to Manhattan.

Lanie, a thirty-three-year-old from Missouri who's an avid Craigslist user, agrees that the site is edgier than other dating sites but, she says, "Because it's anonymous and people can post ads for just about anything, it's both liberating and scary. Like, if I wanted to have someone to come over and piss on my floor and then let me spank them while they cleaned it up, I could." Though Lanie has had her share of adventures, part of the reason she's drawn to Craigslist are the infinite prospects for hooking up that she'll probably never pursue. The immediacy of Craigslist and the fact that it requires no membership and no profile is appealing as well. So although both Lanie and Ruth express trepidation about Craigslist, they also acknowledge the importance of their own responsibility for making the experience safer—by doing a quick background check on their suitors using whatever information they provide and doing a simple Google search.

Lanie and Ruth have both used paid online dating services in addition to Craigslist. Still, Craigslist maintains its appeal not just because it's free, but also because its users can write whatever they want in the posting field, using as many or as few words as they feel inclined to write. The boards are staff- and community-moderated, so there is some degree of control over what gets posted. However, the anonymity, combined with the fact that there is no requirement that a photo be included in a given post (though there is an increasing expectation on this front), continues to make the site appealing to people who love the written word. I'm not trying to claim that the majority of the site's users are literary giants, but Craigslist does attract people who prefer the written to the visual, perhaps mostly because of the promise of anonymity that a text-based site provides and that photographs deny, no matter how abstract or grainy. Lanie is one of the people who finds words more stimulating than images and says, "I prefer the text nature to the pics and vids features of other sites. I think they gunk up the purpose of the thing. I want to know about a person first. And if I want to see a cock shot, I'll ask for one."

Originally, all casual encounters on Craigslist, including paid ones, were listed in the Casual Encounters section of the website. But starting in 2004, a separate "Erotic Services" section was established after the community complained about the excessive use of Casual Encounters by women who were seeking "generous" men to keep them company. Even with the addition of the Erotic Services board, things get stirred up on Casual Encounters due to the fact that there are still women who post looking for generous men, and that plenty of men mention that they can be generous, or suggest that a shopping trip could be part of an encounter. The kinds of encounters that many men on Casual Encounters are seeking are of the "no strings attached" variety, the kind of encounter that would be quite simple to have with a sex worker. So the fact that they'd rather find these women on Casual Encounters can stem from their desire to get a more "real" experience with a so-called civilian, even though there's no way to know what a woman on the other end of a post is really trolling for. Many men would balk at being called johns and prefer to think of their desires as well-intentioned, noncommercial fun. Some even express revulsion at the suggestion that they might consider hiring a sex worker for the type of fun they're looking for. This might sound unscrupulous, but I admit that even when I'm not looking for action, I peruse Craigslist's Casual Encounters and occasionally jump into the fray and suggest that the sexually frustrated men on the boards hire a professional. The resulting flame wars and degree to which the men take umbrage at this suggestion is hilarious, but also telling: Men who don't pay for sex see themselves as entitled to Craigslist hookups. Though their sense of entitlement might be particular to Craigslist, it's likely that these types of outbursts are probably reflective of the way most men on any dating sites feel. They don't want to be seen as trolling for free sex, even if that's exactly what they're doing.

Though Craigslist can in fact function as a dating site and is not just intended for casual hookups, the focus on the casual sex aspect of the site stems from the fact that the site is really based on an impulse-buy mentality: The poster has a desire, acts on it by posting about it, and hopes for the best and quickest outcome possible. Lots of sex workers use the site on slow days, and I've talked to plenty of women who confirm that this impulse-buy mentality is helpful for their business; men who find them on Craigslist want to see them immediately, while men who seek out sex workers via other forums are generally more patient. Thus Craigslist, even in the forums that present themselves as being spaces for more-serious dating ads, lends itself to the person who wants immediate results, which is less often (but not never) conducive to more-serious dating endeavors.

## Social Networking:
## The Dating Sites That Weren't

Online social networking, in the broadest sense, involves any space where people congregate and interact around common interests. Each community is structured differently and functionality varies, but the spaces can include instant messengers (AOL IM is considered to be its own realm of social networking), chat rooms, message boards, blogs, personal profiles, and the ability to "friend" other users and gain access to their profiles as well as their friends' profiles.[1] Some social networking communities are business oriented, while others are purely social, though increasingly there is a bleed between the two as the trend shifts toward job recruiters opting to search social networks to see what potential hires are up to in their free time.

According to Susan Mernit, casual social networking through chat rooms and free sites like Craigslist, MySpace, and Tribe usually doesn't meet the needs of those who are particularly goal oriented in finding a romantic match. Rather, these sites provide spaces for women to flirt with people and, moreover, to flirt with the idea of meeting someone without actually investing money or creating a profile explicitly designed to attract people they would like to meet in person. Unlike people who pay for memberships on dating websites, people who use social networking sites usually don't have a clear goal. Like Kis Lee's experience in opting to use instant messenger because of the stigma she felt was attached to dating sites, some women explore social networking sites as a way to avoid owning up to being an online dater; being a member of a community that isn't explicitly about dating or sex is an easy way to mask one's true intentions or curiosities about dating and sex online.

Free sites also create opportunities for the ever-popular online activity: browsing. Browsing on interactive websites is often called "lurking," which refers to the activity of a member of the community (or someone who is not a member but views whatever pages are available to them) who does not make his or her presence known but pays close attention to what is unfolding within a given community.

Tribe, like Craigslist, was founded in San Francisco, and to this day caters very much to the Bay Area and events surrounding the communities there, despite the fact that it's coded to direct visitors to a URL with the nearest relevant city according to a visitor's location: So when a person from Austin, Texas, types tribe.net into her browser, she gets redirected to http://austin.tribe.net/welcome. Though the site has personal profiles and allows members to contact one another privately, the bulk of the site's interactions occur in groups (tribes) that are structured around interests as diverse as polyamory (6,597 members), Mountain Dew (25 members), alternative money and economics (644 members), and entomology (190 members). Tribes about relationships and dating primarily act as support networks, and especially in the case of highly active groups like the simply named Polyamory Group, have frequent posts by both women and men about their relationship conundrums. However, members of these tribes also meet one another in person. Just like Paige and Cameron's relationship evolved from their interaction on a hacker message board, individuals may continue a thread of a conversation privately and ultimately decide that they want to meet.

On sites like MySpace, which revolve more heavily around the personal profile and claims to have hit ten million members in August 2006, friendship networks and links between people are paramount. Ostensibly, a user can meet a friend of a friend through MySpace and be secure in the knowledge that the friend once removed is a good person to know. Since the site is full of comments and other visible interactions that make relationships traceable, it can also feel a lot safer.

Though the stated goal of sites like MySpace is to meet people, regardless of whether the relationships become real-life interactions or remain online, one of the common uses for the site is to keep tabs on other members. It's unlikely that too many people would admit that this is their principal reason for using the site, but plenty of people use MySpace to look up past and present boyfriends, girlfriends, or partners. Sometimes referred to as "the soft stalk," looking up partners can help a woman piece together information about someone she's interested in, or find out what someone she used to know is up to. In many cases it can instigate anxieties that may or may not be valid. Flirty comments left by strangers or not-so-far-removed exes can blow the cover on indiscretions, give the seeker more information than he or she was ready for or really need to know about their date, and stir up completely unfounded paranoia.

In addition to lurking around the profiles of current and former dates, women use profile searches to dredge up information on people they are only considering dating. For some women, what they find on a potential date's profile could be a turnoff. "I met this guy, and he gave me his email address," says Una, an urban single girl in her early twenties. "So of course

I looked him up on MySpace. His profile was awful—the design was so bad I could hardly read it, and his writing was almost unintelligible." Una ultimately decided that the profile was a deal breaker for her, and she didn't go out with him, though she also couldn't admit to him why.

For many profile lurkers and potential dates, the most telling piece of someone's profile, other than whether there are pictures of the person tangled up in someone else, is how they answer the "relationship status" question. On nearly all profiles, members must select an option that best describes their situation from a drop-down menu, which is sometimes—but not always—straightforward. On MySpace, the gray-area options include "swinger," while Friendster allows options like "open marriage" and "it's complicated." This selection is important for the potential date, but it's also often scrutinized when a couple is in the early and intermediate stages of dating. Nowadays it's not uncommon that a couple's discussion of their relationship status includes how they're representing their relationship on their nondating profiles. Since people regularly maintain social networking profiles when they're in relationships, this means having to engage in conversation about what to do with their profiles on dating sites. Online relationship status can be a source of stress in a breakup too: While some people switch their status to single as soon as they call it quits, others wait a while to mourn the loss of their relationship. Either way, former partners who check their exes' profiles are sometimes surprised to find that they've returned to single status so quickly; some have even gotten confirmation of a relationship's demise by observing the previously unknown "single" status of their partner.

But there is a real danger that these status markers can be easily overanalyzed or read the wrong way. Ruth, a twenty-five-year-old woman who has met most of her friends online, says that she regularly checks in on her friends' profiles. Once, she saw that a close friend had changed her status to "in a relationship" on MySpace. She immediately called her up and found out that her friend had gotten sick of warding off messages from guys who saw that she was available and changed her status in the hopes that her profile would not show up in searches for single women and that she'd be spared some of the more ridiculous emails. Social networking, whether it's used to date or conduct surveillance missions on people, plays a major role in online courtship, regardless of what kind of encounter a person is looking for.

## The Dating Game

Free chatting, networking, and online profiles are an essential part of the online dating industry, and though the industry itself doesn't see these activities and ways of interacting as part of the targeted behavior function of their sites, they're becoming an important part of dating websites. While all free services feature advertisements that are spattered throughout the pages where members interact, and there are lots of ways to measure that the click-through rate on some of those ads is high, community members aren't proven spenders in online communities—yet. Free social networking sites are oftentimes part of an exploratory process for people who might ultimately get more involved in (read: pay for) online dating services. Many of the people who use free sites like MySpace are young. Internet trend watchers think that the average age of most MySpace users is seventeen to nineteen, while users who pay for memberships on dating sites are older, though their age varies depending on the specifics of the site and its target population. It's too soon to tell whether young MySpace users will graduate to different online communities, or whether the site itself will change as its users get older.

The basic structure of paid-membership dating sites is similar to profile-based social networking sites like MySpace—or vice versa, since dating websites came before the free networking sites. Yet, as many free sites as there are, and as much as people love their free stuff, the paid online dating services market is enormous. According to a study done by the Online Publishers Association (OPA), in 2005 personals and dating websites exceeded their 2004 revenue from subscriptions, though for the first time since the OPA started tracking the revenues in 2001, consumers spent more money on entertainment and lifestyles than dating sites.[2] However, it's important to note that adult website sales and memberships were not included in the study. When dating sites began to be launched a decade ago, some sites permitted profile browsing by nonmembers, but today the vast majority of sites require curious people to sign up and fully complete their profile before they're permitted to search other members. While signing up and creating a profile is free on most sites, a visitor is usually prompted to purchase a membership in order to contact other members and oftentimes to receive and respond to messages as well.

## Vanilla Love

Match.com is one of the most oft-cited examples of an online dating community. Founded in 1998, it's now consistently rated by Alexa Internet, a web-data-analysis site, in the top 150 most highly trafficked sites on the Internet. Match.com has also made ties with media beyond the Internet, having hired pop psychologist and self-styled television self-help guru Dr. Phil to dole out his special brand of "get real" love advice. The site, which claims more than eight million members, boasts that it has "inspired twice as many matches as any other dating site." The initial level of membership to the site is free, though potential users have to set up a profile and fill out the required questionnaire before they can search and browse other profiles. On MySpace, a nonmember can see a member's profile (though not their blog posts, pictures, or videos), but on dating sites no content is available without at least setting up a free profile.

Match.com profiles are multifaceted and give several different levels of searchable information, ranging from "match words" to basic stats to short free-form prompted essays in which members express their personalities more fully. Like many dating sites, Match.com has more than one way to contact a person you're interested in: by email message or a "wink." Winks can be sent by both paid members and free members as a way to suggest that the wink receiver should check out the sender's profile and send a message if there's interest. This intermediary form of expressing interest, which falls somewhere between lurking and sending a message, was designed specifically with women in mind. Though women feel increasingly comfortable being the pursuers of dates online, many still have hesitations and prefer to be sought out. The wink gives women the chance to let men know they're interested without having to go out on a limb and risk the rejection of the dead space following a well-composed email that's never replied to. The wink also serves as a hook for people with profiles who haven't committed to being paid members yet.

Ostensibly for safety and security reasons, but mainly to keep members' correspondences and business on the site, messages go to an inbox that's part of Match.com itself. Posting an email address within a profile quickly gets a red flag from the site's administrators, and in some cases is cause for termination of a membership. However, once potential matches feel comfortable, they can exchange offsite contact information in stages: an IM handle, a private email address, links to other online profiles and projects, and a phone number. Graduating from one comfort level to the next is part of how people go through the process of deciding whether to meet.

Unscrupulous business practices have long been rumored on Match.com and other major dating sites; some of these scams are initiated by the sites themselves, some perpetuated by the sites' members. Match.com has been accused of maintaining profiles with images of very attractive people bought through stock photography houses and using these profiles to contact users with a wink or a message toward the end of the subscriber's billing cycle. The hope is that the subscribers will feel seduced instead of discouraged and will keep their membership for at least another month. The most common subscriber-created scam is often pulled over on men, by so-called "Russian mail-order bride" agencies that are essentially advertising women who need green cards as potential mates. Men are seen as more susceptible to this kind of scam because women very rarely contact men directly through the site, and the attention—especially from a beautiful woman—is welcome.

Women who use Match.com and don't have overly precise needs feel safe on the site, and like Gwenyfyar, a middle-aged woman who lives in the rural Southwest, feel that looking for a relationship online is valuable. Gwenyfyar says, "It's on my time, my terms, and it allows me to meet available men—which is incredibly difficult where I live." Jo, a twenty-eight-year-old East Coast city-dweller, confesses that the thing she likes most about meeting people online is that "you can gauge a person's intellect, to a point, via their spelling, grammar, and general sentence structure. I know, that makes me sound like such a boring nerd lover, but really, I just like someone who can hold their own in a conversation, and the Internet allows you to find out how much you have in common with someone on the scholarly level relatively quickly." In other words, the Internet allows women to be picky in ways that are largely structured around personal deal breakers.

While certainly there are plenty of deal breakers in offline interactions, there are things that may pass unnoticed or be concealed longer in person that are glaring faults online (though to be fair, the opposite is also true). Online profiles usually contain drop-down menu items for details like whether a person smokes or has children. Though people can and do lie about such things, if a profile holder is honest and a potential dater searches according to their preferences on these subjects, an incompatible match can be quickly eliminated. So in many ways, people who use and advocate online dating services feel like things that would be deal breakers can be avoided upfront.

Though Match.com remains an online dating superpower, new sites with features that are culled from other kinds of online social networks have begun to crop up and pull customers away from the more traditional sites (if something less than ten years old can be called traditional). Engage.com, which was beta-launched in June 2005, combines elements of a more traditional dating site (like searchable profiles) with features that social networking sites with younger memberships employ (including the linking of profiles to one another as "friends," as well as a member-rating system). Creating friendships on social networking sites can give women a level of comfort. As with MySpace, the knowledge that someone they know or trust knows someone they're considering dating makes the whole prospect feel safer. With the intention of adding to comfort, but also perhaps inadvertently creating more anxiety, Engage also includes a rating system under the headline "reputation." A user's reputation is based on his or her responsiveness to messages, politeness in responses, and the degree to which he or she is "as advertised." Though the degree of accountability and "realness" these features add to online dating is significant, they also leave much room for error and badmouthing. As it becomes increasingly difficult to remain anonymous online, sites like Don't Date Him Girl, where women band together against lousy dates to warn other women to steer clear, can save women a lot of heartache—but they can also allow a bitter and vindictive ex to ruin someone's online reputation.

## My Life as a Niche Market

Though none of the above sites explicitly shun people who belong to a niche market, they don't cater to them either. "Niche" on the Internet can mean anything from a sexual taste or fetish to a health condition or sex partner preference that a person may structure his or her purchases around. It's a somewhat challenging term because it creates a sharp split between mainstream dating websites like Match.com and the smaller, more specialized sites. The existence of niche sites can actually create more of an obstacle to getting dates than people might think because, depending on the site, it presupposes that people who are inclined toward certain behaviors and preferences do indeed *need* a space where they can encounter like-minded people—creating a sense that perhaps they will be bombarded with messages on mainstream sites to the effect of "Isn't there a place for you people?"

Match.com, for example, allows its members to search for same-sex matches, but the site is heavily geared toward heterosexuals. Bisexuals don't visibly exist on Match.com; you can't search for men and women at the same time. Dr. Phil's advice is rarely inclusive of gays and lesbians, and is heavily focused on the goal of marriage, which isn't legal for gays and lesbians in many places anyway. Other mainstream sites like eHarmony don't even allow people to search for same-sex partners. Shandee, an Ohio lesbian, has recently started using the free lesbian personals site Lesbotronic, in addition to several other nonlesbian sites like MySpace and Yahoo! Personals. Because she has a daughter and is not overwhelmingly social to begin with, all of Shandee's dates originate on the Internet, and she sees personals with a specifically lesbian audience as a great help. Though Lesbotronic is in its infancy and doesn't have the high membership of the other sites Shandee uses, the membership population is much more likely to actually have things in common with her. Like other lesbians on mainstream sites, Shandee has been approached far too many times by men who are interested in threesomes, fetishize lesbians, or simply don't read her profile and assume that all women on the site are looking for men. Though Lesbotronic, like any site, isn't foolproof—a man could pose as a woman to sign up for the site— the community caters directly to the women she wants to meet, so the site plays into her preferences and makes the occasional man-poseur worth dealing with.

Online dating services are also created around communities that need support because they are shunned by the dating community at large. Such is the case with people who have memberships on STD Singles, a website for people who have incurable sexually transmitted infections (STIs) like herpes, HIV/AIDS, human papilloma virus (HPV), and all three strains of hepatitis. Many of these infections are quite common in the general population: Around 80 percent of sexually active people have had one of the one hundred strains of HPV at some point in their lives, and about 20 percent of the population have genital herpes. However, many people who are infected show no symptoms, and as a result don't know they are infected, and so the vast majority of STI carriers mingle with the so-called "general population." But really, STI carriers *are* the general population. Members of sites like STD Singles are a very particular subset of STI carriers: people who not only know they have an STI but are proactive about it and feel that they should be honest with their partners about it. Though it's difficult to pinpoint statistics since the issue is surrounded with secrecy, shame, and misinformation, it's likely that plenty of STI carriers do not tell their partners that they're infected. Unless the infected person is having an outbreak (as with herpes), if safer sex practices are employed, the likelihood of transmission is very low, while the likelihood of rejection by casual sex partners and new dates is fairly high if an infected person chooses to disclose. STD Singles creates a separate dating space that can delude STI-free people into thinking that the population they interact with on other websites is clean, or in online dating lingo "D/D free" (drug and disease free), when this might not at all be the case. Still, these types of sites provide an important support network for people with STIs.

Niche sites like Lesbotronic and STD Singles give both a real and illusory sense of security to the women who use them. Though these communities are designed for particular kinds of people, that doesn't prevent outsiders from invading the community, just as people who belong to a niche market aren't barred from more general-interest communities. That said, curiosity may lure outsiders in, but chances are that they won't stick around long because of the exclusive nature of the demographic for these types of sites.

## In the Name of Sex and Play

Though Craigslist is often seen as the cornerstone of instant gratification on the Internet, there are many more full-blown personals sites that cater exclusively to kinky people and seekers of casual sex. The top sites in this category are Alt.com and Adult Friend Finder (AFF), both of which are owned by parent company Various, Inc. Based in California, the company manages more than twenty personals sites, making it one of the largest operators of dating and social networking websites. Alt.com (tagline: "World's Largest BDSM & Alternative Life-style Personals") and AFF (tagline: "The World's Largest Sex & Swinger Personals Community") both exist solely to connect horny and curious adults with one another.

Both sites prominently feature images of scantily clad women on their front pages, not unlike a porn site. These images are developed and placed with male memberships in mind, though they also cater to visually oriented women who appreciate women's bodies. Once inside the membership areas, there's no question that women rule the spaces. Whether single and looking for connections with men, women, or groups, or part of a couple, women are the ones who decide what takes place. The general trend in swinger culture since the advent of sex-positive feminism has been that the women make the decisions about their comfort level and therefore the sex lives of people they are intimately (or potentially) connected to. This trend has continued online to the umpteenth degree, where adventurous and willing women on sex personals sites become the hub of all attention and can pick and choose between suitors in a way that they may not be able to do offline.

Much like Craigslist, but unlike the more vanilla dating sites, straight men who use AFF and Alt.com consistently bemoan the lack of available women who aren't sex workers. Though sites like Match.com use women to seduce men into maintaining their memberships, the battle of the sexes reaches a whole different level on sites centered on sexuality. Men get frustrated by the lack of follow-through from women, while women find themselves intimidated by the intensity of men and the pressure to meet and play, which men tend to lay on thick early in the game.

Difficulties aside, the people who do end up meeting in person through these sites report a high level of success. And by success they mean getting laid. In the spring and summer of 2006, AFF conducted a survey of its members about their likelihood to have sex with a date from AFF on their first meeting, posing this question: "Based on your past experiences (not your wishes), how far have you usually ended up going on your first date?" The results of the poll showed that 29 percent of respondents went "all the way, baby" on the first date. The figure is even higher for women (42 percent of the 1,825 women who responded) than for men (25 percent of the 8,441 men who responded).[3] Perhaps because the women are the gatekeepers (as it were), they are able to get laid on a more consistent first-date basis than the men are.

## Taking It into Her Own Hands

It seems as if there's a dating or social networking site for every person with every interest. However, some people can't seem to find their Match.comes through the standard route of building an online profile, exchanging flirtatious messages and personal information, and then meeting and dating a Match. com in person. Some women simply aren't satisfied with the idea of being one of many and liken it to being offered up on a menu. As a result, some people, like thirty-year-old New Jersey native Blaire Allison, have put up vanity websites focused on the goal of meeting and nabbing a serious relationship. Allison's website, MarryBlaire.com, carries the tagline "Do You Know My Husband?" and is a slightly tongue-in-cheek but also dead serious experiment in Internet dating. It's also an experiment that, nearly three years into the project, has been unsuccessful in its stated purpose to find her a husband, although Allison has met and dated several men who contacted her through the site. When the website launched shortly before Allison's twenty-seventh birthday in the summer of 2004, it attracted major media attention, earning her a piece in the City section of *The New York Times,* as well as television appearances on *Inside Edition,* MSNBC, and Fox 5's *Good Day New York.*

Allison's presentation is impeccably cheerful and good-humored in all of her media appearances, and her website includes many goofy-bordering-on-unflattering photos with captions like "This is what I'll look like when I meet my husband!" and "This is how I'll look when my husband asks me to marry him!" For the most part, the press coverage of Allison's website fell into the "fluff piece" category, and the tone of the pieces generally amounted to "Check out this zany woman!" Allison's experiment, though entertaining, underlines a frustration with the usual channels of dating both off- and online and is a reminder that formulas and profile Match.coming or not, meeting and dating a life partner is a tricky business.

Though all online profiles are essentially narcissistic shrines to oneself, by stepping outside of the bounds of a profile on another site and creating a website with her name in the URL, Allison has one-upped most online daters. Though at face value the site is about the process of seeking a husband, it's really about Blaire taking her place in the Internet celebrity spotlight. And the site has served this motive well; it catapulted her relationship-coaching and sexy-events-planning business forward and brought her infamy both in print and television media. The website also makes her look like a half-crazed and desperate woman, as well as a bit of a hack: This is a woman who claims to be an expert in relationships, yet she's been unable to maintain one of her own. While some people are generally wary of the possibility of exposure that posting personal content online can bring, Allison has embraced it wholeheartedly. And though her website certainly improved her professional life, it's likely that it's hindered the progress of her interpersonal relationships, the details about which she reports on her site. It's not clear whether Allison was too naive to predict what publicity would do to her avowed quest for a husband, or whether she knew the risks and made a calculated move for her business. Either way, the effect of opening her love life and that of any potential suitor who crossed her path has certainly not resulted in the fulfillment of her stated goal.

## So I Met an Ax Murderer on the Internet

The vast majority of people who pay for Internet dating services are looking to meet potential dates in person, and yet many women have hesitations about meeting in person beyond the possibility that someone might not be compatible. There are legitimate safety concerns: *What if he's an ax murderer?*

When I ask Lanie about the safety precautions she takes for dealing with dates procured from the Internet, she says, "I Google them, check phone numbers, and I let someone know where I'll be, with whom, and their contact information. I always meet in a public place first, and I call my friend to check in. Also, I tell the other person that I've done all that." These are steps independent dating experts and dating websites alike advise and promote.

On their second date (or more accurately, "casual sex rendezvous"), Michaela and Chris, who met through Salon.com personals, got together at Chris's bachelor pad in San Francisco, which was scarcely furnished and didn't have curtains. Michaela remembers, "We were lying in bed and Chris reached over and picked up an object that turned out to be a small ax. I thought, *Oh great, I meet a guy on the Internet and now he's going to ax murder me!* As I fled to the other side of the bed, he got up and started using the ax as a hammer to hang a sheet as curtains to give us some privacy. He was oblivious to the threatening nature of his ax act until I burst out laughing. We still laugh about it today."

As with any new technology, the Internet has churned up people's worst nightmares about strangers. Tons of rumors manifest into urban legends about women meeting men who turn out to be real live convicted felons, rapists, and—yes—ax murderers. The reality is that dangerous people make their way around regardless of the Internet, and the ideas about the inherent dangers of meeting someone online are largely the vestiges of online dating stigma.

## Sex, Lies, and the Internet

One fully legitimate fear of online dating is the fear that a person will not be "as advertised." The most frequently told story of women's dating mishaps goes something like this: "He was definitely *not* six feet tall." Though fudging height by a few inches certainly isn't a crime, it can speak to a degree of insecurity in a potential date, and often gets women pondering what else her date may be lying about if he's willing to lie about something that's so obviously false.

More serious infractions include revelations like "I found out he's married!" The problem of the wandering eye (and roving desire) has spawned a website to deal with exactly that: The Ashley Madison Agency is an online dating service that caters to married people who want to have affairs with other married people, to ensure discretion. The website's tagline reads: "When Monogamy Becomes Monotony." However, just as the existence of an STI dating site doesn't prevent people with sexually transmitted infections from using mainstream sites, married-people matchmaking sites don't keep dishonest married daters out of the mainstream dating pool.

Patty, a middle-aged woman who has used a variety of dating services since divorcing her husband of twenty years, says that just before she met one of her current partners (she is polyamorous), he confessed to her that he'd fibbed a bit about his weight, and that he wasn't just "husky" as his ad said, but that he weighed three hundred pounds. "I really struggled with it because my husband was so trim. How could I deal with this? Then I realized it was bullshit; we had so many things in common. I had to meet him." She ultimately was very happy to have followed through with the meeting, they quickly got very hot and heavy, and they've maintained a relationship. Over time, however, her desire to have a polyamorous relationship—in which each of them would have more than one sexual and romantic partner—became problematic for him, and they've since been struggling with how to make this work.

Ruth, who has used the Internet to meet male and female partners since she moved to New York City, speculates about the differences between the way men and women present themselves. "I found that women are *far* more honest online than men are about their physical appearance, at least to other women. Women are used to being judged on their physicality, so they want you to know what to expect. Men aren't used to the same scrutiny and biased treatment based on their physical appearance, so they don't tread as carefully or as wisely."

Lies or no lies, there's one big thing in the Internet dating equation that absolutely cannot be predicted: chemistry. Even if both people have represented themselves perfectly and are just as witty in real live one-on-one dialogue as they are in writing, there's no accounting for personal chemistry. Although the Internet can help a woman to do a lot of the initial legwork in finding a person worth dating, the only true way to size people up as candidates for a relationship is to interact with them in the flesh. It's this sticking point that sometimes makes people balk and flake out at the last minute on dates they've set up online. Ruth admits to having been that flaky woman on several occasions. She says, "I'd just talk and talk and then never follow through. Because in the end I'd get scared that they were not gonna be what I wanted in terms of chemistry." Although she would feel pangs of guilt at blowing people off, she also says, "I wasn't putting anything real on the line, either," because her interactions with potential dates were essentially just blips on a computer screen, and so she admits to not really thinking of them as real people.

As clichéd as it sounds, the Internet has indeed changed the face of human interactions, and especially patterns of meeting people and dating. It's also changed the ways that people tell stories about how they met and the ways they think about intimacy. Kis Lee, who ended up meeting her boyfriend of five years through Adult Friend Finder, says, "I told my friends that I met him on the Internet, but never said I met him via AFF. He said he's lied to his friends about it, too." Gwen Masters, a thirty-year-old erotica writer from Nashville, got wound into a different set of lies about dating and the Internet with a man she men on Alt.com. For the first several months of their yearlong relationship, Max treated her well and they agreed that although using the Internet to keep up with friends was fine, maintaining a dating profile or keeping up sexy correspondence was off-limits.

Nine months into the relationship, Max started acting strangely and began to question Gwen's whereabouts and contacts—the kind of paranoia, a friend pointed out, that generally stems from the guilt of a cheater. After a little bit of sleuthing, Gwen discovered that although Max had shut down the dating profiles she knew about, he had a whole other online persona that he was using to court four different women, often copying and pasting the same declarations of love from one email to the next. After some very upsetting confrontations, and contact with one of the women Max had been corresponding with, Gwen ended the relationship. Though she believes that Max did understand the difference between physical affairs and emotional ones that could be conducted over the Internet, Gwen says, "He became really dedicated to playing the game. I don't think he knew what was real and what wasn't. But he could get away with it because it was the Internet. He never would have gotten away with it in real life."

Although this example is a clear case of cheating given the parameters Max and Gwen had established for their relationship, for many couples the line between Internet playfulness and "real life" is extremely blurry. This makes the process of meeting people online and bringing them into an offline context complicated, even for people who aren't sneaking around behind their partner's back. Though many people are becoming more forthright about having met partners on the Internet, and some even include this information in their wedding announcements (if they make it that far), a purely sexual encounter just for the sake of sex (Internet or no) is still taboo. Internet dating is often laced with sexual innuendos and can be quite a sexualized process, but cruising online for the sole purpose of hooking up does carry a stigma. The women who spend most of their online "dating" time doing this do have a clear sense of what they are looking for, though, and what kinds of adventures they're interested in pursuing. They also know the power they have in interactions with men who are likewise trolling for sex: Women are in charge.

# CHAPTER 3: A DAY IN THE LIFE OF MY VAGIN

## The Personal Politics of
## Sex Blogging

**B**logs—the shortened term for "web logs," (which is now only used by print publications that don't really know what they're talking about)—have started to give mainstream "old" media a run for their money. Blogs are a lot like sexual fetishes: If you can think of a subject (or especially if you can't), there's one out there. The most linked to and highly trafficked blogs range in topics from popular culture, like Boing Boing: A Directory of Wonderful Things, to politics, like Daily Kos: State of the Nation, to location-specific events and gossip, like the Ist-a-verse network of twelve city blogs that includes Gothamist.com, LAist.com, Phillyist.com, Shanghaiist.com, and Parisist.com, as well as personal blogs like Dooce.

The beauty of the blog is that it's infinitely and instantaneously updatable; user-friendly blogging software has revolutionized the Internet and the way media is done, prompting major print news sources (the "old" media) to cry out in alarm about the threat that blogs pose to "real" media (and then get with the times and start up their own blogs). The fear is that bloggers are much more casual—and therefore unscrupulous—writers than traditional professional journalists. In the eyes of the old media, blogs are threatening because their writers are wannabe journalists without any credentials who pose as authorities on any number of subjects, especially politics. While that may be true to some extent, especially since there's no higher institution monitoring blogging ethics, mainstream media's reaction stems largely from severe technophobia, and the irrational and disproportionate reaction to the blogging phenomenon has actually served to undermine old media and strengthen the credibility of bloggers on more than a few occasions. A recent study on blogs by the Pew Internet & American Life Project reveals the most well-publicized (and feared) blogs are political ones, even though only 11 percent of bloggers claim politics and public life as the main subject of their blogs. By comparison, 37 percent of bloggers report their own personal experiences as the primary topic of their blogs.[1]

People blog for many reasons: to keep track of what they're doing and thinking on a regular basis, to share their thoughts with friends and family and beyond, to develop their writing style, to respond to current events and news articles they find interesting, to forward their careers, and because they are exhibitionists. Women who blog about sex and relationships blog for these reasons or combinations of these reasons, as well as for reasons that are unclear, even to themselves.

In the vast blogosphere, blogs written by women about relationships and sexuality, often with some feminist politics thrown in for good measure, occupy their own little corner.

There is a tiny bit of crossover between sex blogging and mainstream blogging, most notably by Violet Blue, who writes extensively about sex on her own website, Tiny Nibbles, but is also connected to blogs like Boing Boing and writes extensively about new media and technology. Violet is a rare exception, however, because most women who blog about sex get pretty firmly locked into that space and find themselves having to maintain more than one online identity if they want to venture outside of the bounds of sex and relationships without getting snarky comments. Though sex bloggers face many of the same issues as bloggers who don't blog about sex, they often risk a lot to tell the stories they feel compelled to tell about themselves, their lovers, and the world of sexuality at large.

## A Blog of One's Own

The overwhelming majority of the women sex bloggers I interviewed had kept private journals at some point in their lives. It's no surprise that the journal keepers of yesteryear are the bloggers of today. However, I was surprised to hear that so many of the bloggers I spoke to still maintain handwritten private journals in addition to their blogs, and see the two kinds of writing as complementary. Jill, who maintains the sex blog Introspectre.com, as well as its nonsex companion of the same name on Blogger, was one of the few women I spoke to who says that she eagerly abandoned paper journaling for blogging. "Generally speaking, the private diary is for thoughts you do not want to share. For me, that's not what writing is about. I want to rip myself wide open and live as genuinely as possible, so private diaries are not my thing," she tells me.

This desire for self-exposure (in ways both sexy and deeply emotional) is almost a prerequisite for female sex bloggers. However, having an exhibitionist streak is not the only thing that drives women to write about their sex lives; after all, many exhibitionists chose very different ways to show off, like online nudity. Van Gogh Chica, a Latina in her forties who has kept both a sex blog and a more mainstream blog, says, "On my sex blog, I could offer myself up as a scrumptious sex *mami* to be lusted after and admired while also having my thoughts listened to. I was not just a photo spread to jack off to." For bloggers, being seen and understood as multifaceted sexual beings—"not just a photo spread"—is very important.

The vast majority of sex blogs are written by women, and for many of them, their blogs become an outlet to express truths about their sexuality that they have been unable to share with their friends and lovers. Because it's easier for many women to write on their blogs than it is for them to talk out loud about their needs and desires with the very people in their lives who need to hear it, blogs—especially anonymous blogs—can encourage silence to a certain degree. However, they can also be instrumental in helping women get in touch with their desires and learn how to articulate their needs. This might sound a little like psychobabble, but coming to terms with sexual preferences, impulses, and even fetishes takes some emotional processing. And despite the fact that blogs might create a crutch, discouraging women from having difficult conversations with offline friends and partners, my feeling is that at least they're talking (or rather, writing) to someone. Jill says, "I think it's inherent in women's nature to talk about a thing, turn it around, ponder it a while. Sex blogging is like the Rubik's Cube for women. Sex puzzles us, thrills us, challenges our ways of thinking, and we tend to turn to words to solve our emotions, or use our blogs to scream our opinions and viewpoints and thrilling discoveries from the virtual rooftops."

Whether it's due to our inherent nature or whether it's the way we're nurtured and socialized, blogs appeal to many women's desire's to talk about and process intimate issues while removing the potential embarrassment of sitting across from a friend and trying to meet her eyes while telling her about getting tied up and spanked by a partner (and loving it). Though some women do share intimate tales, experiences, and questions with their female friends, many feel that to do so risks the possibility of being judged harshly and seen in a different and negative light. "Before I was a blogger," says Magdelena, a British sex blogger whose blog Myths and Metawhores won the Best of Blogs Best Sex Blog award in 2005, "my experience of friendship with women was pretty fractured and empty because it lacked this erotic dimension. Blogging has actually served to transform my offline friendships, and they are more intimate and much closer than before."

The words "virtual" and "cyber" notwithstanding, the experiences of intimacy women bloggers have with each other online and through their blogs are very real emotional experiences. Kis Lee, an erotica writer whose personal blog is now defunct, says that after a few months of cultivating online friendships with other female bloggers, she realized, "We knew more about each other than most of our friends knew about us." When Lee and some of her cohorts stepped out from behind their blogs to meet in person for the first time, she found it awkward that they all knew such intensely intimate details about one another, but the connections between them remained strong, even if they weren't immediately able to have the kind of in-person discussions that they regularly maintained on their blogs.

Though there's much talk about what the difference is between online experiences and "real life," this line has eroded where emotions are concerned. Jane Crowley is a mostly former blogger who I interviewed extensively about her online experiences. She wrote about her personal life, teen years, sex life, and experiences as a stripper and takes this so far as to say, "There's definitely a split between online and real life, but I almost think that it's backward—real life is only surface, and the Internet cuts through all of that and helps us become more real by giving us a place to confess without having to lower our eyes." This lowering of the eyes is essentially what happened to Lee when she met her blogger friends in real life, and it goes to show that though many women have the potential and the drive to be freer, they still feel the sharpness of societal constraints when they're moving around in the world outside the blogosphere. Something about sharing face-to-face and making eye contact opens us up to witnessing the judgments we expect to receive from others. Which is why for so many women the Internet is a safe space to explore, allowing them to make incremental steps toward feeling out their comfort in the world beyond their computer screens.

It's this knowledge of that world of staring eyes that drove O, who blogs at Eros, Logos, to cultivate the illusion that no one reads her blog. Really, this isn't so difficult to do. After all, when she writes, O feels very alone and involved in her own world, which is constituted of just her and her computer. O often chooses to write late at night, and she finds that when she thinks about her audience, it psychs her out of her ability to write truthfully about her feelings and experiences. She speculates, "I think privacy, and my need for it, correlates with the amount of personal or difficult truth I write about." But she also recognizes that without an audience, and without feedback, she probably wouldn't write the way she does. For many women, blogging about sex is, paradoxically, as much a solitary pursuit that's solely for them as it is a public confession that needs an audience to flourish and grow. Either way, women's sex blogs are a personal and political space for both their writers and readers.

## Sex Is the Bad Word

Amber Rhea has blogged using her real name, with the title Being Amber Rhea, since her blog's inception five years ago. When she started keeping the blog in April 2002, blogs had not yet worked their way into popular consciousness, so her readership was limited to her friends and family. Rhea was starting a master's program in Informational Technology, so the blog was mostly about geeky stuff and her penchant for adopting vintage Macs. Over time, her blog has become both more and less personal, as she's delved into debates about feminism, media, and sexuality on an increasingly frequent basis. Though she still maintains her initial readership, which includes several lifelong friends as well as her mother, Rhea's readership has expanded beyond this small circle and now includes complete strangers, who may or may not comment and make their presence known, as well as people who've become offline friends because of the blog. The pattern of expanded readership and the construction of offline relationships because of a blog—even a secret sex blog—is fairly common. Blogging, like involvement in most Internet activities, dredges up images of a lonely person typing away with only his or her Internet pals to talk to, but blogs have become an integral piece of the social puzzle, not just a pastime for outcasts.

Rhea doesn't identify her blog as a sex and relationship blog, but she doesn't entirely shy away from these topics either. She says, "Blogging about sex normalizes it as part of our lives." Her posts about sexuality are usually set into the context of sex-positive feminism and are often reactions to other bloggers' posts or to articles in the mainstream media. Rhea often relates her ideas back to her own personal perspective and experiences rather than spouting theory; this is a common thread among female bloggers who end up getting a following outside their immediate circles. For Rhea, these types of posts tend to get the most attention and personal attacks of anything she writes. On the blog Bitch | Lab, the blogger affectionately known as Bitch has not had the same kind of problems with personal attacks. Like Rhea, she doesn't consider her blog a sex blog, but she says, "My sexuality online has become more political over the past few years because I don't want to be cowed into being nonsexual. I realized that whatever I do on the Internet, men are sexualizing me."

Though Rhea is sometimes taken aback by the intense reactions she gets to some of her posts, she also delights in baiting readers who she knows will vociferously disagree with her perspective on particular subjects. Although most bloggers receive the occasional commenter or frequent email correspondent who loathes their very existence and mocks their perspective and experiences (there is a certain breed of online-content consumer who just loves to hate), women who don't devote their blogs entirely to sex and relationships seem to attract higher incidences of this problem when they do choose to write about sex. Sex blogs occupy a very definite Internet ghetto, and despite the fact that the women who maintain these blogs put a lot of care into their posts beyond just pictures, goofy quizzes, and links without commentary, it's fairly common that they get scoffed at and seen as a lesser form of blog, especially by other bloggers who do not blog about sex. This is something that many sex bloggers are painfully aware of, and many choose to maintain separate identities online—one for a sex blog and one for a "regular" blog.

Van Gogh Chica chose to do this for a while, and comments, "I felt I needed to compartmentalize my sexuality from my general woman persona in order to keep judgments and retribution away from family, coworkers, friends, and possible partners." On the occasions that she did incorporate writing about sexuality into her general blog, this hunch proved to be true, and people asked her questions like "Aren't you ashamed of yourself?" The readers she had offline relationships with saw this kind of writing as a peculiar and unhealthy compulsion, as well as a way of acting out and getting attention, not as a natural expression of part of her being.

The ghettoizing of the sex blog is something of a two-pronged problem: Writing and thinking about sexuality is seen as an easy way to get attention and not at all a noble pursuit, and most of the people who blog in detail about sexuality and their personal sex lives are women. These two elements are intertwined in a way that serves to devalue women's writing even if it is not always directly about sex, while creating an instant funnel for negative comments toward any woman who ventures to the dark side of writing about sex. Sex writing, even when it's about women's personal experiences, is viewed as a cheap trick to get more hits, links, and controversy. And while this is a valid trick—or criticism, as the case might be—the suggestion that women blogging about sex are inherently cheap and unworthy of attention beyond gawking is shortsighted and sexist.

When I started my own blog, Waking Vixen, in the summer of 2004, I knew from the outset that it would be about sex, but I didn't know how personal it would get. Initially it began as a blog about my experiences working in sex, and it evolved into more intensely personal tales of my exploits. I wanted to keep it somewhat separate from my nonsex life, but that differentiation has almost completely eroded over the past few years. Yet, over that same period of time, the blog has become less personal— that kind of exposure was difficult to maintain while staying emotionally healthy.

Before I knew much about the way the Internet works, I knew that many of my favorite sex blogs were hosted at blogspot .com addresses, so when I decided to launch Waking Vixen, I headed on over to Blogger, which had been launched by the small company Pyra Labs in 1999 and was bought by Google in early 2003. At Blogger, I could create a profile from which I could start and maintain as many blogs as I wanted. I built Waking Vixen using one of the ready-made templates and began writing within minutes. As I wrote, I also began to do Google searches on basic HTML, which allowed me to fiddle with my template, with some minor but correctable disasters along the way. Though I wasn't keeping my blog a complete secret from my offline friends, I didn't immediately view it as a permanent online space for my dirty musings. When I began to get more serious about the blog, I bought my own domain name, and in April 2005 I launched my own website with the blog as the centerpiece, though in my site's most recent incarnation as an effort at a more professional appearance, the blog no longer takes center stage.

The path from free blog to a domain of one's own is a bit rare for sex bloggers, especially because it's common to stick to free software and hosting like Blogger, WordPress, LiveJournal, and Xanga in an attempt to blog anonymously. Free stuff is appealing to everyone, not just sex bloggers, but anonymous sex bloggers aren't just cheapskates, they're nervous about being outed and want to have a speedy exit plan should they need it. Domain and blog-hosting purchases require credit card information, and though online security measures are in place to protect this type of information, many sex bloggers feel that it's too much of a risk to create any link between their sex blogger selves and their legally named selves. Many recognize that sex blogging is never truly anonymous and there's always the risk of being found out.

A woman who blogs under the name of Goose alongside her husband on their shared blog, Goose and Gander, says, "Blogging tends to make me kind of anxious. Our locale is pretty conservative, and people can be excoriated for having alternative sexual views. Some days I feel strong and powerful for having the blog, and some days I feel like I'm taking a big risk."

Bloggers who post using free hosting sites feel the security of knowing they always have the safety net of going dark and pulling their archives. However, in recent years it's become clear that online content is not as easily erasable as people once believed: Someone somewhere will always be keeping a personal cache of a favorite blogger's best posts or a favorite porn model's best photographs, and there are a number of digital library projects, like Archive.org, that are striving to preserve both the content and design of websites as historical artifacts in ways that are publicly searchable. Just as libraries with manuscript collections have saved many seemingly extraneous paper fragments, the Archive.org project strives to preserve ever-changing digital culture in an online repository where the public can look up now-extinct websites. By using a feature on the site called the Wayback Machine, researchers can browse websites that no longer exist or see earlier incarnations of sites that have changed over the years.

It's that illusion of temporary status that usually encourages keepers of blogs to experiment with content—and to not worry about the content restrictions of their paid web host. (Most free blog-hosting sites don't have content restrictions, though rumors circulate every now and then that rules are going to be enforced around adult content, and photo-hosting websites already do this.) Although many bloggers are happy to link to blogs using free services, there are plenty who think that the lack of financial investment indicates a lack of emotional and professional investment.

Linking is one way that the blogosphere is drawn together into a more cohesive picture that demonstrates its interconnectivity. Most bloggers choose to link to other blogs that they appreciate in an effort to share traffic and crosspromote with other bloggers. Linking is a bloggy expression of kinship, and many bloggers create links to sites without ever having had correspondence with their owners. Links are traceable through a few different means, the first and foremost being a statistic or hit counter, such as the ones provided by StatCounter, ShinyStat, and Easy Counter, but also through Technorati and IceRocket, which keep track of links created between blogs. The sex blogging community, which, as mentioned, is primarily made up of women, tends to be very insular. Writers crosslink with women with whom they've forged online relationships, or whose blogs they admire. And within the sex blogging community at large there are even more niche blogs that tend to link to one another: blogs written by couples, blogs by women who like to be dominated, and blogs by women who are just starting to explore their promiscuous side.

Though sex bloggers do plenty of linking to one another, sex blogs are ghettoized by the lack of links and traffic from blogs that aren't all about sex. Sex blogs are ghettoized in two ways: by the blogging software and hosts that the bloggers choose and through the systems of links that bloggers make to one another. To use my own website by way of example: According to Technorati, 122 different blogs have put up a combined 343 links to Waking Vixen.

Only about a dozen of those links originate from blogs that aren't primarily about sexuality. Links tucked in the sidebar of nonsex blogs rarely yield new visitors, though this could be a result of my blog falling at the bottom of alphabetically organized link lists and not just the content of my blog. The name of my blog isn't a dead giveaway as to its content, but many linkers create categories for their links lists and label blogs as NSFW (not safe for work) or with some other designation that lets readers know they're about to encounter adult material. The few times that nonsex bloggers have written posts commenting on or linking to things I've written, they've gotten disapproving comments from their readers about it. When writer Lee Goldberg wrote about me in September 2005 and commented on my blogged-about decision to retire from sex work,[2] his readers had nothing but snarky replies, including such gems as "Is anyone else growing concerned re: Lee's Internet surfing preferences?" and "Thanks for the giggle. I needed it."

Of course, I'm not so foolish or self-righteous to think that everything I commit to my blog is rapier-sharp wit and cultural analysis of great heights, but in this case the responses were flat-out derisive, simply because a nonsex blogger's writing was about sex and turned an eye to writing that came from a sex worker's perspective. This reaction to sex blogging is rooted in a lack of understanding as to why people would want to blog about their sex life. Many people believe sex should be private and analyze why bloggers would bring that out in (sometimes semianonymous) public. It's also related to the commonly held belief that sex is just not that important on a societal level. Though these issues seem to be neatly wrapped up in the minds of people who don't devote lots of time thinking about sex (or at least don't admit that they do by writing about it on the Internet), for many sex bloggers these questions regarding the value of their writing loom large as well.

## The New Face of Privacy

Women who blog about their personal sexualities and relationships often express the thought that blogging is a kind of therapy. After all, like therapy, blogging is very process oriented, since a blogger's narrative often unfolds without a perfect story arc, as life itself happens and as the writer explores how much sharing feels okay. And though a blog can also be a space to vent, bloggers who talk about blogging as therapy tend to gloss over one primary and important difference—that they're not face-to-face with anyone who questions and encourages them to reexamine their thoughts and actions. It's true that some commenters and email correspondents challenge writers to examine certain posts, but for the most part, blog readers are sympathetic (sometimes overly so) to the plight of the blogger. Readers are generally on the blogger's side and oftentimes only gently question the blogger's thinking, if at all. It's much easier for a blogger to shut out a commenter or email correspondent than it would be for her to shut out and disregard a living, breathing therapist.

Another element of blogging as therapy that can become problematic, of course, are issues around privacy and confidentiality. Some blog platforms—like LiveJournal—allow posts to be secured and accessible only by bloggers' "friends." On LiveJournal, friends are other members of the site who have permission from the blogger to view certain posts. Different filters can be created so that bloggers have control over who—even among their friends—has access to which posts. This option for exclusivity creates a level of comfort for a blogger—it's possible to know and control who reads your blog.

Meg, who's maintained a personal blog that focused on more-general life experiences on LiveJournal for several years, recently created a sex blog, The Tales of a Teacher and Slut, on Blogger. She eventually told her LiveJournal friends about it, but says, "On LiveJournal, my writing is very stream of life and not as literary and deliberately composed as on my other blog."

LiveJournals tend to not be as story oriented and are more about keeping friends and family updated on one's comings and goings and relating day-to-day details and idiosyncrasies. LiveJournal also offers the opportunity for a blogger to friend different communities—essentially group journals where members can post thoughts and get feedback, not unlike message boards. Melissa Gira, who started using LiveJournal in late 2000 and then abandoned it save for the communities in early 2004, says, "I enjoyed the ongoing conversational nature of it. Commenting on LiveJournal was so casual, like chatting, not like blogging elsewhere, which was more polished, more part of your image."

A major impetus for having a more polished image and tighter storytelling on blogs beyond LiveJournal is that they are open to the public to read: Anyone can do a Google search and end up on a blog they didn't know existed, or can follow link paths from other blogs and suddenly find themselves learning a whole hell of a lot about the person whose blog they encounter. It's this collision of randomness, visibility, and anonymity that positions sex blogs as the primary online tool that's reconfiguring the way we think about privacy.

Although no one denies that blogs are a public expression of self, many bloggers see their blogs as being very closely related to private diaries—or at least they feel that way until the comments start rolling in and there are signs of life from the great wide expanse that is an online readership. "As soon as you get that first comment," says Madeline, whose blog Madeline in the Mirror details the life and times of a "prim and properly perverted parent," "it affects how you choose to portray whatever you're writing about. It's a sort of diary, but it's edited. I don't write about as much of the bad stuff on my blog as I do in my personal journal."

However aware bloggers are of their audience, many still consider the process of writing to be very personal and private, despite the fact that the thoughts that go into their posts are immediately accessible to the public. For bloggers whose readership includes people they know offline, many prefer a kind of don't ask, don't tell situation so that they can maintain their sanity when it comes to thinking about certain people (family, lovers, and close friends) knowing the ins and outs of their personal lives—particularly when it comes to thinking about and having sex. Selina Fire, who blogs explicitly about sex, but not the rest of her life, at Sex in the City—The Real Version, says, "I prefer that my lovers don't read me, and I feel squeamish when I know friends are reading. If they're going to read, I'd rather they just don't tell me."

For women who blog about sex, there's a constant struggle between feeling proud of and sexy about their writing and feeling societal pressure to be good and keep those things private. Among the women I talked to, this push and pull is evident. Gray Lily, who blogs about BDSM and polyamory on her blog Journey into Submission, says, "I need an outlet to discuss and process what I'm going through." This sentiment was echoed by many other women I interviewed when I asked them why they blog. Though many women maintain that their main priority is their own expression, the public element of blogs is an important aspect as well, and it's both alluring and terrifying. Selina Fire says, "I love when people write and say they are jerking off to what they read." For Selina, depicting her pleasure is an important part of her work as a feminist, though prurient interest reigns supreme over any expression of politics. Gray Lily also strongly believes in the public service aspect to blogging, and says, "I love the fact that people read what I write and that I may be educating some about BDSM and domination/submissive relationships."

However, for both of these women, having their "real life" selves discovered as sex bloggers and depraved souls of the first order would be catastrophic. Both women are mothers who are separated from partners who would not hesitate to yank their children away if they found out about the women's sexual practices; both women have jobs that would quickly have them fired if it was revealed that they create a very full picture of their sex lives on the Internet. Both women, therefore, take serious precautions against being found out: Selina does not blog about her life outside of sex, which makes her less identifiable and helps with plausible deniability—her blog could be a work of erotic fiction that has no basis in fact. Gray Lily occasionally blogs about her children, but changes identifying details about her situation and never reveals where she lives—she also does not form offline relationships with anyone she corresponds with through her blog. Despite these precautions, these women and other anonymous bloggers are taking a risk that would have extreme consequences if they were to be discovered. Both women have thought this through, however, and feel that what they gain from sex blogging—honing their skills as writers and connecting with other people who have similar experiences—outweighs what they perceive as a slim chance of losing everything.

Though she had less to lose than Selina and Gray Lily, Aliza, whose blog Aliza's World rested dormant for a while after it was discovered by her family, was mortified when she got an email from her father saying that he'd discovered her blog. She says, "I was horrified, sick to my stomach. To know my parent had seen explicit photos of me and had read intimate details of my rather colorful sex life was just so wrong." In the immediate aftermath, Aliza didn't talk to her father or other family members for a while, and she felt frustrated that the experience churned up old feelings of guilt and shame about her sexuality. Ultimately, she says, "I did question the benefits of exposing myself so much to the world online, but I still feel it was worth it. My sex blog gave me so much; it gave me strength, confidence, creative energy, support."

## A Tale of Two Blogs

Remember the cartoon that ran in *The New Yorker* portraying a dog sitting in front of a computer? He quipped to another dog, "On the Internet, nobody knows you're a dog." This little bit of comedy leaves out an important nuance of the bigger picture: On the Internet, it's safe to say that no one knows you're a dog *and* a cat. Many people maintain several different versions of their identities online. They may be completely different from one another, or they may maintain overlapping identities that only tell a fuller story when combined.

Jane Crowley started blogging in May 2004 at Dissection of Everyday Life, a blog she still posts to occasionally (though nowhere near her initial rate of several posts a day). In its earliest incarnation, Dissection of Everyday Life documented Jane's daily life as a wife and mom of a young child, her stresses over having given up two previous children for adoption to her husband's parents (which eventually also happened with her youngest child), her tumultuous open relationship with her husband, her work as a stripper, and reflections on her time spent in the army as well as various traumatizing aspects of her teen years. She wrote about difficult and inflammatory things, ugly pieces of herself—drugs, rape, family difficulties—in a harsh and unapologetic way. On the Internet, Jane felt visible for the first time; in her life offline, Jane had always felt taken advantage of; people were unable or unwilling to see a deeper part of her that she desperately wanted to expose but also kept very protected. Her posts on Dissection of Everyday Life often inspired vitriol from commenters and email correspondents. She told me, "Whatever my response was to the negative feedback, it would create even more chaos, which would grab readers, spread the word, and give me the attention I've always had to have."

December 2004 saw the end of Dissection of Everyday Life, which coincided with an announcement that she and her husband were divorcing, though she didn't actually end up filing for divorce until September 2005. Though the prospect of divorce and starting anew was a motive for shutting down Dissection of Everyday Life, Jane also had begun to feel the constraints of having a very public blog. Her husband, her coworkers at the strip club, and several estranged family members counted among her readers, and it was becoming too much for her to manage. She wanted a fresh start, to be able to speak her mind freely, so she decided to split her identities and create a new blog for Jane—Jane Says—as well as a pseudonymous sex blog that she called Layla X. The writing on both Jane Says and Layla X was intense, ferocious, and vindictive at times; it was self-effacing and destructive, but very compelling. In many ways, the appeal of Jane's blogs can be wrapped into one word: schadenfreude, malicious delight in the misfortune of others. All of the evolutions of Jane's blogs and the knowledge of the havoc she wrecked on her own personal life were like an extravagant and beautifully written train wreck—impossible to turn away from, but difficult to look at.

In her first post on Layla X, Jane opened with the following: "It is so nice to have somewhere that is completely, 100 percent private from those that I know. They will never find me here. It is my safe haven, floating around in cyberspace, nearly anonymous, where I can vent about all of my deviant desires that would get me ostracized in the 'real world.'"

Although Jane declares here that her primary motivation for launching a separate space was about her desire to be safe, what she really wanted was to become someone else—a stronger and better Jane. Eventually, she realized, "In becoming Layla, I built up courage by saying the things that I did, and started to realize that Layla was more me than Jane ever was. And I wanted to be that person, without hiding, so I started to blur the lines—to tell more as Jane than I would have before Layla existed, and eventually let it be known that the two were one and the same, until it finally became redundant to have two blogs."

This blurring of the lines and revealing of identities came with a price for Jane. Part of the reason she'd started Layla X was because she realized that her "deviant desires would get me ostracized." And though she became braver and began to embrace these desires as an integral part of her, the world outside of her head didn't experience this revelation in quite the same empowered and integrated way. The people with whom she shared Layla X—a few lovers and a trusted coworker—began to steer clear of her and regard her as a liability. She wanted people to see her differently because of the blog, to acknowledge the true parts of herself that she felt she had to hide. "I wanted them to see that there was something in me I wasn't displaying—that I had a brain, emotions, that I had lived and was still living." Jane admits that sharing the URL for Layla X was both an exhibitionistic and aggressive gesture. "It scared people to know that I might write about them, and creating fear in people can create a sense of power that I wanted more of once I'd had a taste. It probably sounds bad, but it's true, in my case."

For Jane, Layla X took over in a powerful and terrifying way, but also in a way that was ultimately extremely cathartic. She shares that she feels sad, however, that "some people will still see me as Layla all the time, whether they understand her or not—walking sex, always on, abortion, drugs, sex, heartbreak." She goes on to say, "I can't say that I wouldn't do it again, if I could go back. I needed to let it out so that I could eventually have a reason to let it die—rather, so I would feel less mournful when I inevitably laid it to rest." For Jane, becoming Layla X both took her away from herself and brought her closer to where she wanted to be. Her story is exemplary of the way that online exposure can be both a risk and an adventure, threatening and healing.

Though Jane didn't face the same kind of risks that Selina and Gray Lily did around their online identities being made public, exposure did change things for Jane. In her case, it's clear that although she claimed that online privacy was important to her at Layla X, her online writing adventures were meant to be discovered. Whatever claim some bloggers lay to privacy and anonymity, exhibitionism and a desire to be known and acknowledged do play a role in online expression. Though it's unlikely that most sex bloggers want to be known, need to be seen, as intensely as Jane did, there are many compelling elements to Jane's story that ring true to many women who choose to expose themselves online.

## The Ripple Effect:
## Sex Blogging and Relationships

Jane's blogs were extremely revealing. She included, for instance, details about her sex life with her husband and others. But they were also revealing for what she did not write about in these relationships and encounters. It wasn't until the fall of 2005 and her impending divorce that she ever mentioned that her husband had been physically and emotionally abusive toward her. This speaks to the fact that even bloggers who are extremely open and self-revealing conceal some aspects of their day-to-day lives and emotional experience, particularly when it comes to their relationships with others. A blogger may have a desire to portray her relationship a certain way, but the choices to keep some things out of their blogs also stem from concerns about safety and privacy. When it comes to bloggers who share aspects of their relationship, readers, like friends, are loyal to the person they read, ensuring that the partner always gets the short end of the stick. Bloggers can oftentimes develop quite a loyal following, to the degree that partners of bloggers risk being outed and having their privacy invaded without the same benefits and support that a blogger has in the blogging community.

Many women who blog their relationships and sex lives feel torn between telling their personal truth and protecting their partners, even as their partners become their exes. Rhea struggled with this on her blog, Being Amber Rhea. She says, "When my husband realized he was transsexual and declared that he was going to pursue gender reassignment, we decided to divorce. It was a very painful time, but I don't think it would have been fair to write about, because I'm not anonymous and it would have affected him." Rhea knows that posts about what she went through during that time would have made for a good read, but she wasn't able to process her emotions about the whole thing in a coherent way—and she still doesn't think that blogging would have helped matters any. Rhea tries to carefully consider any topic that involves another person before she posts about it. Sometimes the posts have been worth it and sometimes they haven't; she worries about being passive aggressive by blogging issues that she has difficulty talking about face-to-face. In general, Rhea strives for an honest if not intimate and complete perspective on her life and relationships on her blog, which she sees as an integrated piece of the way she does communication with friends, family, and lovers.

Many bloggers don't feel at all obligated to share more than a sliver about their relationships on their blogs. Freya, who writes erotica that's often based on real-life experiences on her blog Freya's House of Dreams, says, "I write about this narrow part of my relationship, and I'm not really going into all of what I am or what he is—what we are as a couple." Freya maintains that her blog is not a sex and relationship blog—it is not meant to mirror her experiences in the world and inside of her relationship, but instead is a literary and erotic exercise that she's interested in as a writer and as an erotic being. Although the blog is important to Freya, her relationship is the higher priority. "I like to think of my blog as a sort of love letter to him, but I'm careful to keep the full context in my private life," she says.

Though both Freya and Rhea welcome their romantic partners to read their blogs, many women prefer to keep their blogs away from their partners so that they can have a space to process elements of the relationships and get support and feedback from their readers. Always Aroused Girl maintains her blog—and the extramarital relationships she writes about—without her husband's knowledge. Her blog is a tale of her erotic frustration in a marriage completely devoid of sexual attentions. About two years ago, she began looking outside the marriage to get her needs met while her husband sought out therapy, but he has not progressed much, and she feels more frustrated than before. Though she takes the risk of her husband learning of her exploits and her inner thoughts, she says, "Honestly, I would not be horrifically upset if he did find it at this point, as our relationship is already in such dire straits. If I were outed, I would say, 'That's who I am; that's what I did; like it or not, it's who I am.'"

For most women, a personal blog only remains a secret for so long. Kis Lee used her blog to write about boyfriends in the past, and it was a source of conflict in her last relationship. Initially her boyfriend knew about the blog, but didn't know its URL. Eventually he got curious and looked it up; she knew he was reading because she found his IP address in her site statistics. Yet, neither of them talked about the fact that he was reading. Soon budding friendships with a few other bloggers turned into offline meet-ups for Lee, and that's where things got awkward. Lee brought her then-boyfriend to a blogger party and says, "After we met the other bloggers, he hated that I still blogged about our personal life." Though she resisted his requests and continued to blog about their relationship, Lee did make a concession and only blogged about the positive aspects, leaving out the more challenging stuff. Since they've broken up, Lee considered discontinuing her blog because she's uncomfortable with the idea of her ex checking up on her. Ultimately, though she didn't feel entirely ready to abandon personal blogging, she took the blog down and now only maintains a professional blog. Through the experience, she has realized that she should handle things differently in the future.

She knows that completely concealing her blog from a future boyfriend would be more challenging than it's worth, and says, "Once you're online, I don't think you can expect privacy." She doesn't think she'll blog about her next relationship because "I don't want my next boyfriend reading my thoughts. My last one read my blog posts a little too carefully."

Some women exist somewhat uncomfortably on the other side of this phenomenon when their relationships and sex lives are blogged about by other people. For Sabrina, blogs held a strange mystique. A private journaler herself, she didn't understand why people would want to put their thoughts and experiences up on the Internet for anyone to read and engage with. Then she received a blog URL from Jefferson, a man she'd flirted with online. She told me, "I assumed his intent was to arouse me. I was totally turned off and more uninterested. I was grossed out by the blog." In the buildup to their first sex date, he blogged about their conversations, and she felt that he'd misinterpreted her in some ways. But she was surprised to find that she actually started getting turned on by the wanton sluttiness of the blog and Jefferson's descriptions of his many partners and his bisexual sex parties. She even began to enjoy reading what he wrote about her and seeing the comments people left on these posts. However, as things developed between Sabrina and Jefferson, and the relationship expanded beyond just their sexual encounters, Sabrina has found it increasingly difficult to read about Jefferson's exploits. Though she knows the blog exists for entertainment and titillation, she sometimes finds herself becoming enraged when she finds out about a new lover or a night of debauched fun through the blog rather than directly from Jefferson. She also finds herself drawn into tracing the stories of Jefferson's other lovers, particularly the ones who have their own blogs and blog about him on them.

Once a lover's blog is discovered, it's difficult to turn away from it, even if it causes distress for the reader. I admit that while I'm not exactly egotistically combing for mentions of me anymore, I have a tendency to drop by former lovers' blogs now and again to see what they're up to, even though it has no bearing on my current life. Just knowing the blog is there—living and breathing and maybe as evidence of an ex-lover's triumphs, defeats, and fornication buddies—is too much to bear. I must look. And I'm certainly not alone. This is even more compelling when wounds are fresh or when one is in the midst of a relationship with a blogger. Though there's a gap between the blog and the life it features, and though most sex blogs aren't written expressly for the people whose sex lives it highlights, it's difficult to resist reading between the lines when you become one of the primary players in someone else's blog.

Avah, who's a more recent addition to Jefferson's stable, had been blogging in a variety of venues since she was a teenager and created her sex blog, Designing Intimacy, after and because of meeting Jefferson through his blog. Since starting her blog and the relationship, she has felt very much a part of a blogging and sexual community that's brought fun and its share of complications. She admits that she enjoys reading the blogs of people peripherally associated with Jefferson, but that it also makes her feel insecure. She says, "It's hard enough being with someone who's involved with so many other people, but seeing the proof of it all in writing just exacerbates it really."

Although Avah is anonymous to people outside of Jefferson's circle, she is a real person involved with real human drama inside the circle, and much of this brims over onto the blogs. The interconnectedness of these blogs and lives serves to prove that the people wrapped up in them are indeed involved with flesh-and-blood drama. There's a duality to blogs that focuses on intertwined relationships, because people are blogging about encounters from many different angles and levels of involvement. This can result in storytelling getting orchestrated by several different writers, but it also reveals the inner workings of blogging as a process: There are always many sides to a story, and the intricacies of those stories can take on a life of their own when they're being constantly maintained and updated in the blogosphere. Though different versions of the same tale can be complementary, they can also conflict with one another, and it's undeniable that blogs become a liability in many relationships. Even though they are a tool for communication (if not always direct) and a space for hashing things out, they're a potentially volatile element as well.

For some couples, coauthoring a blog can be a good solution to the perils of the Internet. Though group-authored blogs aren't exactly a revolutionary concept at this point, couples' sex blogs tend to be quite different than single-author blogs. For one, they are rarely as introspective—blogs authored by one woman often tend to reflect an inner monologue, while couples' blogs tend to be more narrative and conversational. Since blogs are so often littered with private confessions and explorations of desires that the blogger may or may not ever reveal to partners, a coauthored blog, by its nature, creates a different kind of space. Many women who blog solo relish in their ability to write about whatever they please—though some later change their tune if they are discovered or if they reveal themselves to people they know. Writing with a partner shifts this paradigm and creates a shared space in which both partners' individual voices get lost a little bit, while they also create a new space for communicating between themselves and the world.

When they decided to start their own blog, Goose and Gander had been reading other sex blogs for quite a while. Goose says, "We were beginning to explore our kinkier sides and decided to chronicle it together." They conceived of their blog as a space in which they could write and process their feelings and experiences as they moved along their kinky journey, but they also saw it as a way to reach out to their local kink community and make friends. They each post to the blog with about the same frequency, though this varies depending on their schedules and inspiration. They decided that it was important to them to talk about whatever they write about on the blog before it gets posted—with the exception of recipes or other short and silly posts. Goose also notes that the blog itself has become a communication tool that complements their other modes of communication. She says, "Gander tends to be less verbal than I am, and I tend to be less of a writer, so in some ways we've been able to use the blog to bridge the gap."

Idyllic as this may seem, a coauthored blog certainly has its pitfalls and limitations. When sharing blogging space with a partner, a blogger is more likely to consider how her partner feels about what she's writing, and might be more inclined to talk directly to him or her about any issues they are having rather than venting on the blog, for example. This limitation might contribute to better communication in the relationship, but it can actually censor what might otherwise have been included in a post. Co-blogging can also serve to limit a woman's voice, which has negative ramifications for many women who are involved in co-blogging ventures.

For Hiromi and her former husband, Brett, their now-defunct blog, called Panties Panties Panties, propagated and made public an already abusive space that had previously been private. The blog was based around their extensive and highly specialized collection of undergarments, and each post featured photos of Hiromi (with her face obscured) modeling panties and usually some back and forth banter between the two of them. They started the blog in February 2004 and pulled it offline in late January 2006. At that time, Hiromi started to blog solo on a new site, Hiromi X. At first, Hiromi was vague about the particulars of her separation and divorce, but as time has passed she's begun to write more openly about her eight-year marriage and her husband's abusiveness. She's even shared her more harrowing personal versions of some of the stories that were told on the shared blog. In the comments, many of her readers who followed her over from the old blog to the new one have expressed their sorrow and discomfort over the fact that they wholeheartedly enjoyed (and masturbated to) the former blog. The new knowledge of what the experience of Panties Panties Panties and the marriage was like for Hiromi has been troubling for many of her commenters. Hiromi has continued to assure her readers that she knows and understands that they would have behaved differently had they known the true story in an attempt to assuage their discomfort. Hiromi's story is an example of the truism that people online aren't always what they seem, but the real experiences behind Panties Panties Panties demonstrate the fact that as revealing as sex blogs can be—whether they show bare boobs or emotions—it's difficult to really know what's happening behind the blog.

## Identity Terrorism and the Battle of the Blog

Though interconnected blogs can erupt into blog drama, one story I came across was particularly harrowing and traumatizing to the people involved. The women who shared their stories with me asked that they and their URLs remain anonymous because the threat of harassment is still so palpable.

George and Carolyn started off as strangers who were both readers and commenters on two separate women's blogs: those of Natalie, who writes about her relationship with a married lover, and Rebecca, who writes with her lover and co-blogger Richard in what amounts to a long-distance love letter between a pair of far-flung (and otherwise married) lovers. None of these bloggers had ever met in person, and they became friends through their interactions with each other, exchanging blog comments, emails, instant messages, and phone calls. As it turned out, George and Carolyn lived close enough to one another that their friendly commenter flirtation turned into emails and phone calls, and eventually became in-person dates and a full-fledged relationship.

Shortly after George and Carolyn became a serious couple, Carolyn began her own sex blog at George's urging. George stayed on the sidelines, only occasionally giving her suggestions on blog templates or proofreading her posts. She dutifully recorded their sex life, and George was her biggest fan. When they ran into trouble—they couldn't figure out how to install a blogroll, for instance—they called on Rebecca and Natalie, who were both happy to troubleshoot with them by phone. Though Carolyn and George's sex life flourished on the blog, in real life it began to suffer. George was suffering from chronic arthritis as a result of Lyme disease and was using Vicodin, which may have contributed to his crankiness and short temper.

While Carolyn kept herself devoted to writing her blog, George became quite the passionate emailer, keeping regular correspondence with both Rebecca and Natalie. One day, after Rebecca and Natalie had written posts with glowing praise for Carolyn's writing, Natalie's own server crashed for a few hours. During the downtime, she got an email from George that read, simply, "What is your problem? Why did you delink us?" Slightly shaken by the brisk tone, Natalie wrote back that her whole server was down and it wasn't a personal slight—no one she had links to was getting traffic through her site that day.

A few weeks later, posts from both Rebecca's and Natalie's blogs got included in the Sex Blog Roundup on the popular porn blog Fleshbot.com, which drove several thousand visitors to their blogs in a short period of time. This new interest in their blogs and the promise of many new readers sent George over the edge. George had apparently been putting together details about the women's personal lives beyond their blog personas. To show that he had knowledge of their offline selves that could wield a scary power, George sent a short email to Natalie's married lover, which read, "It seems like you and Natalie are having a lot of fun." He also posted a comment to Rebecca's blog that used her real name and mentioned the city she lives in. Both women were deeply shaken and couldn't understand where George's hostility was coming from. They conferred with each other and then separately contacted Carolyn, who claimed to have no idea what George was up to. Carolyn later told the women that when she confronted George, he had no recollection of having sent the email or posted the comment. Things escalated rapidly, and Natalie and Rebecca attempted to extricate themselves from involvement with the couple, which they initiated by removing their links to Carolyn's blog.

George responded with even more vicious attacks, and Rebecca and Natalie began to believe that Carolyn was egging him on. They made a mutual decision to refrain from responding to any comment and to sever ties completely. And then George stepped it up a notch. He emailed Rebecca and Richard, her online beau and blog partner, and told them that he had Rebecca's home address and telephone number. He threatened to call her husband, who he named in the email. He then made good on a threat he had made to Natalie—that he would email her lover's wife. He composed a very casual note to the unknowing wife, saying he was an old friend of her husband's who was trying to get in touch with him. The wife innocently forwarded the email to Natalie's lover, who was horrified at George's audacity and realized the fact that George's knowledge could wreck serious havoc on his family life; this brief hello email was merely George flexing his muscles and showing what he was capable of unleashing.

Natalie and her lover feel that George holds the key to their happiness or misery. George apparently knows this as well, and is quite happy to keep them, along with Rebecca and Richard, in this awful limbo, in which marriages and relationships could be crushed at any moment. Ultimately and perversely, this entire story of woe seems to boil down to blog traffic and popularity. It seems ludicrous and impossible that this could be the case, but George's ultimate requests of both Natalie and Rebecca have been the same: Relink to Carolyn's blog, promote it, and leave nice comments, or delete the blogs and disappear from sex blog culture.

Is it possible that Internet popularity and the dissection of a hit counter could really be this powerful and seductive? Perhaps Carolyn's blog provides the glue that gives George and Carolyn the meaning and structure they crave in their relationship and can't get otherwise. Most likely, it's not the pursuit of Most Popular Sex Blog status alone that's important to them; the Internet is not so different from a highly interactive video game with competitors set to be offed. As intimate as Rebecca and Natalie could have become with George and Carolyn, their humanity was in a sense negated. Who's to say whether George would have been capable of doing what he did had he known Natalie and Rebecca in person, but one has to wonder if these types of faceless interactions create situations that would be prevented—either because Natalie and Rebecca would have seen George for who he really was had they met him in person, or because George might not have been so heartless if he had acknowledged them for more than an occasional voice over the telephone or blips on a screen. George and Carolyn didn't lose their marbles because of the Internet, but the Internet was certainly a catalyst.

Rebecca and Natalie both felt particularly antagonized once there was real-life information being exchanged and pulled onto the Internet. Prior to that, things seemed relatively benign. Rebecca says that she won't lash out at her harassers or take Carolyn's link off her and Richard's blog. "They are in my real life, and if I take a stab at them, they will fight me back in real life." Just as in a video game, as long as the encounters stay on-screen, it's still a game of strategy, and it still feels that much safer to Rebecca, even though Carolyn and George have taken this video game mentality a step beyond the virtual space and succeeded in posing a very real threat to the people whose lives they're affecting.

Is this a cautionary tale? Yes and no. I'm not going to suggest that a woman should never share her private information with someone she meets online. Being somewhat cautious when meeting new people should be a given. What can be taken from this story is a lesson about self-monitoring: There will always be vicious people like George and Carolyn in the world, and online interactions can make things even worse, because it's impossible to have the same sense of someone that you would have in offline personal interactions. And it's also important for anyone who uses the Internet as a tool for their own self-understanding and self-expression to wrap their mind around the fact that there are real people behind most online content—except the stuff made by bots trying to sell you something. Real people can't be clicked off or delinked like names on a screen can.

Women who are exploring sexuality and orchestrating relationships outside of traditional monogamy—with or without their partners' consent—need to remember that decisions about sexual conduct that exist outside of the accepted norm come with a risk. This risk is not inherent in a woman's choices, and I'm the last person to point fingers or declare that cheating women are doomed to be punished, but the truth is that the cultural makeup of our society bends things so that women pay the highest price.

## Living and Breathing Sex

Since 2005, two new forms of personal media have begun to encroach the high status that blogs hold on the Internet: podcasting and video blogging, or vlogging. These two forms of multimedia have become increasingly popular, with the user-friendliness and availability of audio recording and editing software, prosumer video cameras (the medium point between professional and consumer-level electronics), and the simplicity of video-editing programs like iMovie (which comes installed on all new Apple computers). Podcasts are essentially Internet radio programs that can be of any length and don't need a station to call home. Instead, they are distributed through podcasting networks, the Apple MP3 program iTunes, and via RSS (Really

Simple Syndication) feeds that alert subscribers whenever there is a new podcast available (RSS is also used to deliver feeds of blog posts). Vlogs are deliverable in similar forms, especially since the advent of the video iPod and the latest version of iTunes, which can download and play MP4s, the video counterpart to the MP3 music file. Though both podcasting and vlogging have had an impact on the Internet, the sex blogging community has been a little bit slow to catch on: Podcasts and vlogs about sex certainly exist, but they aren't being created at the same rate that new blogs are.

Vanessa, a woman in her midthirties whose blog and podcast are on her site, Talk to Vanessa, started podcasting at the encouragement of a fan of hers who listened to her live audio chats and stories done by webcam (though without an image) on an adult dating site. As both a blogger and a podcaster, Vanessa has found that she gains different insights into her fans depending on the medium, and, she says, "The same people who comment about how hot my podcasts are and how hard I make their cock will make a totally different kind of comment on a blog post—a more considered opinion, suggestion, or anecdote." For Vanessa, podcasting is a complement to blogging, and won't be a replacement.

Though she enjoys sharing her personal sexuality through the different intimacies of her blog and her podcasting, Marie B. has chosen to keep her personal blog password-protected at LiveJournal, while also doing a more political and educational podcast, The Post-Modern Geek's Guide to Sex. Marie treats the podcast like a radio program, with different news and culture items as segments instead of one erotic tale. Podcasting was a way for Marie to negotiate her desire to be involved with sexuality on the Internet without revealing too much of her private self.

Violet Blue's podcast, Open Source Sex, her blog, and her increasingly frequent vlog posts all meld together in a mix of personal, professional, and political. The presence of her voice or her image when she's against the backdrop of her apartment creates a different kind of intimacy than the text blog does. She tells me, "Something about the immediacy of sound, my voice in their ears, and the way I get flustered or giggle really draws people into a closer space with me—at least, that's what they tell me in emails and comments."

Though there are claims circulating on the Internet that say that blogs are on their way out now that multimedia is becoming a more significant piece of user-generated content, this is an oversimplified prediction. Violet says that both podcasting and vlogging "have already integrated themselves into the media stew of the blogosphere and dissemination of information that people shop through to find what they want." The ways that these media become integrated into personal sex blogs, however, is slightly different than the way they are handled in other areas.

I think that sex blogs will continue to exist in similar numbers to those that we have witnessed cropping up over the past few years, and that they won't be replaced by various forms of multimedia for a variety of reasons. Women who start sex blogs do so as a way of finding their sexual voices, and some say and describe things on their sex blogs that may previously have made (and may still make) them very pink in the face to say out loud to another person. Sex blogging is a very public process, often more public than writers realize until the blogs are discovered by someone who they really don't want reading them, but the act of writing is a very private, introspective act. For some, sex blogging may be a stepping-stone to wrangling with other kinds of media in a sexy way. But this is not always because blogging provides a relatively safe space, or one that feels more anonymous than having your voice or your image floating around on the Internet (whether this is actually true or not).

Sex blogging is, in fact, much more discreet than other kinds of media making. To blog, a woman doesn't need anything other than her computer and an Internet connection, and she can do it from anywhere. To podcast or vlog, she needs more stuff, stuff that's both expensive and conspicuous. A good number of people who write blogs do so in secret, and it's tougher to explain a pile of audiovisual equipment than it is to explain a slavish devotion to sitting in front of one's computer. Furthermore, some bloggers keep their blogs secret from their live-in partners. (A live-in partner would make it pretty challenging to record sexy audio and video missives.) So maybe other blogs will go away, but my prediction is that sex bloggers will continue to sit tight in our little sex-ghetto corner of the Internet, spinning (sometimes tall) tales of exploits and desires.

## Face-to-Face

"When I started blogging on LiveJournal in 2000, no one I knew offline read me. All my online friends were these MIT hacker guys and goth IT [information technology] geeks and New Agey witches with online covens," says Melissa Gira. "Half the people I knew offline were still asking, 'What's a blog?'—so it felt private."

In the short time that's passed since the turn of the century, the visibility of all kinds of blogs has increased a hundredfold. Many previously anonymous people have been outed, and blogging ethics have been debated. Female sex bloggers have begun to come under closer scrutiny as some go public and get book deals to write about their exploits: Belle de Jour (the high-class call girl), Jessica Cutler (the slutty congressional staff assistant), and Abby Lee (the unwillingly outed British "sex fiend" [her words]) are among the more high-profile writers who struggle to maintain their privacy while also making something meaningful out of their blogs and the people they have met along the way.

In late 2005, a group of sex bloggers based in New York City decided it was high time we all met in person. In February 2006, we had a gathering, which was the first of many Perverts' Saloons, in which we've mostly had very civilized teas with cute little finger sandwiches and the occasional man in a G-string. Whenever I've told this story of (relative) offline harmony to sex bloggers in other cities, many of them can't imagine venturing out to meet other sex bloggers en masse. But many women have started to meet each other one-on-one—for conversation and note comparisons—and often for sex. Though the NYC sex bloggers might be peculiar in some ways, when I brought nine of the local ladies together for a group interview for this chapter, we talked about the effect that meeting each other has had on all of us. We each went from being characters on a screen to being actual human beings with a lot more in common than just sex. Everyone had the peculiar and uncanny experience of already knowing each other's intimate details before ever having met in person, coupled with a level of respect and understanding for what it is to be a sexual woman and a blogger—which is a not-too-common experience.

I'm not going to get up on my blogger soapbox and say that sex bloggers in any proximity to each other should meet up and hang out, but I think that it does demonstrate that as much as sex blogging is about the stories and the orgasms, it's also very much about women connecting—with lovers, with friends, and most importantly, with themselves. The sex blog is an end in itself, but for many women it's also an important tool for sexual exploration—both theoretical and practical.

# CHAPTER 4: I AM WOMAN, SEE ME NUDE
## The Rise of Female-Produced Independent Porn

**P**orn often goes hand-in-hand (or cock-in-hand, if you prefer) with creepy, sex-starved middle-aged men, often referred to as "raincoaters." But in these days of online porn, we may as well declare the raincoat brigade dead (long live the raincoat brigade). Since I'm a child of the eighties and didn't grow up walking past peep shows in Times Square, I have only my seventies-film-tinted goggles with which to consider these men—porn consumers from the past. I imagine them shortish, fattish, and hunched over in their beige trenchcoats, like disheveled, horny detectives seeking out the coin-operated booths in peep shows with neon signage and sticky floors.

Where are the women in these tales of jizz and glory? They are contained by video screens, behind the glass in live show booths, at home doing whatever dull and drab nonsexual things women do. But just as video killed the radio star, Internet porn killed the raincoat brigade. But electric loverland didn't just get these dudes off the streets; it created a new marketplace that, if not completely shame-free, has drastically altered the conditions under which people seek out porn and has therefore changed who looks at, stars in, and produces the new pornography.

Granted, the Internet can't take sole credit for a magical and massive sexual revolution. The sexual revolution that has been grinding along since the 1960s has a lot to it, too. Starting in the 1970s, women like Annie Sprinkle, Scarlot Harlot, and Veronica Vera found empowerment and joy in a sex industry that was constructed largely around men's desires and on women's backs. In their view, the potential of the sex industry lay in the power and sexual adventurousness of women whose desires were finally being realized (most significantly, by themselves). As the adult film industry harnessed the power of VHS in the early 1980s and began worming its way into people's homes in conspicuously oversized boxes, adult theaters began to close in droves. It's no coincidence that this time period witnessed more female performers stepping away from the world of filmed nudity for hire and behind the camera to become directors and producers.

The newfangled approach to making smut, dubbed "couples porn," came of age in the 1980s under the tireless efforts of women like Candida Royalle, Veronica Hart, Nan Kinney, and Debi Sundahl. Royalle and Hart carved out a niche in the heterosexual market, while Kinney and Sundahl were pioneers of lesbian smut made by and for lesbians. Though much ado is made about the content of these films—the action is generally considered more sensual, concentrating on relationships and interactions of body parts other than genitals, the stuff that "women want to see"—the production side is also impressive. At a time when women in the adult industry were almost exclusively talent, feminist auteurs stepped up and began to produce content they thought other women would appreciate, while treating their female performers with an understanding often not afforded them when they went to work for men who had never appeared naked on film or video.

In bits and pieces, as technology marched forward and female and feminist attitudes about porn changed, women began to take more and more back from the adult industry—and not just in a cultural, "take back the night" kind of way, but in a very quantifiable, green-colored way. By seizing the means of production—here I'm picturing a girl squeezing her boobs together and pinching her nipples, so fear not the Marxist talk—women over the last decade or so have started to remake, question, challenge, and enjoy the adult industry in a way that perhaps is only possible with the assistance of increasingly user-friendly and inexpensive technology.

The most high-profile story of a woman's success in the adult industry online is Danni's Hard Drive, which, now more than a decade old, is one of the most oft-cited early and big successes of an adult website run by a woman. Danni Ashe's promotional site, Billion Download Woman, boasts that when Ashe launched her site in 1995, she had $8,000 worth of equipment and an HTML how-to book. In addition to being the original model for the site, she learned how to manage the technology of the site as it grew. Ashe's success and her rise through the ranks from model to site owner to model manager to executive of a multimillion-dollar enterprise is unusual, but it sets the gold standard for what the Internet has made possible for women in the adult industry. In October 2006, the company was sold to Penthouse for $3 million in cash and stock options.

Small-scale, women-run businesses are a mainstay of the online porn industry in the cultural sense. The idea of a woman running her own site seems more personable and sexier than a corporate entity. Though the good old boys still have the industry mostly in their pockets, independent women's sites get a lot of attention, both prurient and financial. Like Ashe, women who run small sites often learn to do everything themselves, from setting up a tripod or enlisting a friend or romantic partner as their photographer to coding the website and managing the back-end credit card processing and interacting with the site's members. The somewhat ludicrous freedom of choice on the Internet has led to the development of niches that are sometimes difficult to imagine even in jest, but has created a window of opportunity for many women with the entrepreneurial nudie spirit.

On the other side of the screen are the women who might be referred to as the neoraincoat brigade—browsers and consumers of online porn. The idea of the lonely, shifty-eyed masturbator has perhaps always been a caricature of the quintessential porn consumer; I suppose it's possible (though not likely) that such men were being deployed to the local porn superstore to fetch smut for their feisty wives. The fact remains that men were and still are the majority of the market for porn, and non-sex-working women were and still are rarities in the world of brick and mortar porn shops—peep show or not. However, the Internet has created something of a safe space for women to explore and experience porn without having to face a clerk and a porn store full of men peering indiscreetly over the female specimens gracing the video section.

## Lady Look a Lot

The Internet has ushered in an age of casual porn browsing for all kinds of people, and with the advent of porn and penis-pill spam, porn can actually be difficult to avoid. Whereas the porn consumer of yore might have spent plenty of time obsessively scrutinizing box-cover art in an adult bookstore or leafing through an adult catalog with the kind of attention usually reserved for forensic investigations, in the age of the Internet, a potential consumer can sample the product before buying, or, as most often seems to be the case, sample the product without buying at all.

Though it's difficult to know exactly what percentage of porn paysite memberships are purchased by women, women are definitely spending time (if not money) browsing porn sites—sometimes with intent to masturbate, sometimes for curiosity's sake. Says Allison, a twenty-three-year-old from Philadelphia, "I started looking at porn online in a joking way when I was about fourteen. I've more recently started looking at porn in an arousing way . . . say maybe since I turned twenty-one." For almost all the women I spoke to who are under thirty, browsing free porn on the Internet had been a common pastime as a teenager. Though some young women told tales of discovering their dad's or brother's stash of glossy skin magazines featuring women in compromising positions, most of them were much more taken with images they found online, especially once they discovered they could do searches. Though the magazine stashes were a novelty, and maybe even well loved by some, many found that they became quite stale after the first few cover-to-cover trips, especially compared with the endlessly updated bounty of the Internet.

While many porn consumers are wary of their magazines being found by family or friends, weblinks are in fact just as easily discoverable, as Becky's family found: "When I was twelve, my brother got busted for looking at porn on the computer, and my parents banned him from it. But the links were still saved in the browser. I was home sick from school one day, and I looked up the sites."

Lauren, like Becky and other women who came of age in the 1990s, learned the joys of Internet porn through online bookmarks made by friends or family members. "At fourteen, I was surrounded by other hormonally charged teenage girls. We wanted to see what the big deal was. I had one friend who would look at boy/boy because she just wanted to see what a penis looked like and we were sick of watching HBO and Showtime and never seeing a penis," Lauren said.

Porn seeking for these young women was a combination of unfamiliar hormones and tingles from "down there" as well as a basic curiosity more often driven by the desire to see "what the big deal was" rather than by overt sexual desire. The young women I spoke to told similar tales of getting past the early stages of stumbling upon porn and starting to seek it out for themselves. At that point, there were a variety of options available to the intrepid and wide-eyed budding young porn connoisseur of the 1990s. People in chat rooms were cited as great resources: They provided large and unwieldy GIFs or turned women on to websites with entire caches of nudie pictures.. Another common discovery was the dirty written word, found on a variety of erotica websites.

## Dirty Words

When I started interviewing women about their porn-viewing practices, I was thinking exclusively about pictures and videos, and not at all about written erotica. But after more than a few women shared stories in their interviews of seeking out and writing erotica online, I started to think more about text and wonder how the word and image intermingled for women who enjoy both. Initially I assumed that there were some clear moments in which women might prefer text over images or vice versa, but this turned out not to be the case. Taryn, a lesbian who told me that she often has a difficult time finding authentic lesbian porn because of the massive chunk of the adult industry that produces girl/girl content for straight men, said, "I was interested in written erotica way before visual porn, partially because it's usually more erotic and less smutty, and the erotic part of sex was—and still is—easier for me to appreciate and be turned on by. Sometimes porn just isn't sexy or erotic—it's too much. Written erotica feels safer."

Written erotica is often perceived as the domain of women: It's lines of print novels like Harlequin Romance; it's evidenced in the rise in popularity of annual erotica anthologies for women, like Susie Bright's *Best American Erotica* and Tristan Taormino's *Best Lesbian Erotica*. Though it's difficult to give exact numbers—there aren't census figures on the population of the erotica-reading and -writing community—Rachel Kramer Bussel, *Penthouse Forum* editor and hostess of the monthly New York erotic reading series

In the Flesh, confirms that most writers and probably consumers of written erotica are women. Most collections of erotica are, indeed, aimed at a female audience, and the websites whose content is focused on erotic writing often promote a female perspective. Adrienne, who has devoted herself to running the Erotica Readers & Writers Association (ERWA) over the past ten years, says that the ratio of men to women interested in written erotica has changed considerably over the years because of changes in society: "Erotica has gone mainstream, and women are no longer frowned upon for writing erotica. A guesstimate would be that seven in ten published erotica writers are women, and probably more now that several of the big romance publishers are rolling out new imprints dedicated to erotica for women, by women." It's more difficult to know who's consuming the material, but chances are that the readership is mostly women.

The increasing popularity of written erotica among female readers and writers is often attributed to the popularly held assumption that men are more visually oriented than women. The truth is a little more complicated than that. Adrienne believes that this representation is part of a trend that evolves and devolves and resurfaces. She says, "I think it's just the social pendulum swing. Men were allowed and women weren't, so the ratio was heavily male. Now women are allowed, and they've eagerly leapt into porn—be it visual or written—with eyes wide open and keyboards clacking like mad." Though it's certainly useful to look at this trend as part of a larger phenomenon, it's also useful to heed what Taryn said about the availability of appealing visual material: It doesn't exist in a significant quantity. And though women are certainly moving into the realm of producing visual smut and shaping it in new ways (with no small thanks due to the Internet), writing erotica has significantly less overhead than producing films or online content. Since it doesn't entail the use of real bodies, written erotica can break free from many of the constraints that come with working with talent, and the physical and emotional issues of doing so. Characters in erotic stories don't refuse to have sex with each other because they think their scene partner smells bad.

However, a woman's desire to read erotica doesn't necessarily preclude her wanting to see pictures of naked people. For the women I talked to, the relationship between their online explorations of written and visual smut was pretty complex. Taryn's early exploration of written erotica had to do, in part, with her nervousness around whether women in visual porn were enjoying themselves, as well as feeling dissatisfied by porn that pretends to show lesbians but isn't intended for a lesbian audience. For Taryn, written erotica is sometimes preferable to visual porn because it allows her to cast women she's attracted to in the roles instead of being force-fed the sex industry's ideal women and sex acts. Emily, another avid reader of erotic stories, discovered written erotica before she discovered online porn. Though she had explored both written and visual erotica in print before she went online, Emily didn't really look for visual porn until more recently, because she felt shy about it.

There isn't an obvious division between the word and image for these women as they search for content online. Often the type of content they're looking for is based on their mood, or it's simply the first interesting thing to show up in their search. Taryn sometimes prefers online written erotica to images because, she says, "I've found written lesbian erotica to be much more prevalent online, and much easier to find and browse for." Emily admitted that her choice between the two mediums is based on her attention span more than anything else: "When I'm online I'm usually doing many things at once—as far as windows open, chatting, whatever—so reading is less intense than watching. And for some reason, I've just grown to prefer watching porn—it's much more visceral and hard to ignore."

## Smut Scavengers

Endless browsing and discovery is a key aspect of hunting for porn online, and though most of the women I interviewed said that their early online porn discoveries and adventures almost always occurred by accident, most of them have honed their skills and become more specific in what they look for. Since some of those female pioneers of film and video started to make videos and films in the 1980s, the concept of "women's" and "couples'" porn has risen in popularity: The joke has become that anything with a soft filter on the lights and a plot about relationships must be women's porn, and that the target audience for so-called women's porn is really gay men, because the men are attractive enough to meet gay standards.

Though women's porn gathered quite a bit of notoriety and scorn starting in the 1980s, the idea of what porn for women is has become much more nuanced since the advent of the Internet. Karen Jones, who runs a site marketed toward women called For the Girls, says that a focus on and concern for women's pleasure is the hallmark of porn made for women. The women I interviewed generally agreed with this sentiment and said they wanted to see porn featuring people who looked like they were enjoying themselves—though they didn't always make a distinction between porn for women and porn for men. Jones was very decisive in saying, "Ideally you could feature almost any kind of sexual act—BDSM, anal, fetishism, whatever—so long as it gives primacy to female pleasure and acknowledges the female audience."

However, as well defined as my interviewees' tastes in porn are, they all say that they aren't especially likely to buy porn online. For some it seemed too risky, with credit cards and identity theft running rampant on the Internet; for others, their curiosity about Internet porn is more than sated by free samples, or they feel like they want porn they can hold—DVDs or books— instead of files on their computers.

Karen Jones turned her dissatisfaction as a porn viewer into a career as a site owner. Though there were a few women's porn sites active before her sites launched, she thought she could do better than what was out there. She and her business partner, a woman who shares Jones's passion for woman-friendly porn, also found the money and lifestyle of adult webmistresses very appealing, since it meant they could work for themselves, look at naked men all day, and make good money. Jones's first site, Grandma Scrotum, was launched in 2000 and remains a free site with sex tips and advice as well as erotic stories, all infused with a grandmotherly (but also filthy) sense of humor.

For the Girls, which offers straight women a large collection of sexy photos handpicked to appeal to them, was launched in 2003. The site contains about 40,000 photos, with new images added in weekly updates as photo sets, which are a sequential—and sometimes narrative—series of anywhere between ten and eighty photos in which a man strips his clothes off or in which an already nude man strikes a variety of alluring poses. About half of the photo sets are pictures of solo nude men, while the other half includes heterosexual hardcore with a sampling of fetish, cunnilingus, group sex, and amateur content. They have recently started adding more and more videos to the site, which allows members access to streaming moving-image files of a variety of porn scenes, and they have a program for content access through paysite plugins, cross-promotional deals orchestrated by third-party companies that help increase the value of a site membership by promoting access to other related sites that a member is likely to be interested in.

Unlike the other independent businesswomen I interviewed, Jones's content is almost entirely made up of photo sets she purchases rather than content she self-produces. After two attempts at producing original content, she and her partner realized that taking their own photos of models would be an expensive and time-consuming process. "We can get similar results buying cheaper sets from established photographers. We could buy fifty photo sets for the amount we spent on one shoot," Jones says. Because For the Girls shows men who are attractive by mainstream standards, they have found that photo sets are fairly accessible as long as they take the time to edit photos that will be perceived as gay.

The content that Jones and her partner seek out is generally made by photographers who shoot and sell gay-male content. The reason for this stems from the fact that images of men for straight women are not the mainstay of the demand for pictures of naked men. Jones says, "If a guy looks stereotypically gay, he won't make the grade. Essentially we're picking photo sets that have been shot for a gay audience, but we take out the 'open bum' photos." The irony, of course, is that they're running a porn website for women that's constructed with porn made for men but edited to be more woman-friendly, or more in line with what women want to see—no spread butt cheeks, no globby cumshots to the face. By opting out of the expensive task of producing porn themselves, For the Girls faces a challenge around framing existing content in a way that they find palatable and in a way they think other women will gravitate toward, but it also gives them lots of creative control and room to experiment with what works and what doesn't.

## Breaking the Mold

Many people complain about the lack of diversity of porn in general. If you ask someone to describe a porn star to you, chances are that the three most frequently used descriptors would be "blond," "tan," and "busty." And although Internet porn is tinged with this type, one of the most celebrated (and bemoaned) aspects of Internet porn is how it's democratized the adult industry in a massive way. Before it was easy and relatively cheap for women to produce their own content, the vast majority of adult content was produced by men and featured cookie-cutter porn girls. Adult print publication *Genesis Magazine* puts out a "Top 100 Porn Stars" list every year that caters to the video-watching public, and it serves as a reminder of what the porn star template is. The vast majority of the women praised by *Genesis* got their starts in the print and video business rather than on the Internet. Though that line is permeable for some women—as it's proven to be for Joanna Angel, an Internet alt porn star who nudged her tattooed and brunette self into the number 42 slot in the 2006 *Genesis* list—for the vast majority of performers, the Internet and video industries are very different.

While the popularity of Internet porn is certainly not going to turn the blond porn girl into an endangered species, it has opened the floodgates for all kinds of women to explore their erotic fantasies and entrepreneurial goals. The fact that consumer electronics like the home video camera are both cheaper and easier to use than ever before means that women are signing up for webcamming accounts, doing erotic chat for spare cash, self-photographing and selling the images to websites, modeling for a variety of sites, or starting their own naked web businesses.

Though the clean-scrubbed, cute, young, and innocent "girl next door" has always been a source of fascination in the adult industry—Hugh Hefner built an entire brand around her—she is not really an accessible or realistic archetype. With the rise of amateur video porn, like Homegrown Video, founded in 1982, many real-life couples (the actual people who live next door to you, who you may not really want to see naked) have begun to self-produce and submit videotapes of their exploits. Home video technology made this shift in porn-making possible, and webcams and digital cameras have propagated this trend and made porn production even cheaper. Today, purchasing videotapes and storing them is practically archaic. Though Homegrown Video maintains brisk video sales, they also have a subscription-based website where members can view content online. With the development of the Internet, many more average Janes have begun to not only appear naked on the Internet, but also to successfully market themselves and make a living from their web projects as independent and often sole proprietors of their businesses.

Because technology has become more accessible, cheaper, and easier to use—including webcams that refresh every thirty seconds, user-friendly software for designing websites, cheap digital cameras, and digital-video-editing suites that come standard on many Mac computers—women have taught themselves how to build their own websites and have learned the best ways to capture images and market themselves online.

## For Fun and Profit

Dawn Marie, who lives in Phoenix and bills herself as a real wife and mom next door on her website Dawn Marie's Dream, has been posting naked pictures of herself online for the past eight years. Her first website, Net Angels, which was online for about five months, was created as a solution to the problem of her husband traveling for work and wanting to see her and interact with her sexually while he was on the road. Though she was initially nervous about the pictures being online, she started receiving positive responses from people in a chat room where she and her husband spent time. This was the impetus to launching her own website. Dawn Marie's marketing pitch is straightforward and honest—she's a believable wife and mom, and not in the glorified, pornified MILF (Mom I'd Like to Fuck) way either. She's the genuine article, not an actress. This authenticity is a key feature of independent online amateur porn sites that are managed by the people who appear on them.

Dawn Marie runs her current site in collaboration with her husband, who manages the technology at the back end of the site and does all of their photography. Dawn Marie's site is hardcore, but she says she doesn't do anything on camera that she doesn't do in her private life—and vice versa. Many of Dawn Marie's sexual adventures with her husband and with other men, as well as solo, are captured for posterity and made accessible for her members.

Like many long-term commercial sex ventures, Dawn Marie's site blurs the line between business and pleasure. Though her goal, of course, is for many people to visit her site, the nature of producing content for websites like Dawn Marie's is very private—there is no set with a film crew, just Dawn Marie and her husband, often in their own home. This setup easily lends itself to a sometimes accidental and sometimes intentional kind of intimacy that creates a different level of connection (or at least, assumed connection) between the model and her audience. When Dawn Marie started getting naked online, she wasn't especially business minded about the project, which was more about playing online and maintaining a connection in her marriage. However, Dawn Marie says, "Once we made the decision to include others in our fun, we decided to set it up as a business, and it is our main source of income now." For Dawn Marie, running the business hasn't diminished the fun aspects of the website, but she keeps to a content-production schedule and has become more attuned to the market and the desires of her viewers.

In the world of women who run their own websites, Dawn Marie—who's now been married for more than twenty years—belongs to a particular culture of women who work on their sites with their husbands. Though some of these women show sex scenes between themselves and their husbands, as Dawn Marie does, husbands are often an off-camera presence. They act as photographers and webmasters and are the Internet version of the "suitcase pimp." Suitcase pimp is a derogatory term for a male partner of a porn actress who is the driving business force behind her career; often it's assumed that he stays behind the scenes because he failed at performing on-screen or because he's pushing his wife to do scenes to support his lifestyle. For Dawn Marie and her husband, decisions about the site are made together, and though they view their site as a business venture (it became Dawn Marie's full-time job in 2002), she says that it's both a form of income and a source of fun for them.

Some of that fun involves other men, though not women, because Dawn Marie doesn't consider herself bisexual. Playing and shooting content with other men is an occasional thing for Dawn Marie that helps to diversify her content, but it's also in line with her sexual preferences. Online adult businesses run by couples are often an offshoot of swinger or hot-wife sexual lifestyles. Swingers are romantically monogamous couples who have sexual experiences with other couples or singles, and are usually part of a swingers community. Swingers often, but not always, attend parties with other swingers. And though the portrayal of swingers' events in popular media tends to focus on overweight middle-aged white people in a heaving pile of orgiastic flesh, their events are more often than not "off premises," meaning that though people attend to meet potential partners for sex, they don't necessarily consummate the act right away.

The hot-wife fetish is considered a subset of swinging and is when a wife is encouraged by her husband to have sexual experiences with other men. The husband may just enjoy watching, or he might prefer to arrange the meetings but not be present, and rather hear detailed descriptions of the events later. Both swinging and hot-wife play fit in nicely with missions of some women's websites because sections dedicated to the exploration of these lifestyles may be primary features; these sites also give members whose lives are unlike the models' the ability to peer in at something a little or a lot different from their own lives. For women in the swinging community who run sexy websites, their play community often becomes a source for meeting people to make content with, and thus work and play are generally closely related.

There is certainly a rift between women who run sites with the assistance or cooperation of a male partner and those who go it alone or with the assistance of other web girls. Husband/wife teams who run adult sites are often perceived by solo women as being casual about their businesses, and in turn these teams tend to regard solo women as being purely business minded and not interested in the personal sexual development that is available to them with a quick digital snapshot and the click of their mouse. Though neither perspective is completely off base, the reality is that the two different kinds of sites have a lot in common, especially the longer they exist.

Trixie Fontaine, who lives near Seattle and calls herself an indie webwhore, launched her first paysite, Tasty Trixie, through iFriends, a person-to-person chat and camming site, in 2001. A year later she launched Tasty Trixie using her own host and an account with credit card processor and monthly rebill champion CCBill, the industry standard for payment processing. She launched the new site, self-designed and coded, with 24/7 spycams as well as camshows and a personal blog. It still exists in this form today, though she's added a few other sites to her empire. Fontaine had no prior web design experience, but she learned the mechanics of it out of necessity, and says, "It would have taken more time and denied me more control to hire someone. I'm very glad that I learned the basics of web design, photo editing, coding, et cetera. I've seen a lot of girls try to start up sites with someone else doing the webmastering, and it rarely works out."

Fontaine's webwhoring grew out of her experimentation with chat rooms and hooking up with strangers for sex. When she stumbled onto iFriends and discovered that women were making money for less work than what she was doing for free, she was immediately intrigued. She took a leave of absence from her pink-collar job to launch her website and see what the possibilities were, assuming that she'd have to rejoin the world of the straight job. She never went back, though, and instead became intent on success in the online porn industry. Five years after the launch of her first web venture, Tasty Trixie, as well as a few other sites that feature Fontaine and her now-boyfriend Tucker, is the sole source of income for both of them.

## Indie vs. Mainstream

Though Fontaine participates in some adult website forums and has attended several conventions like the Internext Expo, an annual porn convention with specific focus on the online aspect of the industry, she finds, "Most people in the Internet porn industry don't really get what we do, even though there are lots of sites similar to ours—homemade. We are such a small percentage of Internet porn sites that most people in the industry don't understand us." It only takes a few clicks on Fontaine's links and the links of other independent web workers like Dawn Marie to reveal a seemingly infinite list of women who get naked for pay on their own sites. Still, the number of independent sites pales in comparison to the vast number of sites run by companies that purchase content, like For the Girls, or that support their businesses through affiliate programs, like the one provided by the Bang Bros Online network. If site owners aren't interested in creating their own content, an Internet porn venture is extremely easy to launch through a page that features affiliate links. Bang Bros Online, a company that's given the world such sites as Assparade.com and FartHammer.com, runs a successful affiliate program that provides support for webmasters. This includes promotional tools and access to free content, which reduces webmasters' overhead in managing their program and only involves guiding their customers toward other content that Bang Bros' websites host.

A business powered by affiliate links is made up of a very simple webpage with links to porn sites on it. Each time a surfer clicks on a link and then becomes a member of that linked site, the owner of the site that brought the customer there makes money—often as much as half the monthly subscription rate for the life of the membership. Each link has a special code built into it that remembers the visitor; it will also recall which site referred the surfer for up to a month afterward, which means the surfer doesn't have to click and sign up for membership immediately, and the affiliate site owner will still make money off of them. Affiliate sites are challenging to keep afloat and profitable because so many of them go the easy route of being a link-dump site, meaning places where the only content is weblinks that are organized with no rhyme or reason. The better affiliate link sites provide a minimum of free content; in fact, many of the sites that offer affiliate programs make it a policy to provide some content for free to help webmasters entice potential subscribers.

The business model for sites that function as content malls, or only provide links to affiliates and aren't built around a personality, is very different from that of sites that are linked to a personality—particularly a woman who's instrumental in running her own site. This is mostly because the big sites don't appeal to viewers who seek out personable porn. They also operate on a much larger, more corporate scale. Though the less personal sites don't create the opportunity for easy money that many people believe they do, the potential for earning and gathering members is much higher among the mainstream sites because their content and appeal is much broader and less of a niche.

On the content-production side of things, many websites buy content from photographers and content brokers who select and purchase photo and video content in bulk, repackage it, and sell it to third parties. These sites can then name the models and write bios for them, none of which have anything to do with the actual person in the photograph. In these types of setups, the gap between model and consumer is vast. As impersonal as it seems, however, this business model is a function of the rapid-fire demand of adult entertainment online, where large websites that post multiple updates every day are responsible for an output of content that is impossible for a website run by one or two people to maintain.

Thumbnail gallery post (TGP) sites, like Mia Movies, occupy the gray area between purchased-content sites like For the Girls and affiliate programs like Bang Bros Online. Mia Movies is updated every fifteen minutes with a dizzying array of explicit thumbnails. Clicking on a thumbnail brings the curious surfer to a short free video clip that's supposed to entice the viewer into pulling out a credit card. TGPs make money the way affiliate sites do, but instead of abbreviated sample sets, they provide an assortment of unrelated samples. TGP galleries are designed for the impulsive porn surfer who is clicking maniacally in search of the porn clip of the moment.

Though independently run websites cannot compete with megasites that have frequently updated content and many models, they do have the advantage of authenticity that some porn consumers crave. Several of the women I interviewed say that they specifically look for sites where the models' personalities, and not just their boobs, are detailed in their profiles, blogs, and message boards. Even though independent sites are a small sector of the marketplace, and don't pull in huge sums of money like many of the larger, more impersonal sites do, they are popular enough that many of the women who run them are able to make a living doing nothing but working on their sites. And this is in large part due to the fact that their consumers become loyal and rabid devotees.

Independent sites can be the answer to the problem of cookie-cutter porn, since many of these women work for themselves. This is usually because they're unable or unwilling to subject themselves to the beauty standard of mainstream porn fare. The trend toward more-authentic girl/wife/mom-next-door porn started with amateur videos in the early 1980s—the Internet can't quite take credit for that trend—but porn content has become ever more specialized online. Now consumers can Google or sort through links and suggestions on message boards to find exactly what they're looking for. Many independent women find niches they enjoy (or at least tolerate) and cater their content accordingly. As a result, the web has seen the rise of many fetishes you've never heard of and that might not exist as fully as they do without the Internet.

## A Bloody Business: Independent Period Porn

Though Fontaine is extremely business minded, her sites are also reflective of her real life, due in no small part to the fact that she appears on cam around the clock. Early on in her career, Fontaine realized that it was important to her to not act the part of the perfect lady and pretend that bodily functions, mood swings, and ugly moments were absent from her life in some attempt to be her subscribers' fantasy porn girl. Fontaine comments that the spycams "humanize us and remind people we're *regular* people who do *regular* things, and that sex is only part of our lives—not all-consuming." Because of her choice to portray the real aspects of her daily life, and since her site proclaims that her cams are 24/7 with frequent updates, she feels that it's natural to do photo shoots while she's on her period; she didn't see any particular reason to hide her blood. However, her credit-card-payment processor, which handles payment processing for a slew of adult sites, viewed the depiction of menstruation themes in adult material as obscene. As a result, Fontaine says, "I had to either delete all of my menstruation porn or move it to another site. I guess pure, unmitigated anger and resentment led me to create and run Bloody Trixie."

As a rule, menstruation is generally not something that's seen in porn, which is a peculiar omission in an industry that fetishizes everything from shoes to stuffed animals to excretory functions. Though credit-card-processing companies seem to have no problem with double- and triple-penetration sites, bukkake, and electricity play, most of them regard menstruation and other forms of blood play as out of bounds, citing obscenity violations as well as safer sex concerns—though anal cream pies and the like are at least as risky. Adult webmasters also tend to regard menstruation sites with disdain (I've even read posts where webmasters refer to Fontaine's site as "sick shit"), which in many ways underlines the ways that the adult industry is set up to fetishize but not appreciate the female body and what it is capable of.

Despite or perhaps because of this taboo, the Internet—by sheer force of size, diversity, and perversity—has created space for menstruation fetishists to meet one another and exchange photos and links. The vast majority of these websites do not focus on menstruation as a sexual interest or fetish, but rather are sites run by men that focus on the refuse of menstruation: soiled underwear, dirty maxi pads, and tampons. Though it's not an adult site, the online Museum of Menstruation and Women's

Health typifies this fascination with the products surrounding menstruation. A score of menstruation message boards and adult sites have popped up; these too focus on used menstrual products more than they focus on bloody pussies themselves. Though this apparent disinterest may seem to some that the focus is in the wrong place, it is in keeping with the traditional trappings of fetishism, where an object becomes the erotic focus. Menstruation products are the earliest point of contact for men who become menstruation fetishists.[1] Big Tunaman and Pixel Pete, who ran a period porn website and a menstruation forum in the early 2000s, focused the vast majority of their content on used products.

The women I interviewed about period porn—Furry Girl of Erotic Red, Candy Poses of the now-defunct art project See Candy Bleed, and Fontaine—don't place primary focus on menstruation products, but rather on menstruating women and blood. Fontaine and Furry Girl both agree that men who fetishize used products or blood-stained clothing get off on being grossed out and often combine their fetish with other shock-value fetishes. All three women want to challenge the shape of the market. Furry Girl sees period porn as a part of the bigger picture of women's sexuality, and says, "I want red sex to come out of the closet, which is why I do not frame the site in the degrading and absurd ways that most of the other menstrual sites do." Furry Girl emphasizes that while having a period is part of women's sexuality, menstrual products don't make most women feel sexy.

When I ask each of the women about the challenges they have faced in running their websites, Furry Girl recounts a particularly poignant experience: "When one large adult company launched a site devoted to raping and assaulting 'sleeping women,' most adult webmasters were chomping at the bit to promote it. When I finally launched Erotic Red, almost everyone I heard from in the industry verbally attacked me with everything from cries of stuff like 'you're fucking sick in the head' to accusing my one little site of being capable of triggering a wave of sexual repression in our nation that would put us all out of business." Poses adds to that sentiment, noting, "A lot of times the people who find it disgusting continued to look at the site, despite warnings that specifically stated what was in it."

Though Furry Girl continues to add new content to Erotic Red, Fontaine and Poses have shut down their sites. Fontaine's site no longer accepts new members because of troubles with billing companies, while Poses opted to shut down her free site after she began to suspect that her brother's friends had discovered it. Even though women who produce porn are generally at risk for all kinds of social and legal stigma, adding a taboo subject to the mix can create all kinds of unforeseen problems and difficulties.

Menstruation fetish websites and forums tend to attract people who write in solely to express their disdain for the participants. Fontaine, Furry Girl, and Poses have all witnessed these kinds of criticisms of their own work because they are active in other sexual communities and commercial efforts online. Because each of the women is outspoken about issues surrounding women's sexuality, beauty standards, and sex work, they have continued to come under fire for their period porn. While running their websites is a full-time business pursuit for Fontaine and Furry Girl, period porn is also an important political issue for them, even though financially it's probably not worth the amount of work and stress. Fontaine, however, is intense about her right to do as she wishes with her body: "I like making porn that disgusts other people; I really do. The more society tries to censor and limit our freedom of speech, the more it makes me want to do whatever I want to do. The more they apply pressure, the more it makes me want to take a big messy shit and smear it around on my body and take pictures of it. Because I should be able to do whatever the fuck I want with my own body and say whatever the fuck I want and take whatever fucking photos of myself I want."

Period porn is a significant example of the power of the Internet for female pornographers who want to put something different into the world and have a political stance behind it. After posing for product-fetish images for Tunaman's site, Fontaine got more serious about Bloody Trixie and moved away from the constraints of working for someone else and his requirements and began to celebrate her flow more freely on the site, which she launched in 2004. Furry Girl and Poses likewise decided to break with the tradition of menstrual-product-fetish imagery and celebrate their periods in a way that concentrates on their flow instead of the products used to catch the blood. It's interesting to note that negative publicity and links trashing them and their work have generated a significant amount of notoriety for all three women and their work.

## Alt Porn to the Rescue

While independent female porn producers are not always political about their work—Dawn Marie says she definitely doesn't identify as a feminist and is uninterested in debates about porn and objectification of women—the burgeoning alt porn subculture has been a location for the rise of fiercely feminist women in pornography. Alt porn performers and content producers are extremely aware of the meanings and struggles around getting naked for strangers, and though many of the women involved in alt porn culture have turned their passion into their business, most of them started out more interested in culture and politics than in the financial opportunities of Internet porn.

What is alt porn? A definition of the genre has made its way into the Urban Dictionary, a website that defines both regional and Internet slang:

> **alternative pornography.** *a medium (mainly online but also occasionally in print) consisting of an alternative to mainstream pornography; websites that often offer communities where members can communicate with models, breaking down barriers and exploitation by featuring models who are real people. Often feature men and women of subculture and considered woman-friendly and sex-positive.*[2]

As the genre grows, the word "subculture" is increasingly employed to describe alt porn models and the websites they appear on. Subculture seems to be a catchall term that refers to the fact that, for alt porn models, tattoos and body piercings are de rigueur. Since alt porn went mainstream (well, for online porn at least), which was marked by the VCA Pictures (owned by Larry Flynt) funded movie *Art School Sluts*—which hit stores in fall

2004, followed by the establishment of Vivid Alt, a division at Vivid Entertainment specifically dedicated to the genre in 2006, tattoos and body piercings have in fact become the marker of the alt porn "look."

SuicideGirls is by far the best known of the alt porn sites outside of the bubble that is the Internet. Founded by Missy Suicide and Spooky Suicide (who is now more commonly referred to by his legal name, Sean Suhl) in 2001, SuicideGirls features softcore pinup photos of tattooed and pierced women who maintain profiles and blogs on the site; the site is adamant in insisting that it shows pinups, never porn. This not-porn claim is fairly prevalent among photographers and models alike when sexy but somewhat clothed ("implied nude") content is involved, and there are many not-porn sites that feature girls posing sexily while wearing lingerie.

Though SuicideGirls attracted controversy about its modeling contracts and other policies as early as 2003, the site came heavily under fire from its models and the alt porn community in the fall of 2005, when several of the models expressed dismay at how the site was being managed and how the girls were being treated. Rumblings of discontent began in the spring and summer of 2005 during the SuicideGirls burlesque tour and the practice period before it, during which Suhl is alleged to have berated the models on a regular basis. Ultimately, the girls claimed that they were not paid the money they were owed for the burlesque tour DVD they participated in. This was followed by the complaint of general exploitation and unfairness regarding multiple facets of the company's policies and practices. Though the site pitches itself as a female-run, feminist expression of sexual empowerment, many models who quit or were forced to have their profiles archived in 2005 beg to differ. In the late spring of 2006, the site's owners sold some of its content to other porn sites, which then posted words like "she loves it from behind" under the models' images; needless to say, there was a lot of outrage in the alt porn community as a result.

This outrage stems from the fact that the women who self-define as SuicideGirls regard themselves and the site as having alternative values and being supportive of (DIY) do-it-yourself efforts and a punk rock, anticorporate ethos. The anger surrounding the sale of content to sites with more of a porn bent to them underlines the fact that many SuicideGirls had too much faith in what they thought was the good word of the site's founders and perhaps didn't pay close-enough attention to the contract they signed (which gave all ownership and resale rights to SuicideGirls). Now that their images are out in the world of mainstream porn, some of the models are coming to terms—and are very uncomfortable—with the notion that getting naked on the Internet is considered porn. Over the last several years, the tangle of feminism, porn, ethics, and capitalism has become increasingly complex for women who work in alt porn, and the flurry of anxiety and drama surrounding the release of company-owned content by SuicideGirls typifies this.

Alt porn models and webmistresses have a variety of opinions about their work—its political potential, its place in the adult industry, and its financial possibilities. Furry Girl, who runs the websites Furry Girl, VegPorn, and the aforementioned Erotic Red, set on the path of creating her own sites shortly after her first modeling experience: "I first posed for a huge amateur porn megasite in May 2002, and the experience assured me that I should be working for myself. The photographer was a fumbly, sleazy guy with a hard-on and a face dripping with sweat, and I couldn't believe he was being paid 150 percent of what I was for our day shoot. I needed to cut out the middleman." Furry Girl is now the webmistress of all of her sites, and her main goal for all three is "to promote an inclusive and playful standard of sexuality."

Molly Crabapple, a twenty-three-year-old professional illustrator and former SuicideGirl, has gained a lot of perspective since being in one of the first big waves of SuicideGirls to quit the site in fall 2005 and being quoted in the *New York Press* as saying that "SuicideGirls is the Wal-Mart of alt porn."[3] Though disappointed in the failed DIY ethos of SuicideGirls, Crabapple has an acute understanding of the business of nude modeling, and her sets for SuicideGirls were just three photo shoots out of hundreds she did during the few years she was working as a model. She is adamant that the modeling she did for SuicideGirls and others was not porn. She drew the line at spreading her legs: "I never did any explicit nudity. Spreading your legs seems like such a small thing, but one spread shot destroys your whole 'art model' cover story."

While SuicideGirls was not what Crabapple and other models had hoped it could be, Crabapple is certainly not sheltered from the realities of the nude modeling industry. Spread legs or no, today she is ambivalent about her time spent posing naked for money. Although she spent a few years model-ing during her student days, she feels that nude modeling, while temporarily very lucrative, was a dead end. When Crabapple began to get more jobs as an illustrator, she stopped doing nude modeling, quit SuicideGirls, and shut down her modeling portfolio website. When I ask her the million-dollar question on every feminist's lips—Does modeling naked make you feel empowered or degraded?—she answers, "Degradation means posing for some vile rich dude who's insulting you the whole time. Empowerment means a fat wallet later."

Furry Girl's websites are very firmly rooted in the DIY ethos, and as a model and site owner, she's very aware of the challenges that face alt porn models. Her sites make the model policies accessible; they state that models receive $100 per model per set of photographs that are accepted to appear on the site. She is acutely aware of the repercussions that doing porn can have on a woman's life. The FAQ for the models includes very clear language that photos will not be removed from the site once a model has signed a release and submitted a set because a lot of time and energy goes into preparing a photo set and promoting it, and the contract must be upheld. Furry Girl advises wannabe models: "If you're already concerned about what your parents/coworkers/conservative friends would think if they found nudie pictures of you on the Internet, you probably shouldn't be doing porn anywhere, even on nice indie sites run by nice people." This underlines one of the more intense ramifications that models don't always consider: Once a naked picture is online, it will exist somewhere, stored by someone, indefinitely. Many photographers and webmasters on corporate sites bank on the fact that models don't think about this, so Furry Girl's straightforward concern about the issue is rare and valuable.

Furry Girl's sites have clean designs that don't immediately scan like porn sites—except for the naked pictures. One of Furry Girl's claims to fame is her acceptance of models with a variety of body shapes and sizes, as well as varying gender presentations. Furry Girl herself is outspoken about her unwillingness to shave her body hair—not as a titillation factor, but as a personal choice. On VegPorn, many of the models are not conventionally attractive. Some are overweight or, in the lingo of the adult industry, "not height-weight proportionate," and many are genderqueer or transgendered. The site features all of the models together on the same page without differentiating between their genders or appearances. Furry Girl's sites illustrate the Urban Dictionary definition of alt porn to a tee—and though alt porn found in the DVD sector of the adult industry increasingly masquerades as different while really just portraying skinny white girls with tattoos, fake nails, and excessive makeup, the Furry Girl empire sticks much closer to the origins of alt porn while also succeeding as a profitable business venture.

Another alt porn webmistress who helped shape alt porn in its early forms is now-retired Lux Nightmare of That Strange Girl, who is generally credited as being the first alt porn producer to offer photo sets of both men and women on her website. Like Furry Girl, Lux was intent on showcasing models of a variety of shapes and sizes on her site, which launched in September of 2002 and shut down in February 2005. She modeled for other people before deciding that the best way to do porn on her terms was to start her own site, where she could not only control the content but maintain ownership of her images. Lux was never able to make

That Strange Girl into her primary source of income; though it did take up increasing amounts of her time and energy over the years that she operated the site and sustained itself financially, it didn't become the cash cow that is (mythically) expected of Internet porn. Lux's inability to make her site profitable may have been because of a lack of demand, or it may have been a reflection of her capabilities as a businesswoman, about which she says, "It's laughable how unfocused I was on money. I didn't have any real sense of this as a business and started out purely focused on the mission." Money tends to be a struggle for all alt-porn-site owners, not just because as business owners they're trying to eke out a living and often need more money to keep afloat outside of the mainstream, but also because oftentimes the driving force behind the work they do is not always the money.

Anna Logue, who launched her site Nerd Pr0n in 2003, is focused on creating porn that doesn't look like and isn't managed like corporate porn because, she says, "Corporate porn sites tend to pull more dirty tricks like popups and blind links, and they also mass-produce porn in a way I find kind of disturbing." She recognizes the challenges that face female content producers, and not just the ones creating content that pushes limits, but all independent women who must deal with the fees associated with credit card processing. Before Logue ran her paysite, she was liberally posting nude pictures of herself online and began shooting amateur sex videos of herself and friends. When she first started she was in her teens, and money was not the sole driving force behind her desire to get naked online. However, the decision to make the leap and start her site was linked to finances: "I was broke, extremely broke, and needed to be able to feed myself. I was already posting a lot of nudes online, so I thought I'd just take it a step further and start charging." In addition to the joy of being able to get naked for fun and profit, Logue says that one of the primary benefits to working on her own porn site is that she gets to indulge in her reclusive tendencies. Many of the other women I interviewed concurred with that sentiment. Although porn performers are perceived as outrageous and outgoing, one of the things many online adult performers like best about exposing themselves on the Internet is that they can hide out in their homes and keep contact with other people to a minimum.

Bella Vendetta's eponymous site has gradually come into existence over the past several years, but it was October 2005 when it became a regularly updated paysite. (In the interest of full disclosure: I am a model on Bella's site.) Vendetta bills it as a site featuring "girls who beat up SuicideGirls"; it is decidedly more edgy than many other alt porn sites. It builds on the SuicideGirls, Furry Girl, and That Strange Girl models, featuring people with body modifications who are unconventionally attractive and representative of a variety of genders and sexual orientations. BellaVendetta has a rougher edge to it than many of the more fluffy alt sites do, and the site features a host of kinks that include necrophilia play, kidnapping, suicide fetishism, and blood play, to mention a few. Like the menstruation sites, Vendetta found it difficult to get a credit card processor to take on her site and has purposefully shied away from a few kinks until she monitors the reactions to the site in its present state for a while. Though Vendetta's goal is to be a fully profitable and financially sustainable business within the next two years—she is one of the few people I interviewed who had a business plan in place—she has so far been unable to pay her models. The site does not go wanting for models, though, and she's able to update with new sets four times a week, with a full update schedule stretching months into the future. When I ask her why it is that so many people are willing to get naked and do all manner of perverse things to themselves and their friends on her site, she says, "I really don't know why they all do it for free. I am always surprised that people want to get naked for free for me—I think it just goes to show how much they believe in the project and feel a part of the community."

Vendetta has been modeling nude since she turned eighteen eight years ago, and during that time she has built up a substantial group of connections to photographers and models, especially based on her involvement in the body modification and suspension scene. Her ability to get people to pose naked for free is largely due to the faith her models have in her as a fellow model, community member, and businesswoman, but even so, it's baffling that her reputation has made people so eager to do for free what many people would not consider for any amount of money. Though alt porn can be considered a business, the models' acts of commercial nudity for no promised financial return highlight a shift in the value of nudity for hire. This is made all the more interesting by the fact that many of Vendetta's models, herself included, have worked in other sectors of the commercial sex industry—in dungeons and strip clubs and as independent escorts—where their degree of "altness" was not cherished, but seen as a liability or a fetishistic element. Thus, for many of these women, modeling for Bella Vendetta more nearly approaches an authentic expression of their sexuality than their paid sex work does, and this authentic expression of sexuality is very important to many alt porn sites and models alike.

For Joanna Angel, owner and leading lady of Burning Angel Entertainment, business and community have melded together in a powerful way that has made her company quickly rise to the top of the alt porn genre, both online and off. Burning Angel started in much the same way as other alt porn sites, with some tattooed girls, some bad photography, and some band interviews. It never hesitated to show hardcore action like some other sites do. One of the keys to Burning Angel's success as a public relations project, other than having a hot girl as the front woman (the power of which should not be underestimated), is that its fans do the promotional work for it. Community is touted as one of the most important aspects of alt porn, and with community buy-in comes lots of attention, and in Burning Angel's case, dollars. "We recently hired a guy to do search engine optimization, and he said we've mastered the most difficult thing: 90 percent of our traffic is from direct type-ins, instead of click-throughs," she says. "This means that our main source of traffic is word-of-mouth, which is pretty impressive for a porn site."

In alt porn, commercial success is both a desired outcome and something that gets easily snubbed. Cries of "sellout!" ring loud when it comes to the successes of Burning Angel and other alt porn producers who have moved off the Internet and into the financial graces of major porn companies like VCA and Vivid. Alt porn people criticize Burning Angel for sliding comfortably into the porn aesthetic; its models may be tattooed, but many of the alt porn performers on DVDs are otherwise conventionally attractive (slim and white). Meanwhile, doing porn as a social or political service is costly financially and socially. So you're selling out if you do succeed, but you're damned if you don't succeed.

## Obscene, but Not Heard

While independent porn producers and alternative models may set the gold standard for what's possible in the adult industry, in the financial reality of the megabusiness that is Internet porn, they serve the primary purpose of getting lots of press and bugging the shit out of other content producers and website maintainers on adult-webmaster message boards. There is an entire group of women I did not interview for this chapter, and their absence is frustrating, but also symbolic in a way. They are the women who do not work directly for a website, but who are hired by photographers who then sell their photos to the highest bidder, and often sell them to more than one buyer. These women drive the porn industry forward at a spectacular rate, while the women interviewed for this chapter, however fascinating, make up a very small portion of the market share. The reason these women are so difficult to interview is because they don't often have email addresses listed next to their pictures and they are not involved in adult industry communities because the industry is a one-time gig for them, not part of a career path.

The average softcore adult nude model is a young woman who may have responded to an online ad for models, posed nude one day, done five or six different sets of photos, collected her cash, and was never heard from again. Softcore nude pictorials and solo girl scenes (sometimes with toys) have been the standard on the Internet for many years because they are the cheapest and easiest shoots to produce. A solo girl does not need to be matched with another performer, and a softcore scene does not require that the model present a test that proves she is clear of HIV, chlamydia, and gonorrhea.

Semianonymous models have always been a part of the adult industry—their faces and bodies fill up scads of adult magazines that have populated the shelves of adult bookstores over the years—but the Internet has made it possible for even more young women to join their ranks through the magic of digital photography. The digital era has also created a new figure: the guy with a camera, or GWC, as they are referred to on online-model message boards. Digital photography has made taking pictures cheaper and much more accessible to the average dude with a hard-on and a desire to photograph pretty young ladies in the nude, as long as he can post a few images to an online portfolio site like One Model Place (OMP) or Model Mayhem (MM) and send somewhat coherent emails. OMP and MM serve a mainstream audience, but they're also spaces where adult models and photographers meet up, even if the models aren't always there with the intent of doing adult modeling. Many photographers—professionals and GWCs alike—approach models on these sites and propose adult shoots regardless of whether the model expresses interest in that kind of work in her profile. This is one of the ways that women who make single appearances on adult sites get recruited these days.

GWCs tend not to have professional portfolio websites and instead choose to utilize MM (which is free), OMP (where posting five images is free but there are also paid memberships), and increasingly MySpace. A little bit of practice with Photoshop and some basic design allows GWCs to portray themselves as serious photographers, even if they're only in it for the naked women, but in many ways this posturing as the real thing mirrors the kind of posturing the models are doing too. Feeling like a model and being admired for physical beauty, whether for pay or not, is something that many young women enjoy. And as adult modeling becomes more widespread and digitized (though whether it's more acceptable than it used to be is a point of contention), more and more young women are appearing naked on the Internet.

A solo girl may or may not have picked a nude modeling pseudonym for herself—but it wouldn't matter regardless because she may show up on different websites under different names. She may be marketed in a million different ways—I've seen the same girl marketed as a college girl-next-door and as a MILF (for the so-called "older woman" category that often includes all women older than twenty-five). The utter lack of information about these models, along with the way their looks are packaged and repackaged according to the needs of the webmaster who buys their images, speaks to their value, and perhaps the value of all women in the world of Internet porn: They are "content."

Though there are amazing women who challenge this notion of women-as-content on a daily basis, and have put their asses on the line to do so, the harsh reality remains that women's participation and power in pornography is curtailed by the churning forward of the industry machine, and the demand for fresh content and fresh pussy, however and from whomever it's obtained. Though many consumers of porn prefer intimate and realistic experiences, which include personality and variation, its scarcity and the stigmas attached to porn consumption—and especially becoming a connoisseur of porn—make impersonal porn the most accessible option. Though there will likely always be porn consumers who will seek out personable porn made ethically by people who love what they do, as long as consumers continue to buy what Anna Logue calls "corporate porn," independent-minded women who run their own businesses and own their own content will not make up the majority of the market—and the content-broker structure will continue to be one of the main ways the industry is driven forward.

## For Love, Money, or Vanity?

The silent masses of adult models do actually give a collective voice to the main reason women do porn: the money. Though for the women I interviewed, making porn isn't *just* about the money, but also about personal and political empowerment and promotion of a positive view of bodies and sexuality; for most women it's simply about the piles of cash that can be made in a short amount of time for work that is challenging but doesn't require an immense amount of talent or skill. A woman using her natural (or artificial, as the case may be) assets for gain is nothing new, but in recent years this commercial form of sexuality has begun to mix in a complex way with beauty, ego, and noncommercial sexuality.

The Internet is a peculiar space in which sexuality is both commodified and exploited for free. With the prevalence of porn online, including in the form of email spam and myriad other spaces that may or may not be intended for adult material, porn has worked its way into the cultural landscape even more so than before. Though the Internet isn't the sole driving force behind this growth, the prevalence of images online has upped the ante and boosted the freedom with which young women get naked or pose in sexually suggestive ways.

On websites like MySpace, young women—some not even of legal age—pose in photos that make them look like porn stars; some even claim the title "porn star" when they are nothing of the sort. "Porn star" has become something of a shorthand for "over-the-top sexy," yet the young women who adopt this style aren't necessarily in line to actually become America's next top porn star. What's unsettling to me is not that women might consider themselves candidates for porn stardom, or a job as some other kind of sex worker, but that the only space available for them to express their sexuality is through imitating commercial sexiness. The Internet makes commercial sexiness more readily available to women who are buying into it—even if they're not buying it.

When I was discussing this topic with Trixie Fontaine, who experimented with her sexuality on the Internet without charging for it before she launched her paysites, she mulled over the possibilities for why young women bare themselves online without pay: "I think they do it: (a) because it makes them feel good to get positive feedback on the way they look, (b) because they have no idea what their value is—that they could be compensated for such things, and (c) because they won't allow themselves to be compensated because they think real women enjoy compliments more than money." Fontaine admitted to feeling judgmental about women who get naked for free, despite trying to live and let live, and I agree with her even though I've tried my hand as one of the very women we are shaking our heads over. Being admired is very compelling.

Do the realities of commodification of female sexuality by porn mean that every woman who chooses to get naked online should demand payment for it? No, definitely not. What they do mean is that it's important to pay attention to the ways in which independent women are attempting to transform the online porn industry and challenge the perceptions of women in porn while also giving serious thought to the ways that porn creates a single-frequency channel for women's sexuality as a marketable entity.

# CHAPTER 5: SEX ON THE OPEN MARKET
## Sex Workers Harness the
## Power of the Internet

S ex work may be the world's oldest profession, but the word "profession," until recently, has been only vaguely applicable to this line of work. It's perhaps more accurate (though less snappy) to say that sex workers[1] are the world's oldest unregulated working population. But for a profession that can stake such a historical claim, the industry is extremely adaptable—and workers have been quick to pursue opportunities provided by the Internet as they arose and continue to change, including but not limited to online porn. Though the porn performers I wrote about in the last chapter, as well as the cam girls in the first chapter, certainly qualify as sex workers, the Internet provides women whose sex work is conducted in person, especially escorts, with new opportunities for advertising, screening clients, and building community with one another.

Because of the shame of societal disapproval and the logistics around the legal repercussions inherent in this line of work, advertising, safety, and access to community are immense challenges to people who work in the sex industry. Over the last dozen or so years, the Internet has allowed for a massive shift as far as access goes, and the sex industry has therefore become more accessible to would-be workers and clients. The sex industry has also simultaneously become more private and more exposed, more professional and more of an identifiable culture. The culture of shame around the industry is very much alive in some respects; however, for many women, shame is being chased out as more and more current and former sex workers out themselves in the media beyond the Internet.

The most obvious example of this outing is in the ways porn stars are obsessed over by mainstream media. Sex worker chic is spreading like wildfire. In certain ways, this is nothing new: Xaviera Hollander, internationally known as "the happy hooker" after her 1972 book by the same name, became a celebrity and symbol of free love in the 1970s. Since then, porn stars, strippers, and high-class call girls have leapt into the mainstream spotlight through sex scandals and tell-all memoirs. For the sex workers themselves, this popularity is not dissimilar to the shiny red apple with a razor lodged inside: As trendy and appealing as sex work can seem to be, the profession is still rife with stigma and many inherent risks. The possibilities of the Internet for sex workers lead to a kind of choose-your-own-adventure negotiation with notoriety and secrecy, where a sex worker can easily become something of a celebrity both within her own community and outside of it if she puts in the effort. Though there are many different kinds of sex workers who use the Internet, including escorts, fetish workers, dommes, and strippers who use online forums for support, the bulk of this chapter focuses on middle-class escorts, the most rapidly growing and visible part of the industry mainly because of the ways the Internet has changed that particular aspect of sex work.

## Print Is Dead

When I was doing public relations for a porn company, people were always surprised that such a job existed. Sure, sex sells other stuff, but, they wondered, doesn't sex just sell itself? The truth is that a lot of deep marketing-thought goes into the sex industry, whether the entity being sold is an independent escort's companionship or couples' porn. However, it's true that marketing becomes tricky when there's no physical product, or when the service that's being provided isn't necessarily legal. Mainstream ad agencies deal with versions of this problem all the time as they market brands and lifestyles, but sex workers tangle with it in a different way, because the thing on the market block is them. Advertising has always been the simplest for street workers, because what you see is what you get—with maybe a few minor and inevitable variations. However, for women who work in dungeons, brothels, and private apartments, or outcalls to hotels, advertising is a very precise art form requiring that they reach a perfect balance between adequately representing themselves so that the client is not disappointed and construing themselves in a way that attracts the kinds of clients they want to see.

For women who work independently, the Internet has opened up a vast new world of opportunity in which different marketing styles can be tried out cheaply and easily—and changed immediately if they fail. It's hardly an overstatement to say that the Internet has transformed the sex industry: the ways businesses are run, the stigmas attached to being on either side of the transaction, the visibility of the industry, and the information available about sex workers who market their services. Many sex workers who worked in the industry before the Internet jumped right on board with Internet advertising as soon as they got a glimmer of the opportunities the web offered. The Internet has also inspired a new generation of sex workers to find their places in the industry and develop opportunities that may not have presented themselves without the Internet.

## The Old Guard Goes High Tech

In 1989, Veronica Monet started working as an escort in Berkeley, California. She advertised in the *Spectator,* a major weekly adult tabloid at that time. The paper was essentially a vehicle for sex workers' ads, which were its major source of capital. Each ad, which typically took up a sixteenth of a page, consisted of a few lines of text, a sort of abstract photo that didn't show the woman's face, and a phone number. For Monet and other independent sex workers of her era, small ads in the *Spectator* and similar papers around the country were the best choice in advertising. Because of the limitations on the information provided, Monet received many more phone calls than she did clients. Oftentimes the potential client would reveal what kind of woman he was looking for and it wouldn't be a fit. Agencies weren't always helpful, and they were renowned for the "bait and switch," in which a photograph or description of one woman is provided and then someone not matching that description at all appears for the job. Certainly the thrill of the unknown was part of the appeal for some clients, though for others the roadblocks to getting exactly what they wanted were numerous.

Monet used the *Spectator* exclusively for the first two years of her career, until a technologically savvy client of hers gave her the heads-up about Bulletin Board Systems (BBSes), an early, nonpublic form of the Internet. After discovering the BBS, Monet continued to use print ads, but she began to give potential clients a password so they could log on to her little corner of the system. The men were able to check out pictures that gave them a much better sense of her than the newspaper ads. Monet made the bold choice to show her face in the photographs she posted online, something almost unheard of at the time. By 1992, Monet was fully exploring the options that the burgeoning Internet technology had to offer.

Likewise, Catherine La Croix, a sex worker who had started in the business as a BDSM phone sex operator in the 1980s, got her start on the BBS in the mid-1990s. She and a business partner (also a sex worker) built the first major woman-owned BBS, Two Babes Online, in 1995. They hosted sixty-four incoming lines and held forums on which people were able to discuss sex. Two Babes Online quickly became a go-to place for people of all stripes to explore their sexuality. But this site became more than just its message boards; it was an early incarnation of a porn site. The images made available on the BBS were posted in many different formats, which meant that a porn consumer had to make some effort to get to know the technology of the system so he or she could sample the wares in order to get the instant gratification that these sites had the potential to provide. Slow-paced and roundabout not-so-instant gratification aside, the BBS proved to La Croix and her partner that there was money to be made from sex on the Internet.

After experiencing the sharp rise in popularity of Two Babes Online, La Croix began to explore the options for advertising offline services on the Internet. She had since become an escort, and decided that the Internet seemed like a good way to pursue clients. Located in Seattle, she was in close proximity to Microsoft. Her foresight that, in her words, "Geeks need sex, too, or even more so," led to a thriving business. Like Veronica Monet, she made the choice to show her face in the photographs she posted on her first website. Though she hadn't shown her face in print advertisements before that point, La Croix had done an appearance on *The Oprah Winfrey Show*, so she wasn't afraid of the level of exposure that might result from her postings. She saw showing her face as an important tool in reaching the kinds of clients she wanted to see. Today, face shots are commonplace among sex workers who advertise online. La Croix notes that the Internet fools people—both sex workers and clients alike—into thinking they're anonymous. In fact, she says, it's quite the opposite. It's possible for anyone posting photos online to be recognized out in public, especially when posting face shots, or pictures with other identifying details, and the IP (Internet protocol) address one posts from is recorded on each website a person visits and viewable if the website's owner keeps track of visitor statistics. So with a little bit of know-how, anyone's Internet use can be traced.

For both Monet and La Croix, the Internet opened up a new, untapped market of tech-immersed, middle- to upper-class men who were spending tons of time in front of their computers and who were looking for ways to interact with women in a structured and limited way because they claimed to have no time for a full-blown relationship. These men began to form the backbone of the online advertisement-driven sex industry. They had money and time to burn on the Internet, which made them ideal guinea pigs for searching and contacting sex workers online. Sex online—something that was previously only accessible and appealing to people who understood the inner technical workings of the Internet—has exploded since the early 1990s, and the Internet has become more widely available and user-friendly.

New York–based dominatrix Jo had been a sex worker before she moved to New York in 1997 but hadn't capitalized on the Internet until she started using the message boards at fetish and BDSM website Max Fisch Domina Guide. Jo launched her website in 1999, a bit later than Monet and La Croix. She doesn't think that the clients she has obtained through the Internet are any different than the clients she got through other forms of advertising. This difference of opinion probably stems from a range of factors pertaining to the different experiences of someone coming to the industry a bit later in the game. When Monet and La Croix first began to experiment with the BBS and online advertising in the early 1990s, Internet access was not as widespread as it would be just a few years later. At that time, the notion of meeting people online was seen as dangerous and sketchy, even though most users were likely to be introverted computer programmers who are more harmless than the average Internet user today. By the late 1990s, America On Line had begun to dominate the Internet and promote a more user-friendly platform, which acted as an invitation for average Americans to get online in droves.

Just as trends in clientele have changed over the years, there have been changes in trends for workers themselves. The change witnessed in the industry was perhaps most jarring for women like Denzi, who became a sex worker in the late 1970s, got out of the industry, and then returned to escorting in the early 2000s and started to use the Internet to advertise. Whereas Monet, La Croix, and Jo all made relatively smooth transitions from print to online advertising, Denzi had a steep learning curve to deal with after having been away from the industry for so many years.

More than two decades ago, Denzi started working at a massage parlor in Tucson, Arizona, at the age of nineteen, staying there until she met a pimp who took her to Phoenix and later to Los Angeles, where she became a streetwalker. After a few years, she escaped her pimp and made her way back to Arizona to finish school. "After getting married, divorced, having kids, and a long career in the paralegal field, I decided to return to prostitution via online escorting," she says. Now forty-eight, Denzi has remade her sex worker persona without a trace of the street worker aesthetic, and notes, "I think I would have definitely started back in sex work without the Internet, but my experience would be far less prosperous without it, I imagine." Denzi, whose tagline on her website, Denzi4u, is "Beyond the Ordinary Erotic Encounter," positions herself as an elite companion with session options that include a sensual Japanese tea ceremony. Like many women who have their own sites, Denzi appeals to a middle-class clientele of gentleman who want to be pampered.

## Class and a New Generation of Workers

One of the most powerful changes the Internet has brought to the sex industry is that it's created a vast and visible middle class of sex workers who cater to middle-class men. Prior to the advent of the Internet, the media tended to portray an extreme when it came to sex workers: The women tended to be either high-class escorts who made upward of $20,000 for a weekend excursion to an exotic locale with a high-status businessman, or downtrodden, drug-addicted streetwalkers who were usually women of color. The number of sex workers who fell somewhere in between those two extremes is difficult to quantify, but there's no question that the widespread infiltration of the Internet into the majority of people's homes has resulted in an increase in the number of women who make up that middle ground. It's populated by women who may be full-time, long-term sex workers, as well as others, such as college students who are temporarily doing sex work or women who do sex work casually to supplement the income they make from full-time jobs in other fields. The scope of the Internet does seem vast, but the majority of the world's sex workers do not use the Internet to do their work.

Documented in blogs and on message boards, middle-class sex workers tell their stories directly and indirectly, detailing lives of middle-class comfort that include homes, families, and friends—just like people in any other line of work. Online advertising venues, message boards, and communities have, in many respects, standardized the industry and brought it to a newly professional level. Without too much effort, a potential client or sex worker can find out what the going rate is for an hour-long session in his or her region; sex workers who charge much higher or lower tend to be criticized by others in the area. Likewise, there are standards for behavior and modes of dress for both online and offline experiences that are increasingly being enforced on message boards and through review sites.

The Internet makes dabbling in the sex industry as an independent worker much easier in most respects, but it's debatable whether the Internet has brought more women into the industry than would otherwise be in it. The Internet makes it possible for the curious woman to explore her working options without having to make the scary phone call to an agency, or go to an interview at a brothel, and she doesn't need to have any direct connection to the industry to try it on for size. Because it is a high-stress, stigmatized, and sometimes illegal business, the turnover among sex workers is immense. Most women don't stay in the industry for more than a year or so at a time. Though they may drift in and out of the industry over the years, it's unusual to find a sex worker who is devoted to sex work as a career.

Catherine La Croix comments, "The web has unfortunately made more women think they can do this because they think it's easy . . . A lot of women don't contemplate the ramifications of this job because of the Internet. What lots of them don't understand is that this is a business, first and foremost." Though sex workers' websites are of course meant to attract clients, they can also have the effect of seducing wannabe workers into the industry under the pretense that the work is sexy, fun, and easy. Speaking about the deceptions offered up by Internet advertising to young dommes, Jo says, "It's easy for them to get the wrong impression because of the way websites are put together. Many women have lists on their sites of things that they will not do because of legal restrictions, but the reality is that everyone in the business does these things once they get to know a client a bit better."

Although interest in sex work has certainly increased since the advent of the Internet, and women who may not have wanted or been able to work independently without an agency or pimp can do so now, the work itself remains the thing that ultimately discourages women from getting into the industry. The Internet has, in Veronica Monet's words, created a class of sex workers with a "pseudocelebrity status," but it has not changed the essential nature of what sex workers do—exchange erotic labor for a living. La Croix is direct: "To put it bluntly, you need much more than tits and ass; it's whether or not you have the mind for it. You have to know who you are, and the way that you see yourself is all-important," she says.

Recognizing the difficulties of sex work is often challenging when women are faced with the ease of technology and increasing availability of both online and offline guides to the ins and outs of the sex industry, as well as intricate support and networking systems. For young women flirting with the idea of entering the industry, the options are both daunting and comforting, as there is no longer the need to do sex work in a void, without the support and understanding or at least email correspondence of fellow workers. Whether a woman ultimately chooses to get into the industry or not, there are many resources available to her online, not the least of which are advertisements posted by other sex workers. Over the last few years, online advertising for sex workers has become a serious business with seemingly limitless options.

## Pitching the Persona

There is a massive number of websites that assist sex workers in advertising to their potential clients. Two of the biggest national sites are Craigslist, which is free for sex workers to post and clients to browse, and Eros Guide, which has a monthly fee for sex workers to place ads and is free for clients to browse. There are many other sites that cater to particular tastes or are similar to these sites with minor variations in design and searchability. While sex workers and clients tend to have their preferred sites, they often use several different ones at the same time, though how widely they cast their net often depends on the associated costs for membership; some sites charge sex workers to post ads, while others charge clients to search them. Craigslist and Eros Guide have each been online for more than a decade, so their national standing is well established. Newer sites that host nationwide ads quickly learn that it is more profitable to cater to select cities and have many ads for one city rather than few ads for each of many cities.

Craigslist's Erotic Services is one of the many pages on the free, public, reader-moderated board, which, like all Craigslist pages, is organized by city. Posters can create text posts of any length, and as of a few years ago, they can also add pictures. Craigslist is a bit of a clusterfuck, though it's searchable by whatever keyword you can dream up. The posts go up on a first-come, first-served basis, and they cycle off the front page of the forum as new ads are posted. The front page features the one hundred most recent posts, which in major cities like New York and San Francisco cycle off at an alarming rate—as quickly as a half an hour after posting. Craigslist's Erotic Services postings are highly sensitive to things like weather, holidays, and time of day, with big spurts of postings near lunchtime and toward the end of the workday. Some of the more amusing posts go up late at night to appeal to high and horny guys trolling the Internet and making less-than-stellar choices about where and how to spend their money (well, maybe stellar for the girls they give their money to). Though the search feature helps make things more exact, Erotic Services doesn't have categories; posters include keywords that they know people will search for, including online escort slang so that they can attract the kind of clients they are most interested in.

Because of the fact that the Erotic Services forum is free to use and doesn't require any kind of registration to post or send messages, as well as the fact that it's attached to a larger website that doesn't have erotic implications (unless you think finding an apartment or trading your bicycle for a TV is sexy), it tends to attract a high number of men who have never hired a sex worker before and have no idea how to go about it, as well as men who are looking for a cheap, fast fuck, and men who don't understand why they have to pay for sexual services. Craigslist is considered by many sex workers to be the bottom of the barrel because of the type of clientele it attracts, but many workers who use other advertising venues as their primary means of getting new clients still occasionally advertise on Craigslist if they have a gap in their schedule to fill.

Craigslist is also popular among women who don't do sex work as their primary source of income and who don't want to spend the money on a monthly ad that will attract more clients than they are willing or able to see. They use Craigslist to post an ad and book a session as their time allows and when their income could use the padding. Chariz, a lesbian in her midtwenties who spent some time making money by wrestling men she connected with on Craigslist in Portland, Oregon, stumbled across the world of erotic wrestling by way of Google. Her work in freelance construction sent her onto the job boards on Craigslist, and after she pursued wrestling as a casual erotic interest, a friend convinced her to try moving her wrestling ad from the Casual Encounters section to Erotic Services. About her choice to do this work, Chariz says, "I probably wouldn't have started wrestling men for money without Craigslist. It was part necessity, but not completely. I've always been able to get other jobs, so if it hadn't been as convenient, I don't think I would have put the time into getting clients." Although Chariz developed a few regular clients who she wrestled once or twice a month, wrestling wasn't her main source of income, and her use of Craigslist to get clients remained fairly casual and dependent on her schedule, as well as her financial needs while she was a college student.

Workers like Chariz are the coveted "non-pro" workers. They're typically young, college-age women (or women who pose as such) who claim to love sex or whatever fetish they're catering to. They often post ads that say something to the effect of "I'm doing this for the extra pocket money," to buy books for school or new clothes or other nonessential items. Full-time professionals are often criticized on Craigslist, despite the fact that, technically, a person who accepts money for sexual favors is a pro. The assumed value of a nonpro is that she's not doing the work primarily for the money, but rather because it's fun and the money is a delightful side benefit. On Craigslist, the message boards and the advertising boards are one and the same, so clients and workers alike declare their disappointment with one another right alongside the ads highlighting the very services the men are seeking out. Whenever clients describe a woman on the board as a pro, they're almost always saying so with a sense of disappointment, because they seem to be perpetually in search of slutty college students who may ultimately agree to a no-strings-attached, no-fees-involved kind of arrangement.

Professionals, however they position themselves, are the name of the game on Eros Guide, which has online advertising branches in more than thirty U.S. cities, as well several in Canada and the United Kingdom. Lily, a thirty-two-year-old from Manhattan, started stripping at twenty-two and later became an escort, placing an ad on Eros Guide in 2001 that was the mainstay of her marketing strategy. Even though escorting was her main form of income, Lily found it worthwhile to advertise herself as a non-pro college student, which was a marketing angle that resulted in her never having to launch a website of her own. She thought a website would make her appear to be the professional she actually was, and that it would destroy her carefully constructed college-girl image. An added bonus was that she could avoid the costs and headache associated with creating and maintaining a website. Lily found that the wording of her ad, as well as the photographs she used, made a big difference in terms of the types of clients she could get: Photos shot from a low angle attracted submissive men, while photos featuring her in conservative outfits baring little skin attracted vanilla clients who were easy to get along with.

Advertisements on Eros Guide are broken down by type of session: escorts, massage, dancers, BDSM/fetish, tv/ts/shemale, men, and tantra; they also have searchable subcategories for hair color, Asian, ebony, Latina, porn stars, boob size, incall/outcall. Though the ad offerings are standard city to city—two hundred words, a phone number, a weblink, and three photographs (all of which are updatable at no extra cost whenever a worker supplies new content)—the ad rates vary by city depending on what the market will bear: In Denver an ad costs $60 a month, while in New York it costs $175.

Eros Guide ads target a middle-class market of men who have Internet access and money to burn. They're for men who prefer an online shopping experience of casual browsing and research before they make a decision. The interconnected networks of Eros Guides in each city make the website ideal for traveling businessmen, because even though the sex workers are different in each city, the website navigation is the same, which lends a sense of familiarity and security to the process. Likewise, some sex workers choose to go on tour and use the Eros Guide network, and the website is set up to put notices up on the profiles of sex workers who are in town on tour for a short amount of time.

Though agencies that employ sex workers use advertising on Eros Guide and other sites, it's usually easy to tell the difference between agencies and independent workers. The easy browsing feature on the site makes searching for independents a more rewarding prospect than it could be if independent workers' sites were not linked in a common space. Lily worked for escort agencies before trying her hand at independent work, which she only did because the agencies she'd worked for were busted. She says, "I'm not sure if I would have gone independent without the Internet, because I just wasn't aware that that was a possibility." Initially, she says, "It was scary to be responsible for doing everything on my own." After learning the ropes of advertising and screening clients, and starting to make connections with other sex workers, Lily began to love working on her own because she was able to control so many different factors—from her image to her schedule to her rates and the degree of interaction she had with clients before deciding whether to see them.

In the trade up from Craigslist to Eros Guide, sex workers gain and lose power and freedoms. On Craigslist, restrictions are put on postings by other members of the community, who can flag noncompliant postings for removal, and occasionally by the Craigslist staff, who may remove postings that blatantly disregard the rules that bar explicit exchange of sex for money. However, the actual structure of the advertisements is totally open to the poster's discretion and can be as brief and vague or as long and detailed (though not sexually explicit) as possible. Ads on Eros Guide look much more put together and typically feature professional photography instead of photos taken with a webcam or a consumer-grade digital camera. Eros Guide ads are also scoured by their staff for any hint of sexual activity; in fact, the word "sex" is not allowed at all. Additionally, the limit on word count puts restrictions on what a sex worker can say about herself, which is similar to the limitations in print ads. However, the advertisements do have the escape valve of a link to the worker's website, where she can say whatever she wants—within the limits of what's acceptable regarding the legal restrictions around the business of sex work. Both websites allow and even encourage a sex worker to operate her own business, whether or not she has her own website.

Both Craigslist and Eros Guide, albeit in different ways, exist as cultures beyond just the listings for sex workers, which makes them not so different from print publications. Their content may be about sex, but it's not always pure advertising. In this respect, sex-worker-advertising sites are increasingly becoming online communities where people hang out to discuss different issues centered on sexuality, but the discussions also deviate from this topic. These advertising/community sites have increasingly begun to look more and more like dating sites, with their articles about sex and off-topic discussions. This design and functionality crossover is an important one—it lessens the stigma of sex work and hiring of sex workers by making it appear more like dating—just with required "generosity" on the men's behalf.

## Dish and Bitch: The Message Boards

If the community and webzine aspect of advertising sites is a bit confusing and nudges the sex industry away from pure commerce and into something else, the world of message boards geared at sex workers and their clients (or providers and hobbyists, as they are called on the boards) is infinitely more complex. Since the late 1990s, message boards have emerged as the more highly interactive counterpart to advertising sites. People who use the boards tend to also use advertising sites, though the reverse isn't always true. Clients who use message boards on a regular basis tend to be very engaged with the culture, referring to themselves as "hobbyists," and referring to the act of hiring sex workers as "the hobby" and the sex workers themselves as the "providers."

The slang that sometimes appears on sites like Craigslist and Eros Guide runs rampant on message boards, to the point that some of the postings are difficult to decipher for readers outside the culture.

The key component of message boards like UtopiaGuide, Big Doggie, The Erotic Review (TER), and Max Fisch are the reviews, submitted by men who have had sessions with sex workers and want to report on them, ostensibly to give other hobbyists the inside scoop so they can make informed decisions about which women they want to see. Though it varies, the boards tend to be password protected. Some, like Max Fisch, are free to read and post on but require registration with a valid email address, while others, like Big Doggie, can be perused in an abbreviated version for free, but require a paid membership on the part of both providers and hobbyists in order to see full reviews or to participate in board discussions. The boards create a space for providers and hobbyists to interact socially outside of private sessions. Explicit advertising is outright banned on most boards, though providers are permitted to post notices about their whereabouts and available days and times. Eve Ryder, a now-retired New York–based escort who primarily used UtopiaGuide, says, "Many of the threads are about guys reviewing girls and swapping tips and such, but interesting stuff is always appearing. I've seen threads there where guys and girls openly debate how tips should work, for example. I've watched girls attack johns who behave badly toward women—openly and with other girls and johns backing them up! Imagine *that* ever happening before the days of boards." In addition to the spaces where providers and hobbyists can talk to one another, most boards also have sections of the sites that are available only to providers or only to hobbyists.

For the providers, the boards are a mixed blessing. Jo, the dominatrix from New York, spent some time as a moderator on the fetish and BDSM message boards for Max Fisch, but she quickly tired of the drama and downright nastiness. She found many of the men to be pushy and annoying: "They were always expressing their preferences, which is generally okay, but they were being very judgmental and had screwed-up ideas about what it means to be a true domina."

Because of the flame wars and general sniping on the site, Max Fisch shut down its community boards and DomBoards and replaced them with The Hang, a more heavily moderated and community-oriented board. Though The Hang is more regulated than earlier incarnations of the boards, it would be naive to expect that people will ever be completely polite on online message boards, especially when dealing with matters like sexual preferences and fetishes, which have the tendency to offend even (or perhaps especially) people who spend a lot of time in a sexualized environment and know what they do and do not like.

The review function of the message boards is the most controversial part of these types of sites. In order to make the reviews a good and sexy read, hobbyists often embellish the truth, which would not be such a bad thing if the changes were only in florid language, but some hobbyists report on sex acts that providers are not actually willing to perform in their sessions, setting a troubling precedent for women and future clients. Some boards bestow special privileges and discounts on hobbyists who have written a certain number of reviews, which results in the writing of bogus reviews of providers hobbyists haven't actually seen as they scramble to boost their numbers closer to whatever quota they are trying to reach. A provider's reviews can certainly affect her business, as many serious hobbyists strictly pay attention to the boards and what their fellow men have to say about the providers.

Eve, an active participant and often agitator on UtopiaGuide, says, "I once posted a review of a client I had after he posted a ridiculous review about me claiming to have done all kinds of acrobatic stuff. I posted what *really* happened, because I just didn't care. You know: 'He was never really hard, and he has a bad back, so I had to be on top for the thirty seconds it took him to come. . . .'" Some of Eve's experiences on the boards were frustrating, to say the least, but overall the boards had a positive impact on her business. During her career, Eve never paid for advertising, but her active participation on the boards—especially when she was argumentative—drummed up plenty of business.

Though Lily recognizes the value of good reviews, she was extremely wary of the review boards and how they affected client expectations, as well as her privacy and reputation. She made her clients aware of her rules: "They weren't allowed to post on TER if they wanted to see me again—that site just has a terrible reputation. I allowed them to post on Big Doggie, but without writing about sex even with the lingo, and it did help my business."

## The False Veil of Secrecy

Beyond the day-to-day minicrises and controversies on the boards, several larger scandals have erupted and brimmed over beyond the reaches of the message board communities in recent years. In the late 1990s, message boards, reviews, and online sex worker advertising in general were a free-for-all. At that time, clients and workers felt that their anonymity was protected on sites like Big Doggie and The Erotic Review, and that they weren't being watched or recorded by law enforcement, or that even if they were, they were safe because they'd developed an intricate-enough slang and a clever-enough disclaimer (which still appears on many websites and which is intended to provide protection from the law):

> *Money exchanged is intended for companionship only and modeling services. Anything else that may or may not occur is a matter of personal choice between two consenting adults of legal age and is not contracted for, nor is it requested to be contracted for in any manner. This is not an offer of prostitution.*

On the boards, which participants view as private, membership-based spaces that are not open-to-the-public forums, explicit sexual acts were often described and dollar amounts provided. As it turns out, law enforcement did start to take an interest in online action. A Florida State attorney launched a two-year investigation of Big Doggie in 2000. The operation, stealthily called "Operation Flea Collar," targeted hobbyists by creating profiles on the site for fake providers. The vice squad went so far as to buy stock images of a lingerie-clad woman around whom they built a website that was a convincing facsimile of a real escort's site—eventually, that is, as it took a little trial and error for them to get clients interested in their provider. When the vice squad felt it had gathered sufficient evidence to definitively accuse Big Doggie of being a conduit for illegal activities, they pounced on the co-owners of the site, Charles Kelly and Steve Lipson, who were charged, along with eleven other men, with more than fifty felony racketeering, procurement, and obstruction charges in July 2002. In December 2002, a judge dismissed charges, ultimately deciding that the message boards were a protected form of free speech.

A big part of the message board scare was linked to the inherent sexism of the legal system when it comes to prostitution: Female workers are the ones most often arrested and made an example of, while the men who purchase their services or facilitate the business stroll away without incident. In this instance, however, the men were being targeted in what is sometimes called a reverse sting. It's interesting to note that "reverse sting" acknowledges the fact that the women are the real targets when it comes to law enforcement around prostitution. It also begs the question: Would there have been such calamity over the message boards in the summer of 2002 if the providers been the targets rather than the clients? Probably not.

Though today Big Doggie is once again the powerhouse it was before the bust, vice squads throughout the country have started to employ online advertising and communities to make arrests. But it's sex workers rather than clients who need to be most concerned about the increasing interest of the legal community in online spaces. Since providers cycle in and out of the industry so quickly, there isn't a strong sense of history or awareness about the types of things they should avoid when pursuing their online sex businesses. New providers often make the same mistakes that providers and hobbyists made half a decade ago: They give too much information about their precise services and what they will and will not do for their rates, while also naively assuming that they're anonymous. Though clients often express concerns about discretion, their worries are mostly about wives and families, while the risks that sex workers undertake are a real and present danger. This danger does not just come from outside the business, either; it often comes from within.

## I've Got Your Back

In the sex-negative, guilt-ridden, judgmental society we live in, the leap in people's minds from sex to danger is a short one indeed. And I'm not even talking about BDSM play, but just regular ol' fucking. Add commerce to sex and you've got a formula for all kinds of fear and guilt, not to mention tsk-tsking and "I told you so's" when a sex worker gets into an ugly situation. Double up this whore stigma with the stigma of Internet weirdos, and you've got a scornful-nearing-gleeful newspaper article waiting to be written. Though many sex workers report never having had a violent client, violence against sex workers is the number one thing that the press pays attention to. This is more often about sending the message that sex and violence go hand in hand than it is a warning that this is something awful that should be stopped.

Despite general assumptions that have led to sex work being voted the job most likely to get you chopped up and stuffed in garbage bags, the non-sex-working public is often surprised to learn that sex workers have elaborate systems for screening potential clients. Though screening and safety systems existed before the Internet—clients were sometimes approved through word of mouth from other workers and discreet but investigative phone calls to the client's place of business were made—the Internet has streamlined the process. Screening serves a dual purpose: to confirm that a potential client is pleasant to deal with and not dangerous or a rip-off artist and to prevent those who work in illegal parts of the industry from getting busted.

## DIY Screening

Most ladies do some, if not all, of their client screening themselves. For the purposes of this book, I'm primarily concerned with middle-class sex workers who use the Internet as their primary source of obtaining clients and who work independently or in collaboration with a few other women. I am not addressing the experiences of street workers who advertise their wares by being present on a stroll known to be a place where commercial sex can be acquired, because they are beginning and ending their transactions in person rather than online. However, it's important to note that street workers, like Internet workers, often have very tight-knit systems of checking in with one another.

Independent workers who work through the Internet rely on several different forms of free screening. Before they even get to that point, they first decide what level of information they require from a potential new client before agreeing to a session with him. Levels of screening vary from worker to worker; it's a matter that can cause cattiness and judgment between fellow sex workers because oftentimes one provider may perceive another as being too lax or overly paranoid. Some sex workers simply require a few exchanges of email in which they assess the client's general behavior and determine whether he brings up anything illegal ("How much for a blow job?") in his initial correspondence. This first level of screening, before and sometimes without the exchange of personal information, tends to be the most basic and can simply be based on a gut feeling in regard to both safety and compatibility issues. Most sex workers are not just concerned with their safety and well-being, but also with their general sanity, and the question "Is this guy going to annoy the hell out of me for the hour we're together?" is usually a much more pressing one than "Is he going to ax murder me?"

For providers who take screening measures beyond gut feelings and correspondence with a client, a simple electronic check is the next step—and a lazy but curious girl's best friend. Just as many women have taken to Googling a potential date's personal information, many sex workers poke around the Internet in search of any and all information they can find about potential clients. Providers Google a client's email addresses, phone numbers, names, businesses, and whatever other shred of personal information the men provide. For the most part, this kind of search isn't going to yield any kind of "this man is mean to hookers" explicit warning, but it may deliver vacation photos, a flan-recipe blog, or boring PowerPoint presentations about a company's gains and losses—all of which contribute to a better sense of who the man is in the real world. If a client is unwilling to provide his real name and the provider doesn't insist on it, his online nickname or handle may be more than useful, because such men are likely to have set up email accounts specifically for their illicit affairs. These handles may lead the intrepid provider to client-and-provider message board discussions starring the man in question.

## Message Boards and Bad-Date Lists

Though message boards have their fair share of both comedy and tragedy as a sparring ground between providers and clients, it's worth going into the fact that they're a valuable resource for women who want to have contact with other providers, and also for those who want to sniff about for signs of insanity or general disrespect in a potential client. More than that, public as well as membership-based message boards serve as an interesting counterpoint to something that has grown out of the ease of information sharing online: the bad-date list. Networks of sex workers, especially call girls, have always tended to maintain their own internal blacklists with the tacit agreement that no girl in their particular circle will see such-and-such a client for whatever infraction they deem serious enough. Those internal support systems aside, the Internet has led to an increase in this type of information sharing.

Private provider-discussion Listservs, like the one run by Prostitutes of New York (PONY), require a reference before a new provider can get on the list, and they often have posts about trends in local and national law enforcement, sex worker news, and the ever-important bad-date list. Providers circulate information meant to assist and protect their fellow workers, and the information can include anything from "He smelled weird and shorted me on my rate" to "This guy was high on something, freaked out, and pinned me against a wall when our hour was up." When possible, providers describe the clients they wish to make persona non grata in as much detail as possible, including images and driver's licenses if they have them, as well as email and phone contacts. Once these details circulate, local sex workers band together and won't see that client, and they'll work to circulate the information to warn other colleagues. Bad-date lists generally do a great service to providers without exposing the clients to the whole world, though there are instances where other sex workers on the list may encourage a fellow provider to go to the police if she's been assaulted.

The popularity and ease of self-publishing on the Internet via blogs and websites has led to the rise of public bad-date lists and blacklists. This is due, in part, to the ease with which workers can put up and update their own sites. While sex workers are unanimous in their support of private bad-date lists, which help to keep providers safe and encourage a sense of community and concern for other workers, there is much debate over the value of public bad-date lists.

The primary argument in favor of public bad-date lists is that by posting even a little bit of a client's information, like an email handle that he may use only for communicating with sex workers, the client is being held accountable. A public bad-date list does not require any kind of registration or exchange of information to gain access. This makes the list a powerful tool for sex workers who are not connected to other workers in their area, but who have Internet access and stumble across the list. Though groups run by sex workers are usually very diligent about their members' privacy, some sex workers are hesitant to trust other sex workers. Public bad-date lists published by sex workers directly serve the workers: The lists supply the information without requiring that the sex worker provide identifying details. Lars Ollson, who runs Don't Fuck with Us!, a blacklist blog for sex workers around Washington, D.C., maintains that "making the list public isn't to shame the client, but to motivate him to fix the situation, and to show that we all talk to each other."[2] Many clients may not be aware that sex workers talk to each other. Away from the comfort of message boards, only die-hard hobbyists spend lots of time in the company of like-minded enthusiasts. (At least as far as they know.) However, intentional or not, if a client's phone number or email turns up in a Google search that leads to a blog that derides him for being mean to prostitutes he hires, that could probably be construed as shaming.

Whereas the private bad-date list only serves the purpose of warning providers about dangerous, unpleasant, or time-wasting clients, public blacklists serve two purposes: warning providers and embarrassing clients. Of course, a client gives up his right to privacy and discretion (the things that keep the sex industry moving along) the moment he robs or physically assaults a girl he has hired. And working girls often win cases against clients who assault them, despite the fact that they're sometimes in the throes of an illegal act when something like this happens. However, some of the incidents that qualify clients for public bad-date lists fall into more of a gray area. On Don't Fuck with Us!, the most common offense is a "no call, no show" (NCNS in the industry lingo) appointment, which is when a client establishes and confirms a date and time but then isn't heard from again—or is maybe heard from after a bit of time passes and he wants to set up another appointment. This kind of infraction, though annoying and disrespectful, comes with the territory of being a sex worker; clients will occasionally flake out due to cold feet, discovery by wives, last-minute change of plans, or a number of other excuses that may or may not be valid. When a client violates the basic etiquette of a session in a way that shows his ignorance of the situation but not his maliciousness, having his information posted on a public bad-date list puts his infraction on the same level as those of guys who push sex workers' limits.

The NCNS client is a close cousin to the time waster. One of the curses and blessings of the availability of ads for erotic hire on the Internet is that it sets up almost infinite opportunities for window-shopping. Because of the absence of face-to-face communication, online window-shopping often extends past looking and into emailing. However, providers quickly get acquainted with the tactics of time wasters and learn to sniff them out. These are guys who ask lots of questions that are thinly veiled attempts at acquiring masturbatory material; they are vague about what they want and when and where they want it. The New York– and New Jersey–area blog Black List is composed almost entirely of lists of the emails of the time-wasting men who populate Craigslist's Erotic Services board.

Though clients, like service providers, are initially careful about concealing personal information, things like phone numbers, which most providers require before agreeing to an appointment, are easily traceable online through reverse-lookup services that give the street address of whatever phone number is plugged into the system. As a result, it's fairly easy to link blacklisted men to their real-world identities: A simple Google search turned up the real names and home addresses of several men on the Don't Fuck with Us! blog. Although men who remove condoms without telling their partner or cross physical boundaries certainly deserve to be reprimanded at the very least, clients with more-minor infractions are subject to blacklist-wielding providers' whims as well, creating a power dynamic based on shame and what could turn into blackmail.

Other than the whole personal-information-posted-online-without-consent thing, a major side effect of public bad-date lists is that men who make good dates fear that their personal information will wind up broadcast all over the Internet. After they've seen some examples of the infractions men commit to land themselves on bad-date lists, I'm sure that many potential clients shy away from making appointments. Likewise, sex workers who mock would-be clients' phone messages and emails on public forums are potentially driving away perfectly harmless clients, who cower in fear from Internet wrath and keep their wallets safely in their pockets. Some might perceive the posting of minor infractions as sex workers acting out in various ways, but the reality is that sex workers are expected to always be well behaved, while clients are not; clients are often less afraid of the consequences of misbehaving because of that old "customer is always right" mentality—not to mention their sense of male entitlement. Public blacklists are a way for sex workers to anonymously lash out at bad and irritating clients. In essence, this functions as a solid counterpart to the posting of anonymous reviews by clients who basically claim that the providers need to be well behaved or be out of business.

Public bad-date lists might have their share of problems, including the fact that they can spur a particularly litigious client into legal action. However, they do serve their purpose well. The freedom to post information about bad clients allows sex workers to alert each other to clients to avoid—the next time this client's email or phone number gets Googled as part of a screening process, it will lead to the bad-date list, which wouldn't happen if the list were on an email list or password-protected message board. Public lists may likewise get the attention of the men who are on them and are either directed to the site—as Don't Fuck with Us! asks providers to do—or find it through vanity Googling, and they will know they're being watched and disapproved of, much in the way that providers know this through reviews clients write.

## High Tech Verification

Posting a client's information online breaks with most clients' top priority: being discreet (or that cringe-worthy common Internet misspelling, "discrete"). Though providers are at a higher risk of attracting the attention of law enforcement than their clients, whether a sex worker is discreet is one of the most common questions posed by clients when seeking out a provider. This question has two unspoken dimensions to it: The first is "Please don't show up at my hotel looking like the hookers I see on TV;" and the other is "Please be very careful with the personal information I give you." Just as different providers have requirements around how much information they need about a potential client before they see him, clients' comfort levels vary from person to person. As the sex industry becomes increasingly professionalized, what information is required is becoming more standardized, which has opened up the market to businesses whose sole purpose is the sharing and protection of information.

The most widely used of these services are Room Service 2000, often referred to as RS2K, and Date-Check, which is popular among escorts and occasionally used by independently operating dominatrices. Both sex workers and their potential clients need to sign up to use the system—and clients have to pay a one-time membership fee. The client is required to submit a heap of personal information, including his full name and credit card information, as well as a home and work address, the name of the company he works for, and his position and title. This information is not passed directly on to the provider, but it must be given for membership so that a provider can rest assured that the client checked out when the website's staff followed up on his points of contact. The purpose here for Date-Check is the approving of the client, which gives providers the security that the client they are in touch with has passed a background check. RS2K creates a buffer between the provider and her client's personal details, which many clients like because it means that their information is not at risk in the provider's hands and they're reducing the risk of transmitting their personal information over the largely unsecured Internet by having to go through the process just once rather than repeatedly. Providers who list RS2K as a verification option sometimes give a discount for their sessions set up using RS2K. In addition to their role as providers of screening, both websites have also evolved into escort-advertising sites, making them sort of one-stop-shopping operations.

Though these sites certainly fill a need and step the escorting business up a notch—out of the shadow realm of strange business dealings—they also create a new kind of middleman between the worker and her client. This can be both helpful and a hindrance. Services like RS2K are a marker of the upscaling of escort businesses and a recognition by business owners that there is legal money to be made from the sex industry. This service, therefore, removes some of the power of interaction from an independent provider. While many providers may be willing, even happy, to surrender the tedious and often frustrating task of verifying a client's identity, it nudges them away from independence and one step closer to signing up with an escort agency or having their hard-earned money soaked up in payments for other "necessary" services.

Lily, whose escorting career started when she worked for a Manhattan agency, took on the responsibility of doing screening herself after going independent and prefers it that way. She says, "I didn't like the idea of putting screening into a third party's hands. I feel like I'm safer verifying a client myself." Other sex workers who use the verification services available feel that the companies offer a veneer of legitimacy. Beverly Fisher, an escort from Denver, Colorado, disagrees with the idea that a third-party service is a hindrance, and says, "I see these services as a help for providers, and they help the clients feel secure, like they don't have to give providers all this extra information."

## Sex Worker Activism

Sex workers and businesses that take measures to protect them demonstrate a commitment to making the sex industry a bit more organized, at least when it comes to the topic of safety and making a profit. However, since the late 1970s, a growing number of people involved in the sex industry have started to argue for and debate about sex workers' rights, supporting causes ranging from labor rights for legalized workers (like strippers in the United States) to decriminalization of prostitution in places where it's illegal to the more general and less quantifiable struggle against the stigmas of being a sex worker in most parts of the world. Just as the Internet has transformed advertising for sex workers, it has increased the capacity for coalition building for sex-worker-rights activists on both the local and global levels. Since the advent of the Internet and its communication tools, sex worker organizations that existed prior to the Internet have adapted to using the new technology, and projects that might not have been possible without the Internet have been launched and carried out.

Prostitutes of New York (PONY), a thirty-year-old sex worker support and activism group that distributes information to its members through a moderated email list that requires a recommendation to join, was once operated solely by sending discreet mailings about events and actions affecting sex workers. Its members maintained a phone tree to notify each other about meetings, as well as bad dates. PONY's website is a one-page informational site without any bells or whistles—or even its own domain—that's maintained its exact same look since it was launched in 1996. The page offers minimal but adequate information about the group; due to its simplicity, it seems as if PONY activities don't take place online. Though it's true that there aren't any public online forums associated with the organization, it has moved most of its written communications services online. This shift has certainly attracted new members who aren't necessarily ready to make contact in person or by phone, or who aren't willing to provide a mailing address, but it has also contributed to the loss of members who aren't technically savvy enough to use the Internet or who don't have access due to financial constraints.

Like PONY, the Network of Sex Work Projects (NSWP) was formed before the Internet became widely accessible and was transformed as the Internet made its way into the homes and workplaces of more activists. Activists Cheryl Overs and Paulo Longo hatched the idea for NSWP in 1991, and formalized it in 1992 to promote sex workers' health and human rights. By 1997, the NSWP Listserv was running strong, and its existence has facilitated international communication and collaboration. Critics of NSWP say that since going online the project has become increasingly American in terms of the voices represented. This is mostly due to the fact that 75 percent of Americans have Internet access, while in many developing countries, less than 5 percent of the population has access. This is certainly a limiting factor, but the gains and time saving that have resulted from the move online have made an immense impact within the activism community. Melissa Ditmore, who works with NSWP, says, "The Internet has brought higher levels of dialogue because the conversation is wider. Language is a huge issue—not only what languages people can use for communication (English is the online standard for international communication), but also the very words chosen. Specific issues, even things about which everyone agrees, have to be presented differently in different contexts. Stronger language is used in some places, while greater tact is required elsewhere." Through the unity the Internet brings, it also underscores international differences.

These differences—both as obstacles and unifying forces—are part of what drove Ana Lopes and her colleagues to form The International Union of Sex Workers (IUSW). The union is a part of Britain's general union, GMB, and its benefits are strongest for its members. In January 2006, for example, the union won its first-ever unfair-dismissal case for a sex worker, against Essex-based phone sex company Datapro Services Limited.[3] In this case, a phone sex operator and IUSW union member named Irene Everitt, who had worked for Datapro for eight years, was fired after having been accused of gross industrial misconduct. The union sued Datapro for her job and won. Though it's not as effective in countries outside of the U.K., IUSW owes its international presence to the Internet. Says cofounder Lopes, "I cannot imagine how my colleagues and I could have founded The International Union of Sex Workers without the Internet. It was and is absolutely fundamental. It was through reading other sex worker organizations' websites that we became aware that sex workers all over the world were demanding to be treated as workers. It was through email and Internet discussion lists that our positions were formed, our policies developed."

Sex workers' activists groups aren't necessarily a unified front, on the Internet or elsewhere. Unions appeal to a small subset of sex workers who do work that can be unionized, like stripping and phone sex, which are legal in most places. For workers whose jobs are illegal or who fear that unionization will take away some of the appealing pieces of the sex industry—its flexible hours and the potential to earn a lot of money in a short time—unionization is not a primary concern. On the Internet, perhaps the most powerful way that sex workers disagree with sex-worker-rights groups is by disregarding them entirely. While the more politically active groups focus on issues like unionization and decriminalization of prostitution, many sex workers use the Internet solely to advertise and connect with other sex workers in a social and business framework that they don't see as political in any way.

Melissa Gira, a San Francisco–based activist and one-woman Internet sexuality phenomenon, is keenly aware of the role that online advertising has played in banding sex workers together in ways that may not seem overtly political to them, but become so over time. Though she began her sex work career as a dancer, Gira didn't begin to discuss the industry with other sex workers until she began doing alt porn modeling online in 1999. At that point, she began meeting people through LiveJournal who were having similar experiences. In the fall of 2000, a LiveJournal friend of Gira's got arrested for escorting, which led to an uproar online, followed by pointed conversations among other sex workers about the wrongs of the sex industry and what they could do about these issues together.

For Gira, a major point of power was her ability to create her own media online. Whereas PONY, NSWP, and the IUSW had all hired people to make and maintain their websites, Gira struck out on her own and built her own sites for creating porn (on her now-defunct site RadicalFaeries), camming (initially on NakkidNerds and then Beautiful Toxin), and blogging (at LiveJournal and various incarnations of her own sites: Sacred Whore and Melissa Gira). For Gira, the Internet facilitated offline sessions with clients, but perhaps more importantly, it created online opportunities for doing business and collaborating with other women. Gira says, "Porn on the web was a way to get all the models talking to each other, and learning to do my own site and run my own business was political for me then." For many women, business and politics weave together in intricate ways. This is not to say that all sex workers who talk to each other online become politicized by sharing their experiences in a sort of "consciousness raising for the Internet generation" scenario. Gira, for instance, had already been working in a politicized environment before making her own website and running her own business; for other women politics don't come into play unless their business is affected. Even so, threats to sex workers' businesses and safety don't necessarily turn most workers into activists overnight (or at all): sometimes because they don't want to spend more time than absolutely necessary on their work, sometimes because they don't want to risk a greater degree of exposure, and sometimes because they just don't care and want to be left alone to do their work.

The younger generation of sex workers—which really just comprises women who are five or ten years younger than the women who started groups like PONY and NSWP—turns to the Internet rather matter-of-factly for advertising, information, and resources. Women like Gira found community on the Internet partly because they were seeking it out, but also because they were already spending social, working, and information-gathering time online. Creating a network and support community among sex workers was a natural progression for Gira and her colleagues.

In the summer of 2006, the swirl of online sex worker activism came to a head with the Desiree Alliance's four-day-long sex workers' conference in Las Vegas, Nevada. Gira and I were both members of the conference's official media team. Gira told me that the conference was "the first sex worker conference in the United States that I know of organized by mostly Internet-based sex workers using the net to organize the conference itself." Stacey Swimme, one of the conference's organizers, echoes a point Melissa Ditmore has made: that organizing online made it possible for an entire group of people to be involved in the organizational process in a way that is actually democratic and responsibility sharing. "Because of the Internet," Swimme says, "we had more community buy-in to the conference. More women felt responsible for and connected to what was going on in the planning stages, so it made for a better and stronger conference."

The strength of gathering on the Internet was very much apparent at the conference, where many conversations among young women about day-to-day sex worker issues like advertising, photographs, and safety hovered around issues connected to the Internet. The women who came together at the conference, many meeting in person for the first time after lengthy correspondence online, were technically adept and overwhelmingly young—though young isn't necessarily a shift away from what sex workers always have been. Swimme believes that "the sex-worker-rights movement would not have moved forward without the Internet, because the Internet links independent workers who are flexible in terms of class, work, and time available to work on activism projects."

Social activism has long been the province of middle-class, college-educated white kids, and judging by the attendees at the Desiree Alliance's conference, the sex workers' rights movement isn't much different. Independence from pimps and harsh economic situations is the norm for sex worker activists— most women who are highly active in the movement don't work for agencies or other kinds of bosses, and many don't have children. Street workers are a minority in the activism scene, though the women who are street workers and involved with activism are not hesitant to make their presence known. After all, they've typically gone through a lot to be able to tell their stories. Most sex workers' rights advocates who aren't street workers are keenly aware of the class disparities within the ranks, and are concerned with diversity and representation, but are also wary of speaking for other women and their needs.

Though it's nearly impossible to characterize an average sex worker, the half-joking T-shirt that reads I SUPPORT SINGLE MOMS next to an illustration of a stripper on a pole is clearly based on the belief that many single mothers enter the sex industry because of the potential for high earnings over a short time coupled with the appeal of a flexible work schedule. It's true that there are plenty of single moms who work as sex workers, and most of their activism is limited to online work, since the need for a flexible schedule is the very thing that prevents them from uprooting and attending a sex worker conference for several days. Their activism may stay online, or their voices may not be heard at all because of the financial and time constraints of earning an income and supporting and raising children. Single moms often choose the sex industry and forego standard middle-class comforts in favor of flexible schedules and an income that isn't fixed. The class divide, especially when it comes to the Internet, is very strong, and when the jump from online to in-person interaction occurs, it becomes even more apparent.

As the Internet has increasingly brought sex workers together, they have formed communities with people in their towns as well as across the globe. They continue to maintain their separate spaces as well, and to be guarded and suspicious of each other in certain areas, which is a natural outgrowth of this line of work. Activism has been part and parcel of the online shift toward being more connected for sex workers, and though the Internet has enabled conversations to happen across the world about sex workers' issues and has allowed collaborations and comparisons of models to happen in a powerful way, sex worker activism online has not just been about chatting and emailing, but about real coalition building. So much about activism and coalition building is essentially about communication, and the ease and speed of the Internet—at least for those who have access to it—brings both communication and activism to a whole new level. In this respect, even sex workers who are not interested in joining activist networks benefit from the work and awareness of other sex workers.

# CHAPTER 6: OUR BODIES, OUR BROADBAN

## Sexual Health and the
## Information Superhighway

**A**s clichéd as it is to say that the Internet is the information superhighway, when it comes to information about health, this metaphor rings true. Eight out of ten people who use the Internet have used it for information about health. (Yes, it's true, health-related topics are searched even more frequently than "boobs.") Women are 7 percent more likely than men (82 percent of Internet-using women versus 75 percent of Internet-using men) to seek out health information online.[1]

Based on my purely unscientific perusal of online forums, it also seems that women are more likely than men to participate in message boards and other interactive spaces where they discuss different health issues. People seeking health information online most often search for a specific disease or treatment, but searches for preventative measures, as well as insurance and alternative treatments, are all on the rise.[2] It's clear from the online communities that form around women's health that the women who use them rely heavily on both the support and information that's provided. In the United States especially, as healthcare costs and responsibilities increasingly shift to the consumer, the demand for health support and information online is surging; increased searches for health information online have a direct correlation with the rising costs of healthcare that individuals must shoulder.

The experience of seeking out and getting healthcare for gynecological issues can feel isolating for women, and often humiliating. Whether a woman is facing something very common (like pregnancy) or more unusual (like transsexualism), many women feel that they face these issues alone. The Internet has created a space where women can look for information and support anonymously without having to speak or convey emotions to a healthcare practitioner face-to-face that might make them anxious and upset. But online communities structured around health topics can be both empowering and damaging: They can encourage women to take command of their health, but they can also steer women away from sound medical advice by providing somewhat arbitrary opinions that usually come from a peer and are based on anecdotal personal experiences.

Women are drawn to several different kinds of health websites: those that are encyclopedic and produced by doctors and other healthcare professionals, message boards that are peer run and moderated, and niche sites that serve specific communities. All of these sites bring with them the usual degrees of cattiness and disagreement we've come to expect online, which can be irritating but can also lead to a different kind of discourse. Especially when personal matters like sexual health are involved, emotions can run high, and when one woman presents her experiences as immutable truth on an online forum, she often comes under attack by others who have a different experience and understanding of the truth. This is a phenomenon often noted in HIV/AIDS-prevention education both on- and offline— often people cling to information that is medically incorrect yet a powerful part of their worldview. For instance, some lesbians maintain that it is impossible to get HIV from oral sex with another woman, and continue to spread this information. Women choose different venues for personal reasons that have to do with what they are seeking, plus the online channels they are most comfortable with and the amount of support and engagement they want with other women who share the same challenges.

## Fallible Authority and Lazy Research

The Internet's version of authoritative health information is WebMD, which was launched in 1998 and features a variety of ways for health seekers to interact with the site, including the search feature (which is front and center), up-to-date news, medication searches, and a list of its top twelve most-searched health topics. In the near-decade that the site has been online, the company has moved beyond the web and now includes medical reference textbooks as well as a monthly print magazine that's distributed to physician's waiting rooms. According to its Alexa ratings, WebMD is one of the top one thousand most visited websites on the Internet.[3]

Part of WebMD's appeal is that it has a portal for health professionals, which boosts its credibility among consumers. However, the site is often criticized for being too littered with advertisements. Though its advertising policy insists that advertising content must be clearly differentiated from informational content, the design of the pages blurs these lines a little. Though consumers have voiced their complaints in public forums, like reviews of WebMD on Amazon, a 2006 study called "Online Health Media Consumption and Impact of Increasing Health Consumerism" notes that consumers are becoming more engaged with all aspects of health websites—including the advertisements.[4] So while some people might express their grievances about the prevalence of advertising, others apparently view it as part of their information-gathering process.

WebMD was conceived as an online resource—it is one of the few companies that made the transition from online to print instead of the other way around—but other print publications and resources have added online portals since their inception. The Planned Parenthood Federation of America, a longtime authority on women's reproductive health issues, has made its website its main source of dissemination of public information, though it still publishes and distributes paper pamphlets to health centers and to people who request them. Most sites that provide public health information realize the benefits of distributing information via their websites: The overhead costs are much lower and information can be updated much more quickly and frequently, and it can be altered if there's a mistake or when new information is discovered or made available.

One downside to this ease of information exchange is that website publishers can be less diligent than they perhaps should be about what kinds of information gets published. Community forums with lots of active participants who are not health professionals (whether they claim to be is another issue entirely) tend to fall into this category. Internet users respond to and embrace information that is accessible to them online, and many people respond to what they want to hear, regardless of whether it's correct. A 2006 Pew Internet study revealed that 75 percent of people who search for health information online do not consistently check the sources or dates of the information they find.[5]

Though there has been plenty of overly dramatized paranoia about the evils of the Internet circulating through mainstream and "old" media, some of these concerns are justified when it comes to health information online. In the mid-1990s, health professionals expressed concern when a woman named Marjorie Phillips launched an online business called New Discoveries, which sold a product that she claimed could cure HIV/AIDS in six weeks. In the 1996 case *Massachusetts v. Phillips,* Massachusetts State Attorney General Scott Harshbarger's claims against Phillips were upheld, and New Discoveries was shut down, setting a precedent for advertising and information online.

Though online health information doesn't go through any approval or examination process, today there is greater diligence around what kinds of information and products are posted and sold, especially with regard to life-or-death matters like HIV/AIDS (but with less attention paid to the ever-prevalent penis-enlargement-pill opportunities). The Medical Library Association (MLA), which was founded in 1898 as a professional organization for people in the field of health sciences information, attempts to monitor the level of information that's online by listing the top ten best websites for health information.[6] It's Consumer and

Patient Health Information Section (CAPHIS) was launched in 2001 as a subdomain of its main website and evaluates health-information websites based on a variety of factors, the first and foremost being credibility. The Medical Library Association's MLANet and CAPHIS offer authoritative information without the bells and whistles of slick design or aggressive advertising, which means that though the information may be better, the sites get about 2 percent of the traffic that WebMD gets.[7] The sites CAPHIS prioritizes are overwhelmingly not-for-profit; in fact, they emphasize the fact that the web suffix ".com" means that those sites are "developed by a for-profit company, which may be selling a product."

Cross-checking sources through sites like these is becoming increasingly easy for consumers to do on the Internet, though not enough people take advantage of this. When it comes to highly politicized issues, it can be difficult to obtain consistent information—and especially support. Despite, or more likely because of, the visibility of Planned Parenthood, information of dubious validity about birth control continues to circulate, especially online. One of the most popular pieces of disinformation that has long been circulated by people who oppose sex education and birth control is that there are microscopic holes in condoms that allow sexually transmitted infections to pass through. Though this is true of condoms made out of lambskin, it's not true of those made out of polyurethane or latex, which are the materials most commonly available. Despite the vigilance of mostly religious groups warning against the ineffectiveness of birth control, a simple Google search for "holes in condoms" reveals plenty of competing claims circulating online. Most of the search results covered the debate, and the links led to articles discussing the differences in opinion between conservative religious organizations and reproductive health communities.

## Community and Confusion: Abortion Support

When it comes to the issue of abortion, the cacophony is such that it makes it difficult for even the practiced eye to easily discern websites promoting pro-life or pro-choice values. Hazel, now twenty-two, had an abortion when she was eighteen and went directly to Planned Parenthood to do so. Hazel didn't do any further research into other providers because, for her, Planned Parenthood seemed like the obvious choice. After her abortion, Hazel felt emotionally distraught, and says, "I didn't regret my decision, but I wanted to talk to someone about how I was feeling both physically and emotionally." She began searching online for communities where women who had had abortions were talking to each other about what they were going through. She was intimidated by what she found: "I kept finding sites that were heavy on judgment and regret, and they were really pretty scary. Ultimately I found some sites for women who had experienced miscarriages, and they were a lot more sympathetic." Hazel's trouble sorting out the politics of abortion-counseling resources is not uncommon.

While many abortion-information online resources are very transparent, such as a website run by Life Dynamics Incorporated called American Death Camps, which likens abortion to a holocaust, or the website for the Whole Woman's Health chain of abortion clinics, which advertises itself as the site of an abortion provider, most are fairly ambiguous, or at least more innocuous, like SafeHaven and After Abortion, which offer support to women recovering from abortions. SafeHaven is an organization that assists women in healing from abortions and is nurturing and supportive of a woman's choice if she's already had one. But dig a little deeper into the site and it becomes clear that the organization is very much against abortion. Support messages are coupled with facts about the dangers of abortion on the Crisis Pregnancy section of the website. The message is clear—that wrong choices can be atoned for, yes, but that mostly, as evidenced by the pages and pages of message board threads about regret and sadness over abortion, that women should definitely reconsider going through with the procedure if they haven't had one yet. After Abortion takes a different approach, stating very clearly that it does not take either a pro-life or pro-choice position; in fact, site administrators put a halt to any politicized or heated discussion along these lines that may erupt on the message boards.

Sites with anti-birth-control and pro-life undertones highlight the failure rates and dangers of birth control methods (all methods except abstinence, after all, have failure rates) and abortion, while pro-birth-control and pro-choice organizations state failure rates more as a footnote to protect themselves from potential lawsuits. Either way, the highly volatile mix of politics and health information is unavoidable when it comes to abortion, and the Internet plays a major role in contributing to the fracas. Rightfully so, most attention paid to the misrepresentation of abortion services happens offline, where women with very real and time-sensitive needs may be shuffled around and given incorrect information when they stumble into a crisis pregnancy center with the intention of getting an abortion. Though the harm of the Internet is less direct—no one is going to be caught in red tape and miss the window of time for a medical or surgical abortion because they're caught up in online forums—conflicting information can be a minefield.

Women on Web is the online project of the international nonprofit organization Women on Waves, which strives to reduce the stigma and silence around abortion and to assist women in obtaining abortions if they live in countries where abortion is illegal. Based in the Netherlands, Women on Waves operates a ship that travels to countries where abortion is illegal, picks up women who want abortions, and then sails to international waters to perform the procedure. The organization, founded in 1999, has high operating costs and is not able to provide its services as often as it would like. Because of this, the organization launched Women on Web in late 2003 to offer online support and access to medical abortion for women to whom they cannot provide in-person medical services.

Women on Web is largely made possible by the development of mifepristone, the "abortion pill" that makes it possible for women to have nonsurgical abortions in the first trimester of a pregnancy. The drug was approved by the FDA in the United States in September 2000 as an abortifacient; it's recommended for use in a regimen with the labor-inducing drug misoprostol. Taken over a period of a few hours, the two drugs induce abortion. The FDA recommends this regimen for use up to seven weeks after the beginning of the pregnancy, which is measured starting with the last menstrual period (LMP). Some doctors will prescribe the regimen up until the ninth week LMP. In the

Netherlands and several other European countries, mifepristone was made legal in 1999 and the mifepristone-misoprostol regimen began to be used there at this time, though the regimen remains unpopular in the Netherlands. Regardless of its lack of popularity, the activists behind Women on Web see it as the best solution to the problem of abortion access in many countries—because it doesn't require surgery and can be administered by a woman in her own home.

A pregnant woman must go through Women on Web's online consultation before she can be deemed an appropriate candidate for its services. She must live in a country where there is no access to safe and legal abortion and not have any health issue that may create complications with the drugs. If the consultation deems the woman qualified for its services, the drugs will be delivered to her door. A donation is encouraged but not required. For women who live in countries where abortion is available, there is a detailed list of sexual health services, including their contact information.

One complication of this service is the fact that a woman must have access to the Internet in order to work with a consultant and get approved—not an easy prospect for women in developing nations. Once women find their way to the site, it is designed to be as user-friendly as possible. The design is basic, and though much of the text is highlighted in hot pink, there is a "discreet" option—a button that makes the text smaller. Although the site's default language is English, all pages can be accessed in Dutch, Portuguese, French, Spanish, and Polish. While the most important activist project of the site is the distribution of mifepristone and misoprostol, it is also engaged in efforts to reduce the stigma of abortion through the portion of the site called "I Had an Abortion," a collection of photos and stories that are constantly being updated. The profiles are visually quite similar to profiles on dating and social networking websites. Each woman selects her answers to the provided profile questions from a drop-down menu of options: reason for abortion, type of abortion, feelings about abortion, whether the abortion was legal or illegal, and her religion. She may provide further information about herself and her choice if she wishes. Within each profile, there are thumbnails showing photos of other women who've answered the questions similarly. This allows the women to be linked to each other—to talk, offer support, or just know that other women who've gone through her same experience are out there—through their similarities.

## Sharing and Caring: Peer Networks

A key aspect of many health-information websites is the message boards, where a site's users gather to share information, support, and personal stories about their experiences. Sites with active message boards are particularly popular with teenagers as they increasingly turn to the web for information about sexual health and relationships. Most of these boards are more about maintaining ongoing involvement with other people around these issues than anything else. The people who run sites for teens are acutely aware that faulty information runs rampant on the web, and each site comes up with its own way of dealing with this problem.

On Scarleteen, which was launched in 2000 as a sex education website for teens by longtime activist Heather Corinna, the voices of the teens themselves are extremely important as both content and guidance for the site. Its mission is to arm teens with enough information about sexuality that they can make informed decisions about the levels of emotional and physical risk they are willing to take. Both young men and young women are welcome, but much of the site's content is focused on the concerns of young women. This content includes frequently updated articles on topics like reproduction, sexually transmitted infections (STIs), and sexual politics, but it's the message boards that are responsible for return visits.

Corinna reports that since launching in 2000, Scarleteen's message boards have had thirty thousand registered users. Most users who register a handle on the site become repeat visitors and participants, though their patterns of use vary. Some users may participate heavily in a thread that pertains to them directly or start a thread about a question they have and then fade into the ether once they feel they've gotten a satisfactory answer; others participate widely across many different threads on all kinds of topics. Scarleteen gets anywhere between fifteen thousand and thirty thousand visitors a day, only a fraction of who are registered users. The majority are lurkers who read and learn from the boards but have no intention of posting comments or responding to threads.

Because of Corinna's concern for giving accurate information, she says, "We have the most heavily moderated sexuality-related board there is. There are at least three moderators on board every moment. About half are peers of the readers in age and background knowledge, and the other half are adult health professionals or students in health education."

Heather finds it challenging to balance the communal, advice-from-your-friends vibe with accurate health information because everyone fancies herself an expert—especially someone who has personal experience with whatever issue is at hand. She says, "It's empowering for people to feel like they know something, which is great, but the feeling often overrides actual knowledge." She and the other moderators on the site spend about half their time correcting false information that gets posted. Heather prefers correcting false information to approving and rejecting content, because she feels it encourages the teens on her boards to self-police their posts and to think seriously about whether their words are based in facts that they can corroborate. Though the process is a little problematic and labor intensive for her moderators, Scarleteen has continued to grow while maintaining the trust of the teens who use the site.

Planned Parenthood maintains a different approach to board management on its educational site Teenwire, which has been online since early 1999. Like Scarleteen, Teenwire includes short articles about teen sexual health concerns. However, the main feature of the site is "Ask the Experts," in which sexual health experts employed by Planned Parenthood answer reader-submitted questions and speak to teenagers' concerns. The site also has two different features that allow visitors to interact with their peers—a once-weekly hour-long chat room moderated by a Planned Parenthood expert and a glorified message board called "In Your Own Words." The site's FAQ asserts that its chat is moderated; questions are reviewed before they are posted, and experts ensure that accurate information is being presented. In Your Own Words allows slightly more freedom for the site's participants than other sections of the site do, particularly where questions that are a matter of opinion are concerned. For instance, on Ask the Experts, it's common to see questions that relate to specific health concerns, such as "Could I be pregnant if I forgot to take the pill one day?" whereas In Your Own Words tends to focus on questions that don't have a clear-cut answer, such as "How do I know if he likes me?"

Because of the fact that Teenwire is run by Planned Parenthood and subject to intense public scrutiny as a result, the site is concerned with preventing the circulation of inaccurate information. Unlike Scarleteen, Teenwire leaves no room for teenagers' trial and error and does not trust teens to dispense health advice to their peers. It's important to note that this is due, in large part, to how the sites are funded: Scarleteen is an independently operated site funded by a combination of Corinna's sweat and tears and individual grants she applies for, while Teenwire has to answer to Planned Parenthood and their complex system of funds and grants—not to mention the related politics. While Scarleteen has made the choice to treat teens' mistakes as teachable moments, Teenwire can't afford that approach. This is a choice that underlies a bigger issue—that health authorities don't always find it easy to trust women (and teenagers especially) with their own choices and the degree to which they are informed or actively seeking accurate information.

It's difficult to figure out whether young women respond better to information produced by peers or by professionals on message boards and other online forums—and each has its own value. According to Ellen Friedrichs, a sex educator and teen sexuality expert who's site is called Sex Edvice, "Kids usually want the fastest and most factual answer possible and don't really care where it comes from or if other teens would find the source legit." The Internet allows young women a space to ask questions that they aren't comfortable asking anyone face-to-face. In both Corinna's and Friedrich's experience, young women who seek sexual health advice online aren't necessarily planning on going to see a doctor in the flesh. Corinna believes that though articles and advice by doctors is important in lending legitimacy to a site, in some cases it may actually deter young women from seeking out a doctor in person: "If someone reads something written by a doctor, they may be less likely to go see one because they feel they've already gotten the perspective of a doctor. Doctors also aren't likely to recommend a second opinion or continued education," she says.

Health advice on the Internet, on the other hand, revolves around the concept of many opinions. Teens especially benefit from the encouragement of continued education, a need that often goes unmet at doctors' offices. And more often than not, the general practitioners that young women see in the crucial years before they begin to see a gynecologist usually have very minimal and not recently updated information about sexual health. Friedrich says, "Despite the fact that we are constantly told to talk to our healthcare providers about sex, for most people the person you see once a year when you have bronchitis is not the person you want to open up to about your inability to orgasm."

Teenagers, of course, are not the only people who are avid users of message boards, nor are they the only group that struggles with the issue of moderation and authority on community message boards. Strap-on, launched in 2000, is "a place for us to talk about personal, political, and other issues related to queer and feminist identities and ideas and queer/punk music."[8] Hosted by Ezboard community discussion boards, the board has four moderators and more than four thousand registered members. The pages of the message board are viewable by the public, but you must be a registered user to post responses. To register, you have to provide your basic information: name, email, desired handle, password, and country of residence. And again, not unlike a dating profile, users can fill in a personal profile that gives viewers more information—except that there's no field indicating "who I'm looking for."

Strap-on has three main thematic posting forums: community, identity, and advice/support. These forums—which consist of user-initiated threads—specifically focus on issues of queerness, gender, and sexuality. Many threads deal directly with health topics like herpes, chronic fatigue, latex allergies, and menstruation, as well as more-immediate medical issues like bleeding during sex and mysterious pain and rashes. Most of the health questions that are posed are opinion-gathering questions, such as the threads debating the merits of various menstruation products or lube preferences, but more-serious medical topics do crop up with frequency.

The women and trans folks on Strap-on have several motivations for turning to an online community for their health information. As active participants in the queer community, Strap-on's users are fairly knowledgeable and in touch with their sexuality, needs, and desires, and many are coming to terms with various issues like body dysmorphia and sexual abuse.

Many of the message board participants feel more comfortable asking their peers for health advice because their sexualities and lifestyles, which can include multiple sexual partners and kinky sex, are often stigmatized and difficult to talk about with healthcare professionals.

Strap-on members have had their share of unfortunate or inappropriate responses to their sexual orientation or gender presentation by healthcare professionals, and some even avoid paying a visit to a healthcare professional as a result. Additionally, many do not have health insurance, so they tend to examine their options as fully as possible before visiting a doctor. Though Strap-on isn't specifically focused on alternative health practices and natural remedies, many of the suggestions for treatments that show up on the site incorporate these methods and discourage the use of doctor-prescribed medicines. Discussions on the message boards tend to promote alternative methods not just because of the expense, but also because of the side effects: Antibiotics can interfere with birth control and can create yeast infections in some women, while many SSRIs (selective serotonin reuptake inhibitors), which are prescribed to alleviate depression and anxiety, can alter sexual functioning and libido.

The existence of sites like Strap-on provides needed community support for people who often feel marginalized by the health community. In some cases, experiences from fellow transgendered people can be more valuable to trans folks than medically accurate information, particularly for people who are seeking answers to health issues that are specifically related to transitioning and other new experiences that are unique to undergoing hormone therapy. Although medical professionals might caution against subscribing to information that's posted on a message board where the people dispensing health advice are clearly not professionals, the power of the community support for women and trans folks who use the site definitely overcomes this warning.

## Crossing Over:
## Transsexuals Seeking Answers

Transsexuals have a very difficult time negotiating their way through the healthcare system when they are trying to figure out what is going on with them and how they can deal with it best. A variety of studies indicates that fully transitioned transsexuals probably make up about 1 to 3 percent of the general population[9]; it's much harder to come by statistics for those who question their gender identity and are unhappy with the body they were born into. Mainstream media, however, seems much more fascinated with (and titillated by) MTFs (male to female transsexuals) than FTMs (female to male transsexuals), which serves to make MTFs seem much more prevalent than they might actually be.[10] Interestingly, FTM transsexuals have found the queer and lesbian community to be more accepting and nurturing of their personal struggles than male to female (MTF) transsexuals. This is largely due to the fact that many transsexual men identified with the lesbian and queer community as biological women before they transitioned. MTF transsexuals also tend to have a more difficult time finding community and support because the lesbian and queer community has been known to ostracize those individuals for invading their female spaces. The womyn-born-womyn policy at the Michigan Womyn's Music Festival is one of the more publicized instances of discrimination against trans women—the policy states that only biological women can attend the festival. Due to discrimination and marginalization among this community, the Internet has been a pivotal space for transsexuals, particularly trans women, as they go through hormone treatments and physical transitions and seek out medical information and unprejudiced healthcare.

Krista Scott-Dixon, one of three editors of Trans-Health, the online magazine of health and fitness for transsexual and transgendered people, says, "The Internet helps to fight isolation, shame, and stigma by showing people, hey, there are plenty of folks just like you." She also believes that offline support and interaction is critical for people who are transitioning. "We definitely encourage people to look for offline support as much as possible," she says. Though the Internet provides a safe haven for trans folk who may not know people in their daily lives who've had similar experiences of feeling so disconnected from their gender and/or bodies, part of the transitioning process entails living life as one's chosen gender—which is something that needs to happen offline.

Now twenty-nine, Hannah began to explore the possibility that she wanted to live as a woman in 2002, several years into her marriage to a woman. After a year of thinking about it and keeping it to herself and researching the possibilities for transition online, she told her then-wife that she wanted to transition. The decision caused a major upheaval in their relationship: They divorced, though they have remained close friends. Hannah's discontent with living as a male was what sent her to the Internet for information about what she was feeling, and it was the community, stories, and counsel she found there that allowed her to entertain the possibility of living as a female. Hannah tells me how the initial exploration opened up so many new ideas and emotions: "I probably spent way too much time online, but it was exciting to discover whole communities of people that had the same feelings as me. And they were transitioning. I knew then that it could really happen." Several of the trans women that Hannah met online during her early stages of transitioning became fast friends, and even though they all hailed from distant parts of the United States, they made a point of getting together in person regularly. Hannah regrets that they have since drifted apart. As they've each pursued their transitions and begun to live as their preferred gender, they've continued to rely on each other, but don't feel as compelled to be in touch so regularly since they're further along in the process and better understand the ins and outs of what they're dealing with.

One of the first sites that Hannah took advantage of was (Transsexual) TS Road Map, an online resource that assists transsexual women in making a plan for their transition and understanding what they're facing: It offers assistance in considering a goal endpoint for their transition, how much surgery they think they might want to undergo, how much time they can expect in terms of recovery and transition, and the expenses that will be incurred along the way. To this day TS Road Map, originally launched in 1996, retains a bare-bones design. Its primary concern is providing emotional support for transsexuals during their transition, and it states that the main goal for transsexuals should be to live full-time as their preferred gender.

One of the most important and powerful things the Internet offers transsexuals is the opportunity to get help connecting to trans-friendly healthcare. Hannah connected with her first doctor through an online friend, but finding the correct hormone balance has been an ongoing challenge for her. She says, "After a while, I couldn't afford to see a doctor [the hormones were covered by insurance, but doctor visits and tests were not], so I started ordering online. I researched intensely online before choosing a reliable overseas pharmacy. I still get most of my hormones this way, and I've never had a problem."

The Internet has certainly made the process of getting hormones and being educated about their effects immeasurably easier than it's ever been. Scott-Dixon of Trans-Health says, "People were often surprisingly well informed fifteen or twenty years ago, since there was a thriving underground information network, but you still had to know that there *was* such a thing, and where to find it, and then wait by the mailbox for the plain brown wrapper to show up. Lots of folks didn't ever find that community or those resources, so they spent decades thinking they were the sole weirdo in the universe." TS Road Map opines that the younger people are when they start their transition, the better chance they have of accepting themselves and being accepted as their preferred gender in the world. With the advent of the Internet, transsexuals have the opportunity to find out what's "wrong" with them at an earlier age and potentially avoid some of the more harmful effects of having to go into adulthood with the pain and secrecy around knowing something isn't right with the body and gender they were born into.

When Hannah began to transition in her early twenties, she found that there was a big divide between the generations of transsexual women. Young trans women had entirely different issues than older ones, so Hannah started to seek out peers her age. She found what she was looking for on a website called GenderPeace, which was designed specifically for younger transsexual women by a younger trans woman named Emily who felt that older trans women dominated the forums in other online spaces. Many of the women who were initially involved with GenderPeace have left it or moved on, perhaps for the very fact that it exists as a resource for younger trans women. The site has changed since its inception—the homepage has links to stories and poems shared by trans women, as well as a link to the forums, some of which are private. Hannah says, "I was asked to join the invite-only forum, where only women who had completed their social transition [living as women "full-time"] were allowed. Everyone on that forum pretty much knows each other, and we've kept the member list small. It's more of a women's forum than a trans forum now." Hannah notes that need for camaraderie with other trans women changes over time, and though she finds comfort in the private forum on GenderPeace, it's the only trans-related website she visits with any frequency today, whereas a few years ago she relied heavily on a variety of forums and websites.

Rachel, now twenty-six, first started to realize that she was transsexual when she was a teenager attending an all-boys private high school in the United Kingdom. Around the time she was sixteen and seventeen, Rachel began to search the Internet for help, though she wasn't entirely sure what she was looking for at first. When she started to realize that her issues were rooted in the fact that her feelings about her gender didn't match the body she was living in, an online friend introduced her to a transvestite who then gave her some links to transgender and transsexual forums. She immediately signed up for some email lists on the topic of transsexuality and began to gain a sense of clarity. Like Hannah, she gravitated toward her peers and tried to join lists specifically for young people. She says, "The lists that weren't particularly youth-oriented I often found to be somewhat creepy. They seemed to be full of middle-aged transvestites who wondered if they might be transsexuals, and a lot of the talk was about how to behave in a feminine manner rather than just doing what was natural to them." When she went away to college at eighteen, Rachel began to pursue her transition in earnest, seeing a psychiatrist and beginning hormone therapy, as well as beginning the resocialization process, which was especially challenging since she hadn't spent much time in the company of girls while she was growing up. During this period, she quickly came out to her parents; she legally changed her name within forty-eight hours of discovering how to do so on the Internet.

The Internet's role in helping Rachel achieve clarity about her gender issues, as well as make her decisions about transitioning, cannot be understated. Rachel found everything she needed to know about the medical and hormonal issues she would confront online, which was invaluable to empowering her to demand the best and most accurate medical attention from her doctors. She says, "I remember going to a doctor and asking if she could refer me for speech therapy to feminize my voice. She said that that was entirely unnecessary and that the hormone therapy would unbreak my voice in time. This is blatantly not true, and that was the last time I saw that doctor, but if I hadn't been able to research for myself, then I'd have had no reason not to believe her." Without access to the Internet, Rachel probably would have had more harrowing and demoralizing encounters with doctors. Because of her access to it, however, she took control of the situation for herself. "With just a little bit of research, I was able to know more about the medical treatment for transsexualism than any nonexpert medical practitioner I was ever likely to see," she tells me.

Rachel makes a point to note that not all of the forums were helpful, and that some behaviors in the forums were potentially destructive. One of the struggles that many transsexual women face is the challenge of proving to a psychiatrist that they are indeed transsexual and would like to be considered for sexual reassignment. This means finding a doctor who will agree to prescribe hormone therapy and approve the pursuit of surgeries that may include facial feminization surgery, breast augmentation, and/or vaginoplasty. Many trans women are very anxious about this process for a whole host of different personal reasons. Though most doctors generally just want to be certain that their patients understand the consequences of this very serious, stressful, and life-altering decision, trans women often see doctors as adversaries instead of allies. As a result, Rachel says, "One thing that happens is 'coaching,' where people on the forums tell others precisely what they have to say to a psychiatrist in order to have hormones prescribed, which I think is actively dangerous." It's possible that some people get approved who maybe ought to spend more time considering what they're going to be putting themselves through. And while the Internet enables this kind of behavior and spreads this type of information more quickly and to more people than it could circulate otherwise, it's inarguable that the Internet has provided more beneficial resources to this community than harm.

Rachel experienced the fast-paced information exchange online. Of her experience, she says, "The Internet groups could be very pressuring, making everyone try to rush through everything as fast as possible. It was taboo to ever suggest that maybe people should stop and think, or that they might want to take things more slowly." Because of the freedom with which information suddenly becomes available to transsexuals who may have previously been living in the dark, not knowing that there was a name for how they felt or that there are others who feel the same way, the Internet can create a kind of knowledge euphoria. Once transsexuals know the possibilities, many of them want to get the show on the road and be on their way toward their destinations. This, coupled with the enthusiasm that other trans women have in supporting their sisters, creates a kind of forward crush that can be motivating for some—Rachel says that she appreciated the push to go and see a psychiatrist—but for others it may come before they're ready to commit themselves. For trans women, as for many women, the Internet is both a blessing and a curse that holds promise but also false hope.

## Getting Connected

Message boards are cornerstones for many health-information-seeking women, but there are other ways that women struggling with sexual health use the Internet to find their own—and each other's—voices in both political and personal contexts. Maliscious Lelo, a woman in her midtwenties from Western Canada, has had chronic illness for nearly a decade. Her blog and other forms of online social networking have become extremely important to her as sites of political organizing, as well as personal growth and exploration. When she began her blog SexAbility in April 2006, she planned to explore issues of sex and disability both in a very personal way and through politicized writing aimed at people with disabilities and the general public, who she categorized more generally as people who don't generally think of people with disabilities as sexual beings. About her blog, she says, "I didn't go online to look for doctors or support services necessarily. Instead, I wanted to find out what it is that other people in similar situations are doing." By using her own struggle to regain her sexual self as a public example, she hoped that readers would learn something and gather strength from reading about her personal experiences.

Six months into her blog, Lelo started developing two different sites that split her work into two distinct spaces. "I decided to make a clearer split between my community activism and my personal activities," she says. SexAbility became the community support and activism site with message boards as the centerpiece, while Scarlet Minx became her personal blog. Straddling the line between these two components in one space proved to be too problematic, as she struggled with her own set of issues while also trying to make clear political and community connections. On sexual health message boards, the bleed between the personal, political, and medical is almost natural; as women discuss their problems getting good healthcare and support, the conversations take many turns. Discussions can turn political when women write about how they're being misrepresented because their health issues are perceived as falling outside of the norm. Often they share personal anecdotes when they recognize problems similar to their own that are cropping up on message boards and blogs.

Blogs lend themselves to more online visibility than message boards (they're more often picked up by Google bots than message boards are) and they create a sense of authority that a more collectively created message board does not. Blogs also get more notice and more incoming links than message boards. The big difference is that the amount of discussion that occurs on the average blog post is far inferior to the discussions that erupt on threads in message boards, where the original poster isn't often perceived as an expert, but as a peer.

SexAbility has very much been a project designed to be visible and provoke thought and discussion as well as share personal stories, and it's a good example of the struggle that many sexual health websites face. Sexual health website managers, content providers, and participants constantly struggle with the amount of energy they should devote to the community they serve and interact with directly, how to address the silent masses of readers who don't ever participate, the space and time they should spend doing public education, and the self-care that needs to happen to let them best handle all the other issues that arise.

# CHAPTER 7: DOING IT FROM A DISTANCE 010101
## The Fantasies and Fallacies of
## Online Sex

A s much as I love and obsess over the collision and/or harmonic unity of women's sexuality and the Internet, pieces about the Future of Sex with pictures of, well, gloriously futuristic stuff (mind-reading devices, computer keyboard implants in people's arms, electro-erotic orgasm field forces, and the like) sort of make me throw up in my mouth a little bit. Why? Because the present is already pretty awesome and futuristic-cool in a way, with trends and technology developing constantly and in the here and now to get people off more quickly and in better and more interesting ways. And as much as future imaginings are cool and interesting, many of the fantasies that get floated are about the disappearance of the need for sex partners—and even the disappearance of bodies themselves. It feels useless and sci-fi-ish to me to try and predict the sex/technology trends of five, ten, or fifty years from now, whether that future is painted as amazing and free or full of doom and gloom. As much as conceptual imaginings of the future make me roll my eyes, I know that these fantasies reveal fears and hopes people have about sexuality and, in particular, about women's sexuality.

The Internet's technologically made spaces are often labeled with the words "virtual" and "cyber," two words that haven't cropped up a whole lot in this book. Both words get thrown around a lot in our culture, and though they've gone out of vogue for most people who work in information technologies, they're still in heavy rotation whenever mainstream media runs a story about the Internet. In that context, virtual reality and cyber-anything are code for "the lurid world of naughty technology." Virtual reality is tactile, and because any kind of new media lends itself to being appropriated and made better and more popular by the adult entertainment industry, sex has become a major element in both the entirely imaginary and real developments of these technologies. In a general sense, these two words simply conjure up ideas of spaces that are separate from daily human experiences.

"Virtual" spaces, indeed, are not real places; you cannot physically be in a virtual space. According to the *Oxford English Dictionary,* the word "virtual" first came into use with reference to computers in 1959. In 1997, the phrase "virtual reality" was added, which is defined as "a notional image or environment generated by computer software, with which a user can interact realistically, as by using a helmet containing a screen, gloves fitted with sensors, etc."[1] Thus, virtual reality, though not a real physical space, is designed in an attempt to bring the body along for the ride. It's experienced while wearing a highly sensitive and wired body suit, in addition to the telltale virtual reality helmet, which has a wraparound screen on the inside of its visor that creates the illusion of looking at a three-dimensional world.

It's a little more difficult to define "cyber"; while virtual reality focuses on the creation of an experience, "cyber" refers to a more generalized culture that's constructed with computers and composed of digital media—untouchable but pervasive. The word "cyber" can be used on its own—as a verb it describes the act of sexy interaction through instant messaging or chat—or as a prefix tacked onto myriad different words, such as "cybersex," "cyberspace," and "cyberdildonics" (a word I'll use a lot in this chapter). The concepts of virtual and cyber are most often visually represented with overdesigned, three-dimensional-looking computer-generated images, especially sexy, vaguely robotic beings donning shiny metal with often-inexplicable wires sprouting out of them here and there.

There was a lot of wink-wink nudge-nudging when the idea of virtual reality first began to stir in the 1970s and 1980s, and after Howard Rheingold's 1991 book *Virtual Reality: Exploring the Brave New Technologies of Artificial Experience and Interactive Worlds from Cyberspace to Teledildonics,* development of these technologies surged.

That last word in Rheingold's title, "teledildonics," has created major waves in information technology and virtual reality. When it came to virtual reality, the question on everyone's lips was "But can you have sex with it?" And the theory of teledildonics answers that question with a hearty yes. Teledildonics are sexual devices that can be operated through the Internet—the ultimate goal being that two (or more) partners can play with each other from a distance, using key commands to operate toys remotely and giving new life to the phone book slogan "Reach out and Touch Someone."

The name of these devices has been changing over the years, however. "Teledildonics" was coined in the 1980s by Ted Nelson, a philosopher of information technologies who was also credited with coining the word "hypertext" in the early 1960s. However, as dial-up Internet connections became increasingly rare, effectively taking the "tele" out of "teledildonics," "cyberdildonics" began cropping up in the late-1990s. Though "cyberdildonics" is used with increasing frequency, many people who followed the first wave of these devices use the historical term "teledildonics."

Perhaps the softest-sounding way to refer to these devices is "Internet-enabled sex toys," a phrase that both says what the devices are and exemplifies the industry's attempt to mainstream their products. Trying to position them in the marketplace entailed getting rid of the word "dildonics." All three monikers—"teledildonics," "cyberdildonics," and "Internet-enabled sex toys"—are used fairly interchangeably, depending on who's talking, what they like best, and what they're trying to get across. I use "cyberdildonics" most frequently because I feel it reflects the current work on this idea most accurately. But whatever you call it, sex toys operated by remote users through the Internet are the source of much fascination, particularly among sex workers who've recognized the money-making potential these experiences hold for them when they choose to create spaces for exploration of sex and technology. I'm not completely drawing a line between what "women" want and what "sex workers" want, as if they were two entirely separate entities, but I was hard pressed to find many non-sex-working women who were genuinely excited about and eager to use cyberdildonics.

## Fucking Machines: Girls and Gadgets

Before I dig into the world of Internet-enabled sex toys, it's important to discuss non-Internet heavy-duty sex toys, which have developed on something of a parallel to toys that can be used via the Internet. They are big and intense and are often made by renegade do-it-yourself engineers who build the devices out of household appliances like power drills and Kitchen-Aids. Commonly called fucking machines by people not known for mincing words, these toys are indiscreet contraptions that exist somewhere on the spectrum between terrifying and orgasm inducing.

Fucking machines are the opposite of the common vibrator. Whereas most vibrators are compact, handheld, battery operated, and designed to enhance a woman's relationship with her clitoris, fucking machines are large, indiscreet, and loud, and most of them are designed solely to thrust dildos in and out of whatever orifice they encounter. The fucking machines like the ones featured on the porn site aptly named Fucking Machines (part of San Francisco's Kink.com network of websites) are featured doing exactly what their tagline touts: "the Humanly Impossible." In any other porn production, a scene with one girl and some toys would be called a solo scene, but the size and intensity of the various machines of Fucking Machines make them into full-fledged scene partners. For straight men, the images on the site represent a kind of ideal; they're able to watch girls be penetrated and fucked without the nuisance of having to look at another man's penis. However, the site is about much more than eliminating unsightly boners; it's about the excitement of watching a girl with a machine, or maybe a machine with a girl, a subtle but important difference. The machine and the girl are both objectified on Fucking Machines, though the perception of to what degree varies from viewer to viewer.

Fixation on the machines captures a kind of adolescent boy fixation on girls and machines, and smashing the two together makes for a confusing mix of hate, love, and industry. In the fusion of female sexuality and technology, the curious and enthralling thing about these toys is the way in which they cast sexuality and technology together in a near miasma of technophobia and technofetishism. The word on the street—or at least, the word coming out in the form of myriad questions posed on the subject by both men and women in sex advice columns—is that men are nervous about the use of sex toys and women are nervous about bringing up their desire to use sex toys because of the idea of participating in "the humanly impossible." The fact that men are nervous about it stems in part from anxieties around their ability to perform and please women, but in fact, fucking machines have created a surprising development: They've allowed this shortcoming to become fetishized. A man may question his abilities—his sexual ego is even likely to be shattered—if he fails to keep up with something small and plastic that operates on two AA batteries, but when up against a machine called the Fucksall, a modified power saw with one-sixteenth horsepower, which of the two has more sexual prowess is a foregone conclusion. The supposed mechanical superiority of the machines becomes a spectacle to behold in itself, one that no longer reflects on the man's physical or sexual capabilities. And he could be massively turned on by this idea.

But what about the woman who is having actual sexual experiences with the machine that's both feared and eroticized by onlooking men? Despite what I've written in this book about women creating their own online (and offline) spaces to experiment with their sexuality, most sexual culture that's for sale is purchased and jerked off to by men. Thus, should they choose to do so, women stand to benefit from the arrangement of men wanting something they'll have to pay to get. Some women are doubtless into machine sex for the fun of it, but there's no question that the machines are most commonly used by women who are machine fucking for money. Most demonstrations of girls with fucking machines take place in porn or swing clubs. (After all, it's possible to move the machines from place to place to do live shows, but it's not especially discreet.) This might be read by some as pandering to male fantasies, and maybe it is, but it's no different from playing out male fantasies in any other sex working environment.

## Dude, It's Virtual Reality

Virtual reality is both the precursor to cyberdildonics and the bane of its existence. In a lot of ways, virtual reality is a cool idea, but not actually a good idea. It's akin to shouting "Look what I can do!" from the rooftops. The concept of virtual reality, as it stands today, is more about the flexing of technological might (especially at conventions and other spaces where the technologically minded gather to praise each other's innovations and strut their own techie stuff) than it is a technology that people can use. The basic goal of sex in virtual reality is to experience the tactile stimulations of sex without actually being physically touched by a partner. And considering that virtual reality suits are ludicrously expensive to make, and therefore not all that viable on the commercial market, they're more appealing as a concept than as a real thing.

In the late 1990s, Vivid Entertainment, one of the biggest adult entertainment companies in the business, was involved in developing a sex suit that got a lot of press. It was tested by models, but never went to market and subsequently dropped off the radar. Vivid representatives refused to answer further questions about it. The suit was essentially a wired wetsuit, made of neoprene, that could produce five different kinds of sensations (tickle, pinprick, vibration, hot, or cold) that could be directed to any of the thirty-six sensors located at strategic places all over the suit—including the genitals, of course. The suit could be used via the Internet, but didn't include a helmet for a visual experience. The goal was to offer a physical experience that would blur the lines between touching someone who is in the same physical space and having a fantasy about touching someone.

The combination of a visual and tactile experience in virtual reality, however, is not so easily produced. Though this full experience is depicted in movies like *The Lawnmower Man,* developers have had difficulty producing it in an authentic way.

It's fairly simple to produce a suit with a visual experience that matches the sensations of the outfit as a set preprogrammed encounter, kind of like a movie that the whole body can experience. However, it's proven more challenging to make the encounter fully interactive with other users who are wearing suits in a remote location. This requires more-elaborate programming to allow a full range of physical gestures and touches, and the technology that is virtual reality is limited by the imaginations of its designers and the ways they can imagine touch.

Vivid spent almost $200,000 to develop prototypes of its suit.[2] To put this in perspective, the budget for an average adult feature by a company like Vivid is $20,000 to $30,000. To justify this expense, they must have believed that it would rake in huge profits as well as mainstream press interest—and it certainly did the latter. The suit was slated to retail for $170, which was considered quite a lot of money for a sex toy at the time. Though that's by no means cheap in the world of sex toys today, either; the industry has been revolutionized since the late nineties, when various companies started experimenting with toys made of materials like medical-grade silicone, steel, and glass.

For all its hype, sex in virtual reality largely remains a fantasy. The addition of a sexual element to virtual reality reveals something very important about technology: It's not a good substitute for "the real thing." The division between online and "real life" is discussed ceaselessly when it comes to people's sexual and emotional involvements, particularly when made possible or facilitated via the Internet, and yet attempts to get physical bodies online have been awkward, almost goofy.

Bodies aren't able to be digitized and streamlined in the way that ideas and desires are. Intellectual and emotional reality persists in being a different kind of experience, one that can enhance (and yes, also harm) a woman's perception of her sexuality. So these constant attempts to bring bodies into the digital realm beg the question: Why? The answer, no matter what form it may take, can basically be summed up as: Because we (think we) can. Perhaps as life becomes increasingly digital, and the technologies of virtual reality become more viable, sexual encounters in virtual reality will begin to make more sense. For now virtual reality is neither an improvement on, nor an enhancement to, the physical experience of sex between partners who are in the same room; moreover, it's actually less satisfying than other forms of remote sex—like phone sex or sex in an online chat room. At least there, words and imagination are the stimulus, and the actual touching part is masturbation, which for most women is pretty darn reliable.

## Remote Control

Cyberdildonics presents the possibility of interacting with a partner in a physical way via the Internet that's entirely different from those attempts by virtual reality enthusiasts. The technology behind cyberdildonics is slightly more viable than virtual reality sex, but the devices have been similarly appealing mostly only to tech geeks and fetishists. Like many new technologies, the first few generations of cyberdildonics were unwieldy, rife with problems, and in many cases not actually cyberdildonics at all. Outsiders tend to assume that people's motivations for using cyberdildonics fall into two categories: the desire to make sexual contact between partners who live apart or spend time apart or the desire, generally male, to live out some sort of online "ultimate fantasy" of sex with a porn star. Although "couples" ostensibly include women, they are nonetheless left out of this equation because couples' involvement has, until recently, been largely a hope of people in marketing, but not a sales reality. The women who are using the technology are those who work in the sex industry, especially women who do webcam shows, and they're the ones who've begun to adapt the toys to their work environments, playing into the remote-control porn star fantasy.

One of the first cyberdildonics devices to get substantial attention was the $369 Virtual Sex Machine (now $100 more expensive), which was designed for users of Microsoft Windows and came onto the market in June 2000. The toy is much more machine than virtual, and though it's technically interactive, it doesn't allow a user to interact with another human being. The device, designed for a male user, is basically a wired cock-size tube that requires software in order to work properly. It comes with several specially made DVDs of women performing various sex acts and is programmed so that the movement of the women in the DVD is matched by the movement and rhythm of the cock tube. Thus, the man using Virtual Sex Machine can have a "virtual" experience that approximates sex with a porn star. This living (though prerecorded) blow job machine was declared the ultimate in male sexual fantasies. "Ultimate" is probably a bit of an overstatement given that it's a far cry from a fully integrated and interactive virtual sex experience, and instead just takes the interactive features of a porn DVD a step further. All it really did was capitalize on digital video's increasing availability and its ensuing reduced production costs to shoot several different versions of a scene for men to get off on.

The toy's steady but lackluster sales have confirmed that men's ultimate fantasy might actually involve a partner with a little more spring in her step, one who would actually be present and responding to stimulations. Aside from never being wildly popular in the male sexual marketplace, companies found out that the concept of the technology itself was off-putting to women. Even though cyberdildonics might seem appealing to women separated from their partners by distance—and those were indeed the customers the companies wanted to reach, both to mainstream and legitimize their toys—it was instead sex workers who responded to the technology as an opportunity and grabbed it. In the mainstream marketplace, men are much more inclined to buy the newest, latest, greatest gadget than women are, and men are more-frequent and more-visible consumers in the sex industry than women are. So, the logical conclusion is that men would flock to sex workers offering sex—plus a new gadget.

In 1999, in collaboration with the webcam site iFriends, an actual cyberdildonics system was introduced, and the connection between cyberdildonics and commercial sex became easy and obvious. The now-defunct SafeSexPlus (though iFriends is still as popular as ever) required the purchase of toys wired for Internet use as well as an adapter that had to be suction-cupped to the computer monitor in order to receive signals from a remote partner. SafeSexPlus was more equal opportunity than the Virtual Sex Machine, with attachments for both male and female users. Neither system encourages women (or Mac users) to explore cyberdildonics for their own edification, unless they are being paid. The visuals on SafeSexPlus's website featured photographs of blond women throwing back their heads in ecstasy, making it look an awful lot like a porn site aiming for men's wallets.

SafeSexPlus offered customers the option to interact with another person, so that the two people could see each other over a webcam via iFriends while remotely controlling a sex toy to stimulate one another. SafeSexPlus worked well for men who were merely curious about remote sex toys because it wasn't necessary to purchase the full system to work another person's remote toy—all that could be done in the online interface. Thus, sex workers who set up cyberdildonics systems would have customers who would not become regular visitors who came just to see what the deal was. Men who were already familiar with the way iFriends worked could experiment on SafeSexPlus using a toy remotely on a willing lady. They might delve in deeper and buy their own set of toys if they really liked it. Both the Virtual Sex Machine and SafeSexPlus, however, are pretty unwieldy systems that aren't sexy in and of themselves, unless the technology itself is the focal point. Sex sells technology and gadgets and really almost anything else you can put a pretty model next to. But in the context of cyberdildonics, users often spend more of their time interacting with the technology itself—getting it to work, positioning it correctly, learning the interface—than they do with the person on the other side of the line. Although computers are asserted as a tool for people, in the case of the early cyberdildonics, the machines themselves often occupied more sexual attention than the women on the tiny screens.

## The Next Generation

During my interview Violet Blue, sex educator and an eleven-year member of machine-arts group Survival Research Laboratories (SRL), tells me, "I was never too interested in sex machines because they were always so poorly designed, crudely made, profit chasing, and unappealing for a user. Things have been changing a lot over the past few years, and a lot of machine makers have come up with some really cool things." The main cool thing is not so much a thing as it is an approach. Individuals like those who run SRL have begun to tinker with sex toys and modify them to turn them into cyberdildonics—with mixed successes. After the invention and intense promotion of devices like the Virtual Sex Machine and SafeSexPlus waxed and waned, the curiosity about the possibilities of cyberdildonics remained, and the next wave of people interested in the toys in the early twenty-first century have tended to be tech geeks who subscribe to the idea that open source culture is the best approach to most new technologies. "Open source" is most broadly used to refer to software that is freely shared, usually over the Internet, but it's also used to talk about hardware whose engineering is transparent and modifiable.

OpenDildonics and Slashdong are two projects, separate until recently, that emerged as a result of conversations about sexual devices and open source culture in late 2004 and early 2005. OpenDildonics manifested as a project of discussions on the message boards on Brum2600, an Internet technology developer support forum. It was a website collective striving to make cyberdildonics technologies more available to people who want to play with and learn about them. The goal of the project is to free budding cyberdildonics technologies from their ties to specific, profit-driven companies (particularly those with a bias toward the Windows operating system).

Slashdong, whose name is a play on the popular technology news blog Slashdot, is written by a man who goes by QDot. The site tracks developments in cyberdildonics, as well as QDot's own experiments and continual modifications to a device called the SeXBox, which started out as a sex toy but has morphed into something much more elaborate. Like OpenDildonics, Slashdong advocates for an open source system with its project FreeSex. The goals of FreeSex, as outlined on the site, are to make cyberdildonics "more accessible, cheaper, and free from subscription services."

However, it wouldn't be fair to say that these sites have made the toys more accessible. Instead, they've made the modification of cyberdildonics accessible to people who know code, are familiar with basic electronics, and are handy with a soldering iron. In effect, they've created user-friendliness for advanced users. Other websites I've discussed throughout this book are very accessible to the average Internet user, from users whose knowledge of computers is limited to basic HTML to those who only know how to access websites by typing URLs into their browsers. Though OpenDildonics is as easy to find as other sites on the Internet, it presents concepts and how-tos that would not be easily understood by the average Internet user. The site does offer how-tos to anyone willing to put in the time and energy to modify sex toys into cyberdildonics, with guides to both hardware and software modifications. It also offers instructions and pictures for modifying a small vibrator—the Pocket Pleaser—into a cyberdildonics device, as well as software for modifying the vibrate feature on a mobile phone.

So where are the women in this picture? Though the inimitable Violet Blue casts her lot in with the machine-lusty, she is one of very few women who's voiced her interest in the machines from the perspectives of both development and play. Nearly all cyberdildonics are designed and built by men, but Blue believes this trend is starting to shift as women begin to tinker with their own designs rather than engaging with toys that might not meet their needs or desires. Blue sees this change extending beyond developers, too. Women are starting to express interest in exploring cyberdildonics for their own pleasure. Blue says, "I think the increase in women cyberdildonics users is analogous to the increase of female porn consumers with the ease and accessibility of porn on the web."

Indeed, women have begun to seek out more and more-varied sexual experiences as a result of there being more options for women to explore porn made for women and increasingly high-quality sex toys. I actually believe that cyberdildonics may be a new frontier for women, despite what I said earlier about being loath to entertain the futuristic images and dialogue people love to talk about when it comes to the Future of Sex. If they're properly integrated into the other aspects of the Internet that women enjoy, I see women latching on to their potential to open up the great possibilities of their sexuality using cyberdildonics. For cyberdildonics to be successful and appealing to the average female online sexplorer, they must provide the opportunity for a woman to actually learn more about her sexuality and not just learn about how the technology itself works. The use of vibrators has become much more popular and acceptable over the past twenty years, just as the use of the Internet for sexual and relationship exploration has over the past ten years, and it's very possible that cyberdildonics will be the emerging sexual technology over the next ten years. However, it's unlikely that women will embrace the technology in their bedrooms (and with their dollars) if the technology isn't able to provide control over female orgasm to the women themselves. Having a remote operator of a sex toy is a fun tease, but it's probably not the most expedient means of reaching orgasm for a woman. While those issues are getting sorted out, sex workers and renegade lady techies like Violet Blue will continue to be at the forefront of these experiments.

In early June 2005, Violet Blue and the fetish model then known as Net Michelle (who now goes by Michelle Aston) engaged in some bicoastal cybercoitus in order to demonstrate the possibilities of cyberdildonics. Blue was at the helm in San Francisco while Michelle was on the receiving end of her ministrations at the Museum of Sex in New York; the whole affair was orchestrated using the technological know-how of Dorkbot SF (tagline: "People Doing Strange Things with Electricity"). The machine they used for the demonstration was the Thrillhammer, which belongs to that rather intimidating world of super–sex machines discussed earlier in this chapter. The Thrillhammer was wired to be a cyberdildonic device, in an effort to further prove the point that cyberdildonics need not be proprietary (manufactured by particular companies and sold through limited means). Both women were accompanied by live audiences: Blue controlled the Thrillhammer, and a webcam was trained on Michelle so that the people attending the event in San Francisco could see what was happening in New York on a large screen accompanying Blue's demonstration.

As could be expected with any technology, especially one still very much in development, there were technical difficulties—not the least of which was the fact that Michelle had accidentally unplugged the Thrillhammer in New York. Once the machine was up and running, Blue confesses that the experience was a little alienating. Aside from the technology and distance aspect of it, she'd never had sex with a girl she didn't know before—plus there was a live audience. But Blue really wanted to give Michelle a good sexual experience, and she concentrated on trying to stimulate Michelle with the Thrillhammer. After the conclusion of the event, Michelle told Blue that she'd had two orgasms.

Another complaint Blue had about the experience had to do with the visuals: The webcam trained on Michelle was aimed only at her vulva. The audience in San Francisco reacted to this as well. Blue says, "The rig Michelle was in was designed only for close-ups of her body parts, and everyone in the room wanted to see the whole picture, more of her body, including her face. It was interesting to see a couple hundred people all disappointed by standard porno close-ups." Michelle affirms that the experience was a good one, and that the machine definitely met her needs, and laughs when she says, "I believe science is a beautiful thing, especially when it is dialed precisely to my clit."

Although the machine was being controlled by Blue, Michelle didn't have any contact with her other than the knowledge that she was the force behind the machine's movements: The camera only went one way, pointed at Michelle for the benefit of the San Francisco audience. In my interview with her, Michelle spoke about her experience with the machine itself, and though she says that she would definitely repeat the experience with a remotely located lover, it wasn't about connecting with Blue, it was about experiencing the Thrillhammer. After all, the scope of her experience was limited to what was going on right in front of her. While the experiment technically worked, after a little bit of cajoling, the demonstration still fell short of a true interactive cyberdildonics experience because there wasn't any dialogue between Blue and Michelle during the demonstration.

The context and the specifics about how the Dorkbot event came about were certainly new and interesting, but the idea of machine and woman as spectacle aren't new: Think of the sexi-ness of nineteenth-century women tooling around in public parks on bicycles, technology between their legs. The whole thing was something of an overproduced live and cam sex show (not that there's anything wrong with that). Cyberdildonics pares down the sexual experience to something very mechanical—put tab A into slot B and vibrate—and highlights some deeply ingrained and horribly unenlightened concepts of female sexuality: that women's bodies exist to be poked at, experimented with, and put on display as something that's part science and part fetish. Perhaps a big part of the reason that so few women have been interested in cyberdildonics is because there's something inherently creepy about them, something that doesn't speak to a woman's needs beyond her desire for reliable and untiring genital stimulation.

Regina Lynn, *Wired*'s sex and technology columnist, says that for the most part, "Women still see these machines as being really weird." Like Blue, she believes that we're at the start of a trend toward cyberdildonics becoming more acceptable. One of the questions women always have for her about cyberdildonics is kind of an incredulous one: "How could you have sex with a computer?" Her answer is, "You're not having sex with a computer—the computer is a tool, another level of interaction with a partner." However, since the various attempts made at interaction (especially the two-way, reciprocal kind) haven't been so successful, this question is pretty right on. For some women, technology can feel like a barrier instead of a communication device that promotes intimacy—especially when that technology has peculiar wires and requires tech support. The sexiness and intimacy of an encounter can evaporate pretty quickly when the technical parts aren't working. Lynn says, "The technology is completely subordinate to the human connection." Some companies are trying to make this statement a hallmark of the experience they promise their customers by placing cyberdildonics into the greater context of human interactions so that the toys become part of chatting and flirting instead of being a mysterious world unto their own.

The paid-membership website High Joy is making an attempt to bridge the gap between cyberdildonics and actual human use of the devices. The company also has a comarketing partnership with Doc Johnson sex toy manufacturers, which produces the devices available for purchase on the site. The site features a cyberdildonics interface while incorporating as many aspects of Web 2.0 as possible on one website, with its "Internet-enabled adult toys" feature being only one of many ways to interact in a social, dating, and sexual context on the site. Amir, one of the founders of the company, which launched its website in 2003, sees cyberdildonics as part of a more highly interactive experience for online daters. He says, "When women seek out men on Internet dating sites, they plan to meet them but have intermediate steps toward that goal, like instant messaging, phone conversations, and webcam sessions, to see if they are comfortable with this person. Using toys online can be another way to learn about the guy before meeting up with him." In addition to being aimed at singles looking to meet and play both online and offline, the site also attempts to tap into the holy grail of the evolving adult industry—the couples market.

The couples angle was initially how Sofia, a thirty-two-year-old yoga instructor in Los Angeles, was drawn into the site. Her boyfriend at the time was living across the country and suggested they try cyberdildonics. He signed them up for the site as a couple and bought toys to go along with their exploration—a Rabbit vibrator for her and a sleeve with a vibrating egg for him. The Rabbit is a dual-action vibrator that offers simultaneous clitoral stimulation and internal stimulation of the vagina with rotating pearls; it was popularized after it was featured on the hit television show *Sex and the City*. Sofia had been using a Rabbit for several years before she and her boyfriend ventured online with High Joy, so she was relieved that at least the toy itself was familiar.

Sofia admits that she probably wouldn't have tried High Joy were it not for her boyfriend's curiosity, but after they broke up she maintained her membership on the site and began to explore different aspects of the community. As mentioned above, the site offers a pretty comprehensive online experience, which includes personal profiles for dating and social networking and chat spaces that can include cams. As a solo woman on High Joy, Sofia uses the site as a dating site, but she isn't against taking things a little further online. Not surprisingly, many of the men she corresponds with get a bit overeager and try to convince her to play with toys as soon as they strike up conversation with her. She says, "I have a strict policy of only using my toy with someone who I have ongoing correspondence with. Random guys aren't welcome."

Although the mechanics of using a vibrator and trying to tell someone else—over the Internet, nonetheless—where exactly they should touch for that extra-good feeling remain complex, making cyberdildonics into part of an interactive experience is a step away from scary thrusting machines with unfriendly interfaces or DIY electronics. High Joy and other cyberdildonics won't ever replace the experience and pleasure of an in-person sexual experience, but they are certainly a way to enhance both online dating and long-distance relationships and add a dimension to phone sex, naughty chat, and webcamming.

## Not the Ultimate Experience

In apparent recognition of the problem and degree to which some cyberdildonics may be off-putting to women, some sex toy companies have begun to create a variety of toys that are pseudocyberdildonics, toys that interact with or respond to computers or other digital media but don't give another person the ability to control them. These toys give a nod to the potential popularity of cyberdildonics, but they don't go overboard with claims about revolutionizing sex, touch, and the Internet as we know it. Which is good, because like cyberdildonics in their current form, they don't. Instead, they are fun gadgets that are well within the understanding and means of most women who buy sex toys, plus the techie shtick lends their designers the freedom to design, market, and package a product that is sleeker and smarter—and less reliant on words like "dong." These toys are also designed to be relatively nonthreatening to male partners—they aren't, for example, penis shaped.

Sex toy packaging and marketing copy of the past few years have often latched onto the idea of cyberdildonics and futuristic toys—indicating the toys are any different from the average vibrator. Words are specifically chosen to suggest that a particular vibrator might be super advanced, amazing, and somehow computer-cool; the shortcut to this would be to throw a lowercase "I" in front of the name of any given vibrator and hope that ladies buy up before Apple Inc. catches on and disapproves of such brand piggybacking with a hefty lawsuit. This trend actually started a few years ago with a variety of iVibes of various shapes and sizes, from pocket rockets to more-elaborate dual-function vibrators—all of which were manufactured in translucent colors to match the colorful iMac computers. Recently, pseudocyberdildonics have gone a little bit more high tech, with several different toy companies creating small vibrators that can be connected to a computer's USB port instead of using batteries.

There are also some developments in toys that are a little bit smarter: The OhMiBod is a toy that's specifically designed for use with the iPod MP3 music player and is even photographed in tandem with the iPod on its promotional website. It's small and sleek and works like a vibrating egg except that it's wired so that it will vibrate to the rhythm of whatever music is playing on the iPod it's attached to. In a similar vein is the Je Joue, which debuted in 2006. It's a smart toy with programmable vibration patterns or grooves that can be uploaded and downloaded from the toy's website—similar to the way songs are in iTunes.

Toys like these take their cues from the idea of cyber-dildonics, but they are modified to be smaller, cheaper, techno-logically manageable, and, most importantly, more woman-friendly than the big, clunky devices that have a strangely aggressive and sinister feel about them. The pseudocyberdildonics packaging even reflects this difference: All are presented with a sense of lighthearted fun. They have smooth lines, nice curves, and a bit of shine to them, and it's no coincidence that many of them are manufactured in light colors, including shades of pink and purple. The purplish High Joy website picks up on this part of the trend as well, while the more heavy-duty toys like the Thrillhammer and its sex machine compatriots (though not technically cyberdildonics) look like the power tools they are and are sold from bare-bones websites that don't appear welcoming for women.

## Safer Sex: Truth or Marketing?

When technologies that enable tactile sensations to be trans-ferred from one user to another via the Internet (or other, offline network) first started being developed in the late 1980s and early 1990s, many of the companies doing the developing staked their claims on the growing popularity and importance of the safer sex movement. These virtual experiences, they crowed, would eliminate the risk of disease and infection transmission, especially important in the era of HIV/AIDS. And hey, if you're going to don an unwieldy and unnatural device like a condom, you might as well put your whole body in a virtual reality suit or pilot a device to poke your friend in the genitals over the Internet. Viewed in the context of other sexual-technology developments and AIDS-fear-based obsessions of this time, the idea of sex without touching makes sense. Though the condom has been made in some form or other for centuries, the HIV/AIDS crisis jumpstarted the invention of a variety of barrier methods, many of which never made it to market because of their sheer unfeasibility in any kind of real social or sexual context. The United States Patent and Trademark Office (USPTO) is a veritable gold mine of unmarketable but not unthinkable safer sex contraptions that include things like a full-mouth kissing guard and a full latex apron (like a splash guard) with a condom built in. There's no question that fear was behind some of these inventions, and we even witnessed their absurdity in pop culture in the movie *The Naked Gun* (1988), where two characters put on full-body, raincoatlike condoms just before they have sex.

Technically, the claim that cyberdildonics offers a solution to sexually transmitted diseases is absolutely true—they're as physically safe as abstinence. However, safety isn't the main reason that people seek out and use cyberdildonics. Regina Lynn comments on this idea: "Safer sex is an added value. It's not the main reason people use them, because that envisions cybersex as the replacement." This, of course, doesn't stop toy developers from putting safer sex at the forefront of their marketing campaigns. This was certainly the strategy of SafeSexPlus; the name of the project itself indicates that safe sex is the main goal, with the "plus" probably meaning whatever hot action a user can find.

When I interviewed Amir of High Joy, he too cited safer sex as an important aspect of what his toys do, though his idea of safer sex is more expansive and includes not just sexual health but emotional and social health as well. Amir posits that using the High Joy as a premeeting bit of sex play can help women be safer and make better choices about men they meet off the Internet. Fear does interesting things to people, but making them stop fucking isn't really one of them—at least not on a massive scale of long-term abstinence, except maybe for the most severe of germaphobes.

## The Machine Ate My Soul and Stole My Partner

Hardware designed for sex brings out the best and worst in people, pushes the limits of communication, unearths technophilic and technophobic lusts, and has the potential to mechanize and commodify female bodies and sexuality. There's a strong argument for the idea that human sexuality beyond the basic impulse to procreate is not "natural" but instead largely constructed by cultural expectations and taboos that are specific to a particular place and time. Given the expanse of human history, sexual and otherwise, it's often hard to believe that there remains such a strong notion that sexual norms are natural, that there's a way sex has always been done.

One of the myths of the natural surrounding sexuality is that a person should just know how to do it and what she wants and how to ask for it. To bring additional elements into a sexual encounter—whether toys, fantasies, dirty talk, or an extra body—is to go against nature and represents some kind of failing, an inability to do sex right. Though the stigmas against the Internet's role in sexual discourse have faded over the past decade, they flare up again when it comes to cyberdildonics. Despite all the talk about the dangers of the Internet, the Internet doesn't become real to people until it has physical manifestations, whether they be potential bad dates or evil machines.

While it's easy to scoff at headlines like "Will Cybersex Be Better Than Real Sex?" which ran in *Time* magazine in June 2000, it's also important to recognize that this expresses a real anxiety—that technology might be better than people—and is therefore threatening. Though this chapter has focused on the tension that exists between men and women as a result of the emerging trends in cyberdildonics, tensions can come about as a result of technology regardless of the type of sexual relationship a woman is having. Thus, developments in technology like cyberdildonics, which are still very much in their awkward teen years, seem to make people shudder in fear or dread of the obviously impending emotionally articulate fuckbot army takeover. The fear of what's possible in the online world is loaded with additional complications because many people can't even begin to wrap their minds around something that's not "real" or emotional and sexual components of a relationship or identity that the physical can't even touch. This is not to say that human sexuality as we know it is doomed by a sinister combination of fucking machines and sexy wordsmiths that will lure away our partners into a mystical land of perpetual orgasms, but rather that if we accept it, the Internet offers the possibility for human sexuality to grow and expand—particularly in the area of communication and expression of desires. And if you've ever read a single sex advice column, you'll know that poor communication is the number one barrier to a good and healthy sex life. When people write in with questions of woe to sex columnists, the advice is almost always a variation of "talk to your partner" or "talk to a therapist."

Until recently, most of the print literature out in the world about sexuality and the Internet has been clinical and academic writing about the dangers of the Internet, but the writing about online experiences done by laypeople and professionals alike on the Internet itself tells a different, more complex tale. The darkness that exists online is not a property that lurks inside our servers and our cyberdildonics; it is inside the people who have found an outlet that helps them to express themselves—for good and evil (and sexy stuff in between).

To say that the Internet is an entity that threatens human society, morality, and nature is naive at best and an expression of displaced blame at worst. The Internet is becoming an ever-expanding part of women's lives—the way they get and create media, share their experiences (and bodies) with other people, and forge relationships both online and offline—but these experiences are driven by people, not machines.

The Internet, in its size and connective ability, is stunning and seductive to women who seek out communication, understanding, and exploration. It's true that it enables some women to live too fast, too hard, but it also enables a lot of "just right" quality of life (sex life included) that wouldn't otherwise be available.

**CONCLUSION**
# Sex Culture and Self-Exploration— For Love or Money?

T here is no way to tie up the conclusion to this book into a neat little bow. I haven't solved the problem of whether the combination of female sexuality and the Internet is a good or bad thing—it's still both and neither—but I never intended to solve it, of course. For me, this remains a complicated topic, both intellectually and personally.

Over the past several years, the Internet has gone from being a space I peeked in on and used in fairly limited ways to send email and gather information to something that's become extremely integrated into my daily life as a space for work, play, and sexual experimentation—sometimes all three at once. I haven't mastered a balance of those three things, and I don't think I ever will. Access to the Internet compelled me to spill out pretty much everything personal and private that many people think should remain behind closed doors. And honestly, even after thinking about it a lot, and after writing a book about how and why other women do it, I'm still not entirely sure what was/is behind that compulsion. I only know I'm far from being the only one to have it.

One of the most trying and complex issues at the heart of this book is the tangle of women's sexuality, Internet culture, and commercialization. On one level, I wholly support the concept of open source culture and software—I want women to be able to blog for free and have their voices heard; I want them to be able to use free email and upload, download, and exchange content that they produce themselves for free. And not just for free—but freely. I want women to feel that they're in control of and engaged with the process of discovering their sexuality and that the Internet is a tool to help them do this and to connect them with other people who are doing the same (or an entirely different) thing. I'm aware of the fact that none of the above-mentioned things are truly free—they come at the cost of being constantly assaulted by advertising in both overt and subtle ways—nor are they truly democratic and accessible to all women.

I also think constantly about what online culture is worth to women, particularly that which they're making and participating in. And I'm afraid of what the answer might be. Because while user-generated content is shifting culture in a major way—so major that those five corporations who own most of the old media in this country are starting to respond and incorporate it into their vision of media, so major that *Time* magazine's 2006 Person of the Year was "You"—I can't help but be concerned about what it's doing to female users who have the exploratory impulse.

The balance between showing off and marketing one's image is a precarious one. After all, many women specifically explore their sexuality online because they have exhibitionistic tendencies and a desire for attention and praise that manifests itself in complex ways—I should know, I'm one of those women— but it's also inextricably linked to commerce. While some women write out impassioned tales on their blogs, post skin-baring self-portraits on Flickr, and swap flirtatious or downright raunchy emails and IMs with other people, other women sell pictures of themselves to porn sites and set up appointments with clients who want to rub their feet and talk sexy in person—sometimes they are even the same women at different times. The Internet has opened up vast possibilities for women who want to play with sex or work with sex, or both. As a former sex worker and current advocate for women (both sex working and not) to be self-determined, I struggle with the complexity of what this means for women—myself included.

As a woman who didn't fully come into her own sexually and emotionally before engaging with the Internet in an intense way, I know that our culture doesn't make space for these explorations and discoveries to happen. As it turned out, I needed this space, and I made it or found it through the Internet. Until I started meeting strangers for sex and meeting up with photographers who shot me in a variety of provocative poses, no one who'd seen me naked had ever called me beautiful. I had no sense of what my body was or what it meant, or what the power of female sexuality could be. It will be easy for critics to point a finger at me and conclude that there's something fucked-up about this, and fucked-up about me, but again: I know I'm not alone. In the process of doing the research for this book, I was astounded time and time again to hear other women, women very different from me, echo similar inner thoughts, fears, and needs. When I first told people that I was writing a book about female sexuality and the Internet, many people assumed that I'd be writing my own story. As it turns out, I didn't need to write my story, because dozens—probably hundreds or thousands—of other women are living and telling similar stories.

Female sexuality is traditionally contained and constrained by many cultural forces. The immediacy of the Internet and the urgency of the women using it is chipping away at these limitations in much-needed ways. Though I have no doubt that some women take this exploration, this urge for freedom and self-determination too far (been there, done that), I also think that these first and second generations of female Internet users will help to create better and safer ways for this type of exploration and work to happen. And I believe (and hope) they'll bend the larger culture to a greater acceptance of female sexuality.

The women I've interviewed in this book, along with so many others, are creating an unprecedented historical record of female sexuality. As a researcher in the history of sexuality, I've spent hours in various libraries trying to piece together tiny yellowed fragments of throwaway culture from the nineteenth century that might give a better picture of the daily sex lives of people in that era. It's hard to do, because until very recently, in the Western world, sexuality was not at all valued as an important key to human nature and nurture. Diaries of sexual behavior, if kept at all, were generally hidden or destroyed by family members; pornography and sexual health information were often burned by agents of the state; surviving reports of sexual interactions are couched in obscure terms so as to be rendered unintelligible to a modern audience. The Internet is changing all of this, and future generations will have a much clearer idea of what we were up to than we have about our great grandparents. Hopefully, the experiences of the women whose stories shaped and informed this book will inspire other women to explore and think about all the possibilities the Internet offers and will empower women to challenge the ways female sexuality is represented.

0100101010000100010101000010001010100001000010101010000

Of course, a book is not a blog, so unfortunately you can't just hit the "comment" button at the end of this page. But I do have a blog, and I encourage you to come on over and visit me at WakingVixen.com. And really, feel free to drop me an email and let me know what you think: dacia@wakingvixen.com.

If you're too lazy to type each and every one of these URLs into your web browser of choice, come visit my site, Waking Vixen, where I have all of these sites listed with hyperlinks that you can click on. Actually, lazy or not, come visit me.

**ADULT FRIEND FINDER (AFF):** Site with profiles mostly intended for people who are interested in hooking up for sexual encounters, though some people use it for dating.
**http://adultfriendfinder.com**

**AFTER ABORTION:** Nonjudgmental post-abortion support site.
**http://afterabortion.com/message.html**

**ALEXA INTERNET:** A decade-old web-traffic tracker. On Alexa, you can type in a URL and learn about who the site is owned by, how long it has been online, what kind of traffic it gets, and what its popularity ranking (in terms of links and traffic) is compared to other sites. You can type in several URLs at once and compare their traffic to one another. Though Alexa isn't extremely accurate, it helps to give a good comparative picture of a site's popularity.
**http://alexa.com**

**ALIZA'S WORLD:** The personal sex chronicles of Aliza.
http://sexyukgirl.blogspot.com

**ALT.COM:** Site used for connecting people who are into BDSM and fetish play. Owned by the same parent company as AFF.
http://alt.com

**ALWAYS AROUSED GIRL:** AAG's blog details her challenging relationship with her husband and her sexual affairs outside of her marriage.
http://alwaysarousedgirl.blogspot.com

**AMERICAN DEATH CAMPS:** Anti-choice website that aggressively keeps track of so-called "abortion mills."
www.ldi.org/DeathCamps/DeathCamps.cfm

**ANACAM:** Musician and artist Ana Voog launched her cam site in 1997 and claims to be the first art/lifecam girl. Her site is still running, and through facing the recent complication of becoming pregnant, she has started to question camming in a new way.
http://anacam.com
http://ana2.com

**ASSOCIATION FOR WOMEN IN COMPUTING:** A nonprofit professional organization for women and men who have an interest in information and technology, dedicated to the advancement of women in the technology fields.
www.awc-hq.org

**THE ASHLEY MADISON AGENCY:** Site that connects married people who want to cheat with one another—its tagline is "When Monogamy Becomes Monotony."
http://ashleymadison.com

**BANG BROS ONLINE:** Popular porn franchise sometimes accused of being misogynistic.
www.bangbrosonline.com

**BEAUTIFUL TOXIN:** Melissa Gira's cam site and experimental space for web-based art and sexuality experiments.
http://beautifultoxin.net

**BEING AMBER RHEA:** Amber is one of few bloggers who write about sex (though not often her own sex life) using her real name on her "regular" blog, which she's kept since 2002.
http://amber.tangerinecs.com

**BELLA VENDETTA:** The eponymous site features Bella and a host of her friends, usually sporting a variety of heavy body mods, in various states of undress. Bella's models get naked for her for free.
http://bellavendetta.com

**THE BEST OF BLOGS:** Annual reader-nominated and voted on awards for blogs in many different categories, including Best Sex Blog.
www.thebestofblogs.com

**BEVERLY FISHER:** Denver-based escort and writer.
www.beverlyfisher.com

**BITCH | LAB:** Bitch writes some of the best and snarkiest feminist, sex-positive posts around. In early 2007, the blog went through a transformation and was re-christened "Queer Dewd formerly known as be elle (Bitch | Lab)." The author remains the same, though the focus of the blog has shifted.
http://blog.pulpculture.org

**BLACK LIST:** A New York– and New Jersey–area blog that is seldom updated but has several extensive lists of emails used by men who attempt to hire providers through Craigslist.
http://providerblacklist.blogspot.com

**BLOGGER:** Popular free blogging application owned by Google and widely used in the sex blogosphere. Setting up an account is free and doesn't require giving any personal information.
www.blogger.com

**BOING BOING: A DIRECTORY OF WONDERFUL THINGS:** Simply put, the largest blog and best example of the chaotic weirdness of the Internet.
http://boingboing.net

**BURNING ANGEL:** Alt porn site that has made its way into production over the past few years, with Joanna Angel at the helm.
http://burningangel.com

**CANDY POSES:** Nude model and blogger Candy Poses kept a blog about menstruation that she pulled but maintains a blog about feminism and nude modeling.
http://seecandybleed.com
www.candyposes.com

**CATHERINE LA CROIX:** Catherine does sex work and sexuality consultation, which she details on her website. She is also the author of the self-published book *On Our Backs, Off Our Knees: A Declaration of Independence by a Modern Sacred Whore.*
http://catherinelacroix.com

**CCBill**: Standard credit card processing company in the adult industry. Allows adult sites to open merchant accounts and does monthly rebilling.
http://ccbill.com

**CONSUMER AND PATIENT HEALTH INFORMATION SECTION (CAPHIS):** Part of the Medical Library Association website that supports librarians in helping patrons to obtain good health information but that can also be sued directly by the consumer.
http://caphis.mlanet.org

**CRAIGSLIST:** The simplest-looking website ever, with blue links on a plain white and gray background, Craigslist has become an Internet staple over the past decade and is now the seventh-most-popular English-language website. Craigslist is a community site where people advertise everything from odd jobs to apartments to intimate encounters.
http://craigslist.org

**DAILY KOS: STATE OF THE NATION:** Major political commentary blog.
http://dailykos.com

**DANNI, DANNI'S HARD DRIVE, BILLION DOWNLOAD WOMAN:** Danni Ashe was granted a Guinness World Record for "Most Downloaded Woman" in 2000. Her website is an Internet porn staple and was sold to Penthouse in October 2006 for $3.6 million. She also maintains a promotional site, Billion Download Woman.

http://danni.com

www.billiondownloadwoman.com

**DAWN MARIE'S DREAM:** Amateur independent porn site run by a middle-aged mom and her husband.

www.dawnmariesdream.com

**DENZI:** Denzi is a middle-aged escort who used the Internet to remake herself after a career in her teens and early twenties as a street prostitute.

http://denzi4u.com

**DESIGNING INTIMACY:** College student Avah blogs about her relationship with her older lover and his network of friends, lovers, and sex parties.

http://designingintimacy.blogspot.com

**DISSECTION OF EVERYDAY LIFE, JANE SAYS, AND LAYLA X:** The three different permutations of Jane Crowley's sex, relationship and life blogs.

http://jane129.blogspot.com

http://janesaysisnolongerhere.blogspot.com

http://layla-x.blogspot.com

**DON'T DATE HIM GIRL:** A controversial site where women post profiles of men who they feel have wronged them, in an attempt to warn other women off dating them.

http://dontdatehimgirl.com

**DON'T FUCK WITH US!:** Run by a Washington, D.C.–area male escort, mostly male workers in and around D.C. list their grievances with various clients, whose aliases and phone numbers they post.
**http://blacklistednow.blogspot.com**

**DORKBOT SF:** One of many city branches of Dorkbot, which started in New York and self-describes itself as "a monthly meeting of artists (sound/image/movement/whatever), designers, engineers, students and other interested parties from the new york area who are involved in the creation of electronic art (in the broadest sense of the term.)"
**http://dorkbot.org/dorkbotsf**

**DOOCE:** Heather Armstrong is a personal blogger; after being fired from her job for blogging, this act became known as being "dooced."
**http://dooce.com**

**EHARMONY:** Billing itself as "the first service within the online dating industry to use a scientific approach to matching highly compatible singles," eHarmony asks new signups to fill out a long and complex personality profile, which is then matched with other members' profiles.
**http://eharmony.com**

**ENGAGE:** Engage is based on the concept of social networking and linked profiles; members play matchmaker and introduce each other in hopes of making a connection.
**www.engage.com**

**EROS GUIDE:** A website with paid advertising featuring sex workers from many cities in the United States as well as several in Canada and the United Kingdom.
**www.eros-guide.com**

**EROS, LOGOS:** O writes erotic tales of her encounters with her lover.
**http://eros-logos.blogspot.com**

**EROTICA READERS & WRITERS ASSOCIATION:** Resource for fans and writers of erotic stories: calls for submission, articles on the craft of erotic story writing, links to sites with stories, and active forums.
**http://erotica-readers.com**

**FLESHBOT:** A porn and sexuality blog run by Gawker Media that was launched in 2003 and rapidly became the go-to blog for snarky commentary on porn and has become a champion of sexuality culture online.
**http://fleshbot.com**

**FLICKR:** An increasingly ubiquitous photo-posting and -sharing website owned by Yahoo! A member can post photos and either keep them private or open to view by "friends" on the site and the public at large. The site also contains code that makes it easy for users to upload their photos to a blog, personal profile, or other website.
**http://flickr.com**

**FOR THE GIRLS:** Based in Australia, Karen Jones and her female business partner run a porn site for women that features both hard- and soft-core content.
http://forthegirls.com

**FREYA'S HOUSE OF DREAMS:** Freya writes stories, fantasies, poetry, and erotic imaginings from her bedroom. Note: She took this site down as of 1/2007.
http://freyashouse.blogspot.com

**FRIENDSTER:** Friendster, the precursor to MySpace, was launched in 2002 and ushered in the age of social networking websites.
www.friendster.com

**FUCKING MACHINES:** Porn site featuring women fucking and being fucked by large machines made from household appliances and power tools and retrofitted for sex.
http://fuckingmachines.com

**FURRY GIRL:** Independent model, producer, and site owner who runs a variety of ethical porn sites.
http://furrygirl.com
http://vegporn.com
http://eroticred.com

**GENDERPEACE:** Designed specifically by and for young transsexual women who feel that older trans women dominate the forums in other online spaces.
http://genderpeace.com
http://forum.genderpeace.com

**GOOGLE:** The mother lode of all search engines can now be used as both a noun and a verb meaning "to search the Internet." Though the search engine is the hub of all things Google, the company has expanded in recent years to include email, maps, online shopping, and myriad other activities and information.
**www.google.com**

**GOOSE AND GANDER:** A blog by a young married couple exploring their sexuality and interest in kink.
**http://thegooseandgander.blogspot.com**

**GRANDMA SCROTUM'S SEX TIPS:** A free sex advice and humor site and the first site launched by Karen Jones of For the Girls.
**http://grandmascrotum.com**

**GWEN MASTERS:** Besides telling me about her online relationship nightmare, Gwen is a prolific erotica writer.
**www.gwenmasters.net**

**H-DATE:** Dating site for people with herpes.
**http://h-date.com**

**HIGH JOY:** Combines cyberdildonics with dating and social networking. **http://highjoy.com**

**HIROMI X:** Formerly a part of the now-offline couples blog Panties Panties Panties, Hiromi blogs about the aftermath of her abusive relationship with her ex-husband.
**www.moronosphere.com/hiromi**

**HOMEGROWN VIDEO:** Canadian porn company that is one of the originators of amateur porn; produces and distributes amateur content both on- and offline.
**http://homegrownvideo.com**

**ICQ:** One of the oldest and largest free, downloadable instant messaging programs. ICQ automatically assigns users a number that acts as their identity for interacting with other members of the site, though usernames can also be attached to this number.
**www.icq.com**

**THE INTERNATIONAL UNION OF SEX WORKERS:** Sex workers union most active in the U.K. that uses the Internet as an organizing tool.
**www.iusw.org**

**IFRIENDS:** Launched in 1998, iFriends is the largest and fastest-growing webcam community in the world, where many women got their starts in online porn and one-on-one interactions with clients. Though there are many sections of the site, the adult cam section is the most popular and the most lucrative.
**http://ifriends.net**

**INTERNET ARCHIVE/WAYBACK MACHINE:** One of the hazards of putting URLs in print is that by the time the slow wheels of paper publishing roll forward, the website may no longer exist. Archive .org, a nonprofit digital-library project, is working to reduce the trouble of disappearing websites. By typing a URL into the Wayback Machine, you can access dead links and see the changes in design a site has gone through over the years.
**http://archive.org**

**INTROSPECTRE:** Jill's blog is sometimes ridiculous and disorganized, but also very intensely personal and a space she uses to process her thoughts and feelings about sexuality.
**http://introspectre.com**

**"IST-A-VERSE":** Network of twelve city blogs including Gothamist.com, LAist.com, Phillyist.com, Shanghaiist.com, and Parisist.com.

**JABBER:** An open source, ad-free alternative to corporate instant messenger programs.
**www.jabber.org**

**JDATE:** Dating site catering to Jewish singles. This is one of the sites that popularized niche dating sites and helped to make online dating more acceptable.
**http://jdate.com**

**JE JOUE:** Smart toy with programmable vibration patterns or grooves that debuted in 2006.
**http://jejoue.com**

**JENNICAM:** Jennifer Ringley launched her cam site in 1996 and shut it down in 2003. She is regarded as one of the first women to run a 24/7 lifecam out of her home.
**http://jennicam.org**
**http://jennicam.com**

**JOURNEY INTO SUBMISSION:** Gray Lily describes her blog as "a BDSM love journal by a thirtysomething, polyamorous, bisexual, submissive, masochistic bottom with a thing for bondage and flogging."
http://bdsmlover.blogspot.com

**KIS LEE, PROFESSIONAL SMUT WRITER:** Though Kis Lee's personal and sex blog is no longer online, these days she blogs about being an erotica writer.
http://kislee.blogspot.com

**LESBOTRONIC:** Totally free dating site for lesbians with a leftist bent.
http://lesbotronic.com

**LIVEJOURNAL:** Blogging application popular with personal bloggers and people who want to be able to limit access to their blog.
www.livejournal.com

**LUX NIGHTMARE:** Founding model and webmistress of That Strange Girl, the first alt porn website to feature both men and women.
http://thatstrangegirl.com

**MADELINE IN THE MIRROR:** Madeline's blog is self-described as "the life of a prim and properly perverted parent."
http://madelineinthemirror.blogspot.com

**MARRY BLAIRE:** Set up by the enterprising Blaire Allison, who tried to catch a husband through the site.
http://marryblaire.com

**MATCH:** Match has become one of the leaders in the world of online dating, especially since signing on television personality Dr. Phil as a love consultant.
www.match.com

**MAX FISCH DOMINA GUIDE:** The premier site for listings and links to the websites of professional dommes around the United States. Also hosts a very active discussion board.
http://maxfisch.com

**MEDICAL LIBRARY ASSOCIATION:** A nonprofit educational organization of more than 1,100 institutions and 3,600 individual members in the health-sciences-information field committed to educating health information professionals, supporting health information research, promoting access to the world's health sciences information, and working to ensure that the best health information is available to all.
www.mlanet.org

**MEEBO:** A web-based instant messaging system introduced in September 2005. Users can be signed on to a multitude of instant message accounts from different applications and keep the messages all within one browser window. Excellent for public or shared computers on which new programs can't be downloaded.
www.meebo.com

**MELISSA GIRA:** Longtime denizen of the Internet. Early cam girl, alt porn model, blogger, and vlogger.
http://melissagira.com
http://beautifultoxin.livejournal.com

**MIA MOVIES:** TGP and video-clip site that links to small bits of free content in the hopes that the surfer will sign up for a membership. www.mia-movies.com

**MICHELLE ASTON:** Fetish model and participant in Dorkbot/ Museum of Sex Thrillhammer (http://thethrillhammer.com) cyberdildonics demonstration with Violet Blue: http://michell easton.com. Violet Blue's account of the experiment: www. tinynibbles.com/blogarchives/2005/06/apres_dork.html

**MODEL MAYHEM AND ONE MODEL PLACE:** Free model- and photographer-portfolio site.
http://onemodelplace.com
http://modelmayhem.com

**MUSEUM OF MENSTRUATION AND WOMEN'S HEALTH:** Website run by a man devoted to cataloging the history of menstruation, feminine hygiene products and women's reproductive health. www.mum.org

**MYSPACE:** Launched in 2003, MySpace has quickly become the premier social networking website and claims to have acquired its ten millionth user in August 2006. Though it is ostensibly not a dating site, lots of people use it for that purpose. http://myspace.com

**MYTHS AND METAWHORES:** Magdelena's award-winning sex and sensuality blog.
http://mythsandmetawhores.com

**NAKKID NERDS:** An early alt porn site that featured scheduled camshows.
http://nakkidnerds.com

**NERD PRON:** A solo site (with occasional special guests) run by self-professed nerd Anna Logue. (Anna's ass graces the cover of *Naked on the Internet.*)
http://nerdpr0n.com

**NETWORK OF SEX WORK PROJECTS (NSWP):** Project linking together sex work projects from around the globe; members' meetings often take place online.
www.nswp.org

**OHMIBOD:** Vibrator that responds to music played by an iPod.
http://ohmibod.com

**OLD BOYS NETWORK (OBN):** Started in Berlin in 1997, the OBN is the forerunner of the cyberfeminist movement, even if it refuses to define exactly what that is and offer up its "100 Anti-Theses," definitions of what cyberfeminism is not.
www.obn.org/reading_room/manifestos/html/anti.html

**OPENDILDONICS/BRUM2600:** OpenDildonics is a pet open source hardware and software project of the participants of the Brum2600 forums.
www.brum2600.net
http://opendildonics.org

**OPEN SOURCE SEX:** Erotica, sex ed, and more podcast with Violet Blue.
http://violetblue.libsyn.com

**PEW INTERNET & AMERICAN LIFE PROJECT:** Produces reports that explore the impact of the Internet on families, communities, work and home, daily life, education, healthcare, and civic and political life. The Project aims to be an authoritative source on the evolution of the Internet through the collection of data and analysis of real-world developments as they affect the virtual world.
www.pewinternet.org

**PLANNED PARENTHOOD FEDERATION OF AMERICA:** One of the oldest and most visible reproductive rights organizations.
http://ppfa.org

**THE POST-MODERN GEEK'S GUIDE TO SEX:** Marie B's sexuality and sex ed podcast.
http://marieb.libsyn.com
http://postmodernsexgeek.blogspot.com

**PRABA PILAR:** An artist focusing on technology and communication, she has produced performances, installations, and interactive projects. *Cyber.Labia,* her chapbook of artwork, musings, and interviews on women and computers, is available as a downloadable PDF on her website.
www.prabapilar.com

**PROSTITUTES OF NEW YORK (PONY):** New York City–based organization for sex workers with a thirty-year history.
www.walnet.org/csis/groups/pony.html

**RACHEL KRAMER BUSSEL:** Erotica writer, blogger, editor, and reading series hostess.
http://rachelkramerbussel.com
http://lustylady.blogspot.com
http://inthefleshreadingseries.blogspot.com

**ROOM SERVICE 2000 AND DATE-CHECK:** Websites that offer client-verification services for escorts.
http://roomservice2000.com
http://date-check.com

**SAFEHAVEN:** Postabortion-support website that disapproves of abortion.
www.postabortionpain.com

**SAFESEXPLUS:** Cyberdildonics toys that could be operated through popular webcam site iFriends. Site is offline now, but archived pages can be found at **www.archive.org** by typing in **http://safesexplus.com.**

**SCARLETEEN:** Founded by sex educator Heather Corinna in 2000, this site offers articles as well as message boards on a wide variety of topics pertaining to teen sexual health.
http://scarleteen.com

**SEXABILTY AND SCARLET MINX:** The political and personal (respectively) blogs about sexuality and disability written by Maliscious Lelo.
http://scarletminx.net/
http://sexability.wordpress.com

**SEXEDVICE:** Sex educator and teen-sexuality-information advocate Ellen Friedrichs.
http://sexedvice.com

**SEX IN THE CITY—THE REAL VERSION:** Selina Fire, a bisexual woman in her midforties, rediscovers her wanton sexuality after a decade-long monogamous relationship with a woman.
http://selinafire.blogspot.com

**SLASHDONG:** Blog keeping track of the latest developments in cyberdildonics. The blog's author, QDot, also features his own experiments and how-tos. The project FreeSex is also part of this site.
http://slashdong.org www.slashdong.org/content/projects/
freesex_network/freesex_the_open_source_teledildonics_
network-000246.php

**SPRING STREET NETWORK:** Initially a sister company to the web and (now-defunct) print sexuality and culture magazine *Nerve*, Spring Street Network took off after starting to attract people who saw themselves as too hip for other online dating sites. Spring Street now offers personals through sites like Salon, *The New York Times,* and Lions Gate Films in addition to *Nerve*.
http://springstreetnetwork.com

**STATCOUNTER, SHINYSTAT, AND EASY COUNTER:** Web hit counters that can track how many hits a website gets, where the traffic is coming from, length of visit and pages viewed, search terms leading to the site, and the internet protocol (IP) addresses and physical locations (usually city and state) of the site's visitors.
http://statcounter.com
http://shinystat.com
www.easycounter.com

**STD SINGLES:** Online dating for people who self-identify as having an incurable sexually transmitted disease.
www.stdsingles.com

**STRAP-ON AND EZBOARD:** User-moderated message board forums for queers and feminists to talk about personal, political, and other issues, hosted and powered by Ezboard.
http://strap-on.org
http://ezboard.com

**SUICIDEGIRLS:** Alternative pinup site launched in 2001 that has brought a lot of attention to the world of alt modeling.
http://suicidegirls.com

**SURVIVAL RESEARCH LABORATORIES:** The beauty and danger of lethal machines for fun and laughs.
www.srl.org

**THE TALES OF A TEACHER AND SLUT:** Blog by Meg, a young woman exploring the workforce and her sexuality for the first time.
http://missslut.blogspot.com

**TALK TO VANESSA:** Erotica and personal stories in both text and audio format.
http://talktovanessa.com

**TASTY TRIXIE:** Trixie started out as a cam girl on iFriends, and after launching her initial site, Tasty Trixie, she expanded her online presence to include sites with her boyfriend as well as a site featuring her menstruation.
http://tastytrixie.com
http://spyonus.com
http://trixieshouseboy.com
http://bloodytrixie.com

**TECHNORATI AND ICEROCKET:** Sites that track links that blogs make to one another.
http://technorati.com/
http://blogs.icerocket.com

**TEENWIRE:** Sexual-health-information website for teens run by the Planned Parenthood Federation of America.
www.teenwire.com

**TINY NIBBLES: VIOLET BLUE:** Sex educator, writer, and sex-tech forerunner, not to mention a real foxy lady.
http://tinynibbles.com

**TRANS-HEALTH:** Online magazine of health and fitness for transsexual and transgendered people.
http://trans-health.com

**TRANSSEXUAL ROAD MAP:** Resource that assists transsexual women in making a plan for their transitions and understanding what they're facing.

**http://tsroadmap.com**

**TRIBE:** Largely a San Francisco phenomenon despite being available on the World Wide Web, Tribe is built more around groups and interests than individual profiles.

**http://tribe.net**

**URBAN DICTIONARY:** A searchable user-generated-content site with entries that define slang words and colloquialisms. Often humorous, always insightful.

**www.urbandictionary.com**

**UTOPIAGUIDE, BIG DOGGIE,** and **THE EROTIC REVIEW (TER):** Message board and advertising websites where providers and hobbyists can interact and hobbyists can review providers.

**http://utopiaguide.com**
**www.bigdoggie.net**
**www.theeroticreview.com**

**VAN GOGH CHICA:** Self-described as "a Latina mermaid in her forties who writes about her life, art, and Zen Buddhism."

**http://vangoghchica.blogspot.com**

**VERONICA MONET:** Veronica is a former sex worker who offers sexuality education and consultations and is the author of *Veronica Monet's Sex Secrets of Escorts: What Men Really Want.*

**http://veronicamonet.com**

**VIRTUAL SEX MACHINE:** Designed by Virtual Reality Innovations and debuted in 2000, the Virtual Sex Machine's champions claimed it would provide the ultimate sexual experience.
http://vrinnovations.com

**WEBMD:** Extremely popular health information resource.
www.webmd.com

**WHOLE WOMAN'S HEALTH:** Pro-choice and women-friendly sexual health and abortion clinic.
www.wholewomanshealth.com

**WIRED:** A magazine launched in 1993 about all things technological. Today both the print magazine and website are very active. Regina Lynn writes their weekly sex and technology column, "Sex Drive."
www.wired.com

**WOMEN ON WAVES** and **WOMEN ON WEB:** Websites that offer international assistance to women who live in nations in which safe, legal abortion is not available by making the "abortion pill" obtainable by mail.
http://womenonwaves.org
www.womenonweb.org

**WORDPRESS:** Popular paid-blogging application that can be paid for and then installed on one's own domain.
http://wordpress.com

**XANGA:** Blogging community similar to LiveJournal in its insularity.
**www.xanga.com**

**YAHOO! PERSONALS:** Yahoo! was one of the first comprehensive websites to offer email, Listservs, news, community message boards—and last but not least, personals.
**http://personals.yahoo.com**

**YOUTUBE:** User-generated videos as well as clips from television and movies are uploaded and shared on YouTube, which has revolutionized online content and really rolled out the concept of Web 2.0. Launched in early 2005, YouTube sold to Google in the fall of 2006 for $1.6 billion—before it had turned a profit.
**http://youtube.com**

# WEB WORDS
## A Glossary of Internet Terminology

**A** **SCII PRON**—Dirty pictures drawn using the ASCII (American Standard Code for Information Interchange), the characters on a standard keyboard. A short-lived, time-consuming, but bandwidth-preserving precursor to pornographic images. The word "prOn" is a deliberate misspelling of "porn" to circumvent spam and other Internet filters that are set against sexual content.

**BACK END**—The code and "stuff" that makes a website run. The job of a webmaster or webmistress is to "maintain the back end." If it is running properly, the back end of a website is not something that a user will ever have to worry about.

**BAITING**—On online forums, message boards, and blogs, the act of a contributor deliberately writing something to stir conversation up among participants. Usually done in a space where the participants are known on some level and aimed at specific participants. Though trolls do this, it can also be done by a blog writer who wants to rankle her readers and encourage heated discussion.

**BLIND LINK**—A shifty coding technique used on some porn sites that deceives site visitors into clicking on a link that takes them to a site they didn't expect to go to. Most often used in porn-site advertising.

**BLOG**—Contraction of the words "web log," a blog is a frequently updated webpage where posts are arranged in chronological order. Most blogs have RSS feeds that readers can subscribe to so they can read updates without having to return to the site to check for updates.

**BLOGOSPHERE**—A term that indicates the vast interconnectedness of all things blog-related.

**BLOGROLL**—A link list on a blog that features all the other blogs a blogger reads frequently. Though these link lists can of course be coded by hand, a blogroll is a special bit of programming that installs links.

**BOTS**—A program written to do automatic tasks, which can range from chatting to trolling sites for information and keywords to add to search engines.

**BROADBAND**—The shortened form of "broadband Internet access." Transmits information much faster than dial-up, which is done via phone lines. Rapidly becoming the premier way to access the Internet, broadband is often accessed through cable lines or through digital subscriber line (DSL) over a phone line.

**BUDDY LIST**—On instant message programs, an approved list of other users with whom communication is approved. A user can see whether other people on her buddy list are online unless they are concealing their online status. Most IM programs automatically add or ask permission to add a user to the buddy list after the first contact between two users.

**CLICK-THROUGH RATE**—A measure used in online commerce, usually per thousand visitors, of how many people click from one website to another via a link. Advertising rates are sometimes quoted in terms of click-throughs instead of weeks or months.

**COMMENT**—Popularized on blogs, many websites with user-generated content allow visitors to post a message saying what they think of a particular blog post, photo, or video. Most comments are visible to the public. Some sites require comment moderation, in which the site owner or maintainer must approve a comment before it is visible to the public.

**CONTENT**—All the stuff there is to read, see, or listen to on the Internet is content. "Original content" means it is generated by assigned content producers, while "user-generated" means that the site's visitors produce the content.

**CYBER**—Culture that's constructed with computers and composed of digital media, usually related to the Internet. Often used as a prefix in words, as in *cybersex*.

**DIAL UP**—Internet access gained through phone lines. Tends to be very slow, but is used in many parts of the world because the only necessary equipment is a computer, a modem, and a regular phone line; broadband requires special wiring.

**DOWNLOAD**—Saving a file from the Internet onto one's personal computer.

**EMAIL**—Electronic mail that can be web-based and accessible from anywhere (popular, free email clients include Yahoo!, Hotmail, and Gmail) or tied to a particular domain and downloaded from a specific server.

**FILE SHARING**—Can be accomplished unwittingly by posting content that someone else then downloads, or through programs designed for this task. The best example is probably Napster, the famous illegal music-file-sharing program.

**FLAME**—Deliberately hostile and offensive postings or comments in an online forum that are designed to get a rise out of other participants. Flames are often written by people whose interests directly clash with the stated interests of a community, i.e. a person identifying as male referring to women in a pro-choice forum as "sluts" or "baby killers." A single flame often erupts into an escalating flame war.

**FRIEND LIST**—On a social networking site, a friend list is an approved group of users who have a heightened degree of access to a user's profile, i.e. on MySpace, users in the friends list are allowed to post comments on a user's profile, on Live Journal friends are allowed to read password-protected journal entries.

**HANDLE**—A stand-in for a proper name that a site user chooses to be known by. Interchangeable with *login* and *username*.

**INFORMATION TECHNOLOGY (IT)**—Dealing with information made accessible or protected on networks of computers. Includes both hardware and software.

**INSTANT MESSAGE (IM)**—Real-time text-based communication, usually done through an IM client like America Online, Yahoo, GTalk, Jabber, ICQ, or Meebo.

**INTERNET**—Computer network accessible by users around the world. There are many smaller networks within the Internet. See also *World Wide Web*, which is a part of the Internet but not the same thing.

**IP (INTERNET PROTOCOL) ADDRESS**—A unique string of numbers that identifies a computer's location on a computer network. Personal information can often be traced through an IP address, and most website statistic trackers record the IP address when a visitor comes to the site, though the web stats can't then trace all the other sites a particular IP address has visited.

**ISP (INTERNET SERVICE PROVIDER)**—A business that provides Internet access, usually for a fee.

**IRL**—"In real life." Usually used to differentiate between online relationships and relationships with people who an Internet user interacts with on a daily basis offline.

**KEYWORD**—A word used in searches that is most likely to get the desired results.

**LINK**—A bit of code that directs a user to another webpage when the user mouses over it and then clicks on it. Usually denoted with text of a different color than the surrounding text. Also called *hotlink* or *hyperlink*.

**LISTSERV**—An email list that distributes messages from individual members to the entire group. Users can usually choose for emails to be delivered individualy, in digest form (one daily email of all the posts from that day), or to log on to the Listserv's site and read the messages there.

**LOGIN**—See *handle*. The verb form, log on, is used to mean the act of filling in one's username and password to gain access to a membership site.

**LURKING**—Regularly visiting a site with comments or user-generated content without participating.

**MEMBER**—A person who maintains a handle or a profile on a site, whether it's a free site or a paysite. Sometimes also called a *user*.

**MESSAGE BOARD**—A public or private forum in which people post messages on a "board" that is visible by other members and sometimes unregistered visitors of the site. When people respond to a post, it creates a thread. Encompasses bulletin board systems (BBS), though BBS require a direct subscription through a sysop and most message boards today are accessible on the web.

**MP3**—A music file that is compressed in size so as to be easily shared over the Internet.

**MP4**—A video file that is compressed in size so as to be easily transmittable over the Internet.

**NEW MEDIA**—A buzz word that describes media enabled by digital technology, especially the Internet.

**OLD MEDIA**—A buzz word, usually used derisively by users and producers of new media, that includes print media like newspapers, magazines, and books, as well as television.

**OPEN SOURCE**—Hardware and software that is readily modified to enable user-generated content.

**OPERATING SYSTEM (OS)**—A computer program that manages the basic functions of a computer's hardware and software. The most popular ones are Windows, Mac OS, and Unix—users are often slavishly devoted to one OS over another.

**PAYSITE**—A website that requires a paid membership to maintain an active username and password. Most porn paysites bill monthly through a third-party credit card processor.

**PIC**—Internet-shortened version of the word picture.

**PODCAST**—Audio files, usually formatted like a radio show, distributed by really simple syndication (RSS) or Atom feeds. Podcasts can also be downloaded directly from a website.

**POP-UP**—Messages, advertisements, and images that pop up outside of the window of the web browser, usually without the site visitor wanting them to (though some sites with photography use pop-ups to view images). Web browsers like Firefox are developed to prevent pop-ups.

**POST**—An entry on a blog or online forum.

**PROFILE**—Information about a user on a website that can be updated by the user. Often contains a handle, an image, or an avatar, contact information, and a summary of the user's interests.

**RSS (REALLY SIMPLE SYNDICATION)**—A feed produced by a frequently updated website, especially a blog, that readers can subscribe to and have delivered via a chosen feed reader or aggregator like Bloglines. Readers who subscribe to RSS feeds read blog posts from many different sites in a centralized location instead of clicking around to many sites to check to see if they have been updated recently.

**SEARCH ENGINE**—A website designed to comb the Internet for whatever keywords a user enters. Google is the most popular, though there are other search engines available, including Yahoo! and MSN.

**SIGN ON**—Process of entering one's handle and password to gain access to an online service.

**SOCIAL NETWORKING**—Websites are increasingly built around this concept, which encourages users to build a profile page and then add other users to their network. MySpace has become the most often cited example of online social networking.

**TEMPLATE**—A pre-made webpage layout, especially for a blog. Most templates are open source and easily changed.

**THREAD**—A topic and its responses on an online forum.

**THUMBNAIL GALLERY POST (TGP)**—Site that provides a limited selection of free porn that is linked to advertising.

**TRAFFIC**—The number of visitors coming to a website. Somewhat difficult to measure precisely, more web statistics offer both the number of page views (clicking around a site) and a number of unique visitors (visits to a site from unique IP addresses within a certain timeframe).

**TROLL**—A person who intentionally threatens an online space with his or her posts, comments, and messages. See also *flame*.

**UPLOAD**—To transfer a file from the hard drive of a personal computer to another computer or to a website or online storage space.

**USER-GENERATED CONTENT**—Usually refers to a website, especially a social networking site, that encourages visitors to create a profile and add content like blog posts, images, and video. Sometimes also called consumer-generated content.

**USERNAME**—See *handle*.

**WEB 2.0**—Coined in 2004, Web 2.0 refers to websites that are highly interactive and often encourage user-generated content and file sharing.

**WEB BROWSER**—The program an Internet user installs on her computer to access and explore the Internet. Common examples are Firefox and Internet Explorer.

**WEBCAM**—A low-resolution, real-time digital camera that allows a user to take frequent pictures (intervals of 30 seconds are common) and upload them to the Internet. Most webcams can be installed in a static position from which they take and send their images.

**WEB STATISTICS**—The measure of traffic and incoming links on a website.

**WEBZINE**—A media form somewhere in between website and print magazine. Typical of print publications that feel the need to go online but don't understand the Internet and haven't caught up with the Web 2.0 way of doing things.

**WIKI**—A website that allows users to edit, update, add to, or delete its content, typically without a required registration or approval process. Wikipedia, a collectively edited online encyclopedia, is the most popular example.

**WORLD WIDE WEB**—Internet services like email and FTP are incorporated into the World Wide Web. When you use a web browser (like Firefox, Internet Explorer, or Netscape), you are accessing the Web. Without the Web, easy public access to and searching of the Internet would not be possible.

**VLOG**—Video blog, usually produced serially at approximate time intervals between each episode. Like podcasts and blogs, vlogs (also called *vidcasts*) rely on RSS feeds for distribution.

## CHAPTER 1: GIRLS GONE WIRED

1. Sherry Turkle. "Computational Reticence: Why Women Fear the Intimate Machine," in *Sex/Machine: Readings in Culture, Gender, and Technology,* ed. Patrick D. Hopkins, 365 (Bloomington: Indiana University Press, 1998).

2. Ibid., 366.

3. Joy M. Callan. "Attitudes Toward Computers: The Changing Gender," *Feminist Collections* 17, no. 2 (1996): 30.

4. NIKAinteractive. "Marketing to Women: How to Attract Women to Online Services," *About Women & Marketing* 9, no. 3 (1996): 3.

5. Deborah Fallows. "How Women and Men Use the Internet," Pew Internet & American Life Project (2005), www.pewinternet.org/PPF/r/171/report_display.asp.

6. Donna J. Haraway. "A Cyborg Manifesto: Science, Technology, and Socialist-Feminism in the Late Twentieth Century," in *Simians, Cyborgs*

and *Women: The Reinvention of Nature,* 153 (New York: Routledge, 1991). This essay was published in an earlier iteration as "Manifesto for Cyborgs: Science, Technology and Socialist Feminism in the 1980s," in *Socialist Review* 80 (1985).

7. Praba Pilar. *Cyber.Labia: Gendered Thoughts and Conversation on Cyber Space* (Oakland: Tela Press, 2005).

8. *Cyber.Labia,* 15.

9. Deborah Fallows. "How Women and Men Use the Internet."

10. Though neither of Jenni Ringley's sites is online today, many of the pages can be accessed by typing the URLs into Archive.org's Wayback Machine.

11. Frequently Asked Questions, JenniCam: http://web.archive.org/web/19990508052112/jennicam.org/faq/general.html.

## CHAPTER 2: HOOKUPS, MATCHES, AND SEX PLAY

1. On LiveJournal, "friend" is used as a verb to mean the act of adding a user to one's friend list, which allows that person to read password-protected posts.

2. "Online Paid Content U.S. Market Spending Report, Full Year 2005," Online Publishers Association, www.online-publishers.org/pdf/opa_paid_content_report_fullyear05.pdf.

3. "How Fast a Lover Are You?" Adult Friend Finder (2006). Full survey results are here: http://adultfriendfinder.com/intgroups/pi143/typoll/acshow_poll_result.html?m=18368060_36517.

## CHAPTER 3: A DAY IN THE LIFE OF MY VAGINA

1. "Bloggers: A Portrait of the Internet's New Storytellers," Pew Internet & American Life Project (2006), www.pewinternet.org/PPF/r/186/report_display.asp.

2. "What's it Worth to You to See Me Put on Deodorant?" Post on A Writer's Life, September 27, 2005. Found online at: http://leegoldberg.typepad.com/a_writers_life/2005/09/whats_it_worth_.html.

## CHAPTER 4. I AM WOMAN, SEE ME NUDE

1. David Austin. "Why Is Period Porn So Rare?" Notes for talk presented at the World Pornography Conference (1998). Posted on www4.ncsu.edu/%7En51ls801/period.html.

2. Urban Dictionary, alt porn: www.urbandictionary.com/define.php?term=alt+porn.

3. José Ralat Maldonado. "Pinup or Shut Up," *New York Press*, October 8, 2005.

## CHAPTER 5. SEX ON THE OPEN MARKET

1. "Sex work" is a phrase that was coined by self-proclaimed whore activist Scarlot Harlot in the late 1970s to refer to the explicit exchange of erotic labor for a mutually agreed upon amount of money, goods, or services. Though "sex work" is often considered to be a euphemism for prostitution, the sex industry encompasses many different kinds of work—stripping, naked oil wrestling, phone sex, domination, and panty hose modeling, to name a few—many of which never involve genital contact and some of which don't involve any kind of physical contact at all. Just as there are many different kinds of

sex work, workers have many names for the work they do. More politically active folks tend to refer to themselves as "sex workers," which is linked right up with socialisty, labor organizey folks (even if those same people don't connect themselves with the struggles of said sex workers). Most women in the industry identify themselves with respect to their specific job: escort, porn performer, dancer, masseuse, dominatrix. Despite the names different types of performers and service workers prefer, I will be using the term "sex work" throughout this chapter, though when quoting workers, I have left their lingo usage intact, and I refer to the workers however they choose to refer to themselves.

2. Lars Ollson and Tracy Quan. "Positions: Are Public Client Blacklists a Good Idea?" *$pread Magazine* (Summer 2006): 10.

3. "Sex Workers: GMB Wins First Ever Unfair Dismissal Case," Independent Media Center (2006), www.indymedia.org/nl/2006/01/832371.shtml.

## CHAPTER 6. OUR BODIES, OUR BROADBAND

1. Susannah Fox. "Health Information Online," Pew Internet & American Life Project (2005), www.pewinternet.org/PPF/r/156/report_display.asp.

2. Ibid.

3. Alexa Traffic Rankings: www.alexa.com/data/details/main?q=http%3A%2F%2Fwebmd.com&url=webmd.com.

4. Monique Levy. "Online Health Media Consumption and Impact of Increasing Health Consumerism," Jupiter Research (2006), www.jupiter research.com/bin/item.pl/research:vision/103/id=97889.

5. Susannah Fox. "Online Health Search 2006." Pew Internet & American Life Project, www.pewinternet.org/topics.asp?c=5.

6. MLANet's top ten best sites for health info can be found at www.mlanet. org/resources/medspeak/topten.html.

7. Comparative traffic graph on Alexa: www.alexa.com/data/details/traffic_ details?site0=caphis.mlanet.org&site1=webmd.com&site2=&site3=&site4 =&range=6m&size=Medium&y=r&z=1&url=caphis.mlanet.org&x=0&y=0.

8. From the FAQ "What's this space all about?" www.strap-on.org/faq.html.

9. Tarynn M. Witten, Esben Esther Pirelli Benestad, Ilana Berger, R. J. M. Ekins, Randi Ettner, Katsuki Harima, Dave King, Mikael Landén, Nuno Nodin, Volodymyr P'yatokha, and Andrew N. Sharpe, "Transgender and Transsexuality," *The Encyclopedia of Sex and Gender: Men and Women in the World's Cultures*, C. R. Ember and M. Ember (eds.) (New York: Kluwer/ Plenum, 2003), 216–229.

10. Joanne Meyerowitz, *How Sex Changed: A History of Transsexuality in the United States* (Cambridge: Harvard University Press, 2002), 9, 148, 276–277.

## CHAPTER 7. DOING IT FROM A DISTANCE

1. The *Oxford English Dictionary* is available online by paid subscription (or for free via your university or local library's subscription) at http://oed.com.

2. Mike Brunker. "Sex Toys Blaze Tactile Trail on Net," MSNBC (1999), www.msnbc.msn.com/id/3078776.

## 01100011100101 **AKNOWLEDGMENTS** 011010110

F irst and foremost, my infinite thanks go to the women I interviewed—without your insights, experiences, and willingness to share your stories with me, this book would not have been possible.

Many thanks to the people who got their hands dirty during the writing of this book: my gracious editor Brooke Warner, for believing in this project and making incisive and smart edits; Amber Rhea for her encouraging comments on the first chapter and helping me with the glossary; Madeline Glass for her comments on the introduction and the dating chapter (as well as late-night instant message support, gossip, and procrastination); Lux Nightmare and Molly Crabapple for reading and commenting on my porn chapter and being generally awesome; Theresa Anasti and Rachel Aimee for their comments on my sex work chapter; Astrid E. Allen for research assistance; Anna Logue for lending her ass to make one fine cover; and Jamye Waxman, my Monday writing buddy and cheerleader, for everything.

For their support and inspiration, I thank the staff of *$pread Magazine,* whose strength and passion over the past few years has changed my life in the most amazing way; Ann Snitow, my advisor at Eugene Lang, who encouraged me to think about, analyze, and write about porn in a whole new way; Violet Blue, who has always had kind words to say about my work and has helped pave the way for what I do; Bella Vendetta, the toughest, hardest-working, and biggest-hearted woman I know; Melissa Gira, whose passion and creativity about sex work, the Internet, and writing makes me want to work all the harder; Jess Davis for being a partner in sex nerdiness; and Libby Lynn, for getting excited about my work and telling me I rock.

And last but not least, I thank my late-night writing companions: ham-and-cheese sandwiches, Coca-Cola, and Rob's funny stories.

**AUDACIA RAY** is an executive editor of *$pread,* a magazine by and for sex workers, and is a contributor to the porn blog Fleshbot. She has a BA in Cultural Studies from Eugene Lang College and an MA in American Studies from Columbia University. She lives in Brooklyn and blogs at WakingVixen.com

© 2006 Niesha Studio

For more than thirty years, Seal Press has published groundbreaking books. By women. For women. Visit our website at www.sealpress.com.

**INDECENT** by Sarah Katherine Lewis. $14.95, 1-58005-169-3. Chronicles the real work and emotion behind the carnal adult sex industry.

**FULL FRONTAL FEMINISM** by Jessica Valenti. $14.95, 1-58005-201-0. A sassy and in-your-face look at contemporary feminism. *

**THE NONRUNNER'S MARATHON GUIDE FOR WOMEN** by Dawn Dais. $14.95, 1-58005-205-4. A light and funny approach to women running marathons, complete with tips and strategies to making your training a success.

**NOBODY PASSES: REJECTING THE RULES OF GENDER AND CONFORMITY** edited by Mattilda a.k.a Matt Bernstein Sycamore. $15.95, 1-58005-184-7. A timely and thought-provoking collection of essays that confronts and challenges the notion of belonging by examining the perilous intersections of identity, categorization, and community.

**INTIMATE POLITICS: HOW I GREW UP RED, FOUGHT FOR FREE SPEECH, AND BECAME A FEMINIST REBEL** by Bettina F. Aptheker. $16.95, 1-58005-160-X. A courageous and uncompromising account of one woman's personal and political transformation, and a fascinating portrayal of a key chapter in our nation's history.

**WHIPPING GIRL: A TRANSSEXUAL WOMAN ON SEXISM AND THE SCAPEGOATING OF FEMININITY** by Julia Serano. $15.95, 1-58005-154-5. Biologist and transwoman Julia Serano reveals a unique perspective on femininity, masculinity, and other gender identity.